A VAQUERO OF THE BRUSH COUNTRY

GEORGE W. SAUNDERS,
friend of John Young for a lifetime—President of the
Old Time Trail Drivers' Association—gatherer of material for
the monumental work entitled *The Trail Drivers of Texas.*

A Vaquero of the Brush Country

The Life and Times of John D. Young

BY
JOHN D. YOUNG
AND
J. FRANK DOBIE

★

ILLUSTRATED BY
JUSTIN C. GRUELLE

PREFACE BY
LAWRENCE CLARK POWELL

UNIVERSITY OF TEXAS PRESS
Austin

International Standard Book Number 0-292-78704-9
Library of Congress Catalog Card Number 81-50222

Fifth University of Texas Press Printing, 1998

Requests for permission to reproduce material from this work should be sent
to Permissions, University of Texas Press, Box 7819, Austin, Texas 78713-7819.

To Lola Lee Hunter, granddaughter of the vaquero and keeper of the family rings.

AND

To the memory of James M. (Jim) Dobie, a cowman out of the old rock, whom most of the other cowmen and vaqueros of Southwest Texas knew and yet remember to admire.

CONTENTS

John D. Young (left),
his father, L. D. Young (seated),
son John D. Young [Jr.] right,
and grandson Hary J. Friend II (standing center).

PREFACE
THE TIME, THE PLACE, AND THE BOOK

SOMEWHERE in Browning's poetry occurs the phrase, "Never the time and the place and the loved one all together!" As a lifelong reader I have often experienced the perfect conjunction of the time, the place, and the book, having first read, for example, *Moby Dick* on an ocean voyage, *Madame Bovary* in a French *pension,* a book on Leonardo da Vinci in Florence, and Mary Austin's *Lands of the Sun* in rainy Paris, exiled from California, so that the effect of her essays was doubly powerful.

Likewise my first reading of the book I am here prefacing came at precisely the time and place of maximum impact—after a good lunch, high in the air, on a flight from San Antonio to El Paso, over the very Texas heartland of Dobie's book.

Habent sua fata libelli—books have their own fates, the Roman said. And so do readers. And when the two coincide at precisely the right time and place, there is then consummated a union second in power and glory only to that of man with maid.

We had come down at San Antonio, en route from Houston, and I got off the plane to stretch my legs. I was bemused from reading Tom Lea's *The Wonderful Country,* and my mind was on the oranges of Bavinuchi, the falling eagle at the pass, and on the black stallion Lágrimas, noblest steed since Pegasus. There I was for the first time in San Antonio—and I failed to remember the Alamo.

I was not completely witless, however, for on the bookstand I spied a Dobie unknown to me, bought the paperback, and regained my seat on the plane. It was *A Vaquero of the Brush Country.* Not a good edition, true, for it was abridged and lacked Dobie's introduction. But it was unmistakably Dobie on every page, in every paragraph, sentence, and word, its prose permeated with the flavor of the writer I have called the best Southwesterner of them all.

So there I was up in the air, reading at random the chapter called "Brush Country," a rhapsody to the mesquite and other kinds of chaparral which still cover millions of acres in that part of Texas; and that prose poetry so excited me that I had to get up and walk the length of the plane and back. I am sure my seat neighbors thought me mad, for when reading arouses me I have to form the words out loud and move with the rhythm of the prose. Don't the psychologists have a phrase for such behavior? *Kinetic empathy.* In this chapter Dobie's imagination became incandescent and yet his language did not melt, which is the peak of creative writing many strive to reach and few attain.

As the plane droned on west, rangeland yielded to badland, and the Southwestern landscape became more barren and beautiful, its colors and configurations increasingly familiar; and then as we crossed the Pecos at Red Bluff Dam I experienced a further conjunction of the place and the book, for I had skipped over to the final chapter called "Trans-Pecos," and as with one eye I read that tribute to the West's most fabled river, with the other I looked down on the watercourse itself, far below its sweetwater source in the Sangre de Cristo range of northern New Mexico.

It was not until later that I got around to reading the whole of this book, the first in the series of Dobie's Texan triumphs. In it are to be found the origins of his later books, *The Longhorns* and *The Mustangs.* Taking the simple narrative of John Duncan Young's reminiscences, Dobie used it as the frame into which he put all he knew of Texan history, range lore, longhorns, mustangs, razorbacks, cattle drives, Mexican banditry, Indians, Billy the Kid and other badmen, with the heroic figure of the *vaquero,* the Texan cowboy, unifying the book.

Although Dobie was a professor in the University of Texas when this book was written, it is free from academicism, which

means making much ado about little and qualifying that little
to an infinitesimal and unreadable point. The *Vaquero,* and all
of Dobie's subsequent books, are fat with facts, with the fruits
of his own research—encyclopedic, not impressionistic. Dobie
formed his own library of range literature with which he docu-
mented his work. I have seen the collection, lining the walls of
his study, and believe it to be the best of its kind.

   To be a meticulous researcher is one thing, to be a graceful
writer is another, and lastly to be a humane being is perhaps the
rarest of all. To be all three, and a native Texan to boot, is well
nigh unique. This prodigious total is J. Frank Dobie. Let his
books be sent far and wide over the earth! Our country and its
language could not have better ambassadors.

LAWRENCE CLARK POWELL

UCLA *Library*
University of California
Los Angeles

A NECESSARY EXPLANATION

THE first time I saw John Young was eighteen years ago in Alpine, Texas, which is near John Young's mountain of marble. He was deep in the joys of constructing, purely in an imaginative and *mañana* manner, a ten-storied marble hotel at San Antonio for the use of old time trail drivers and the cattle people of generations to come. In time I learned that John Young is something of a dreamer—a man of imagination. I learned that he had dreamed in youth of breaking the biggest monte bank in Mexico. I learned that he had dreamed of finding the Lost Nigger Mine of the Big Bend, and had a wonderful story of his adventures in searching for it. Then in the summer of 1925 I learned that he was dreaming of writing a book in a very realistic manner about a very real thing—his own life.

"The story will be mostly about my experiences as a vaquero in the brush of Southwest Texas," he said, "but the trail will stretch to the Platte, circle around Dodge City, and prong out across the Plains up into the Rockies. It will meander all up and down the Nueces, Pecos, and Devil's rivers. It will often cut the sign of *bandidos* from below the Rio Grande, and it will follow the tracks of cow thieves, horse thieves, and Billy the Kid. This trail of mine will lead into immense boneyards that marked the drifts and die-ups of the open range. It will run into the Big Steal, into mustangs, rattlesnakes, bob-wire, and a lot of other things. I'll need somebody to go over the writing and put it into shape."

We made medicine, and John Young began firing in certain episodes out of his career. But the book that has resulted can hardly be considered as the biography of a single man. The rôle that John Young played was not unusual for the range men of his day; it was representative of the unfenced world. My own

xi

interest has been in the genius of that unfenced world. Hence
I have sought to make a book that should be considerably more
than the straightaway chronicle of one range man's experiences,
though considerably less than a comprehensive history of the
range. It is a combination of range adventurings and range
backgrounds, emphasis having been thrown on features little
known to either the public or special students of early cattle
days.

The story of the brush and the brush hand has never been
written, though the cattle industry of America began in the
mesquitals along the Rio Bravo, and the first cowboys were
"brush poppers." These brush riders had—yet have—a technique
entirely apart from that of the plains cowboys; the brush ranges
were and are entirely different from those of the storied plains.
So, sometimes riding with John Young and sometimes picking
a course on foot far behind him, I have sought to open a *sendero,*
as we say on the border—a clearing—that will allow people to
behold some of the secrets that the brush has hidden.

Frequently I have delayed the Vaquero in his ride in order
to make clear certain extraordinary and now obscure practices
of the open range before barbed wire revolutionized it—the practices of the "hide and tallow factories," of the "Skinning War,"
of cattle inspectors and "stock meetings," of brand burners and
brand buyers, and of the manipulators of the "Big Steal." I
have dwelt long on the chaos of the open range and the earth-
quaking effect of barbed wire.

John Young was a hunter-down of bad Mexicans. Hence
a chapter, the longest in the book—a chapter into which he does
not once enter—seeks to tell a part of the dark and unknown
story of that border land between the Nueces and the Rio Grande,
where Texans and Mexicans for generations killed and raided
in a way to make all Indian troubles of the region seem insig-
nificant and to suggest a modern parallel for the Highland
border of Sir Walter Scott. Following this principle of interpret-
ing and picturing backgrounds, I have sought to give a meaning to Cortina, the great *bandido,* to Shanghai Pierce, to Billy
the Kid, to Horsehead Crossing on the Pecos, to the literature

of McNelly's rangers, to the cowboy's bandana, to the Mexican reata, to the razorback hog, to windmills, to the Picketwire, and to many another object that John Young's ride brought him athwart.

Thus the Vaquero sometimes rides his way unimpeded, and again he pickets his horse and goes to sleep while the reader is invited to examine the terrain—the prairie dogs burrowing into it, the blackjack bushes growing out of it, the *Camino de San Pedro* lighting the sky above it. Doubtless this attempt to blend personal narrative with impersonal explanation, which is, however, replete with narrative incident, has resulted in some queer proportions. Frankly, the only guide to proportion has been a wish to include what is pertinent, interesting, freshly illuminating, and authentic—authentic folk-yarns, for example.

A common object of both Mr. Young and myself has been to place in a clear light certain characteristics of ranch people that, on account of the prolific work of sensation mongers and sentimentalists, require stressing. The men of the Western saddle, however untutored in books some of them may have been —were not ignorant. Their profession was one that demanded skill, alertness, resourcefulness, close observation, will power, and fidelity. It was a profession that engendered pride. They were laborers of a kind, it is true, but they regarded themselves as artists, and they were artists. Years of experience, of practice in deftness, and of study in animal psychology were necessary to perfect a top hand. No genuine cowboy ever suffered from an inferiority complex or ranked himself in the "laboring class" along with "clod hoppers" and ditch diggers. He considered himself a *cavalier* in the full sense of that word—a gentleman on horse, privileged to come it proud over all nesters, squatters, Kansas jay-hawkers, and other such earth-clinging creatures. When he left the farm to trail cattle he literally graduated up from it. He was the aristocrat of all wage earners.

In contrasting the mounted trappers who followed Captain Bonneville with the trappers of the north, Washington Irving made an analysis that can well be applied to the mounted cowboy. "A man who bestrides a horse," says Irving, "must be

essentially different from a man who cowers in a canoe. We find
'the Mountaineers,' accordingly, hardy, lithe, vigorous, and active; . . . heedless of hardship, daring of danger; prodigal of the
present, and thoughtless of the future. . . . They move from
place to place on horseback. The equestrian exercises, therefore,
in which they are engaged, the nature of the countries they
traverse, vast plains and mountains, pure and exhilarating in
atmospheric qualities, seem to make them physically and mentally
a more lively and mercurial race than the fur traders and trappers of former days, the self-vaunting 'men of the north.' . . .
Self dependent and game spirited," one of these mountain hunters is "with his horse and rifle independent of the world, and
he spurns all its restraints."

Such was the temper not only of the mounted trapper of
the mountains but of the cowboy of brush and prairie. The
ranch owner was a kind of feudal lord over his range principality,
but he made no attempt to lord it over his Anglo-American
cowboys. The cowboy, then, to be understood must be regarded
as a proud rider, skilled, observant, alert, resourceful, unyielding,
daring, punctilious in a code peculiar to his occupation, and faithful to his trust. His individualism was so marked that he moulded
in his own image, as it were, all aspirants to his occupation; the
novices, not he, changed.

Although there were cowboys mean, vicious, vulgar, dis-
honest, and cheap, even ignorant, they did not fit in; the general
run of cowboys, the great majority who set the standards of the
type, as described above, could not be and were not ignorant or
morally degraded. Yet, partly on account of the same reasons
that restrained Thackeray, a full delineation of the cowboy's
masculinity, a quality interwoven with morality, is not in this
book entered into. Moreover, as every work has of necessity its
limitations, this one, while seeking to avoid heroizing, glozing,
whitewashing, regards the cowboy for the most part only on the
range and in the saddle—the seat of his individuality. A frank
and full—that is, a naturalistic—delineation of the cowboy as a
man apart from his work and yet as a natural product of his
own soil, remains to be done. It will probably be done only in

fiction. Samuel Pepyses have been as rare in the West as in the East. Nevertheless, because of Charlie Siringo's first—not his last—autobiography, *A Texas Cowboy* (1886), and because of *The Log of a Cowboy* by Andy Adams and *Cowboy* by Ross Santee, not to mention two expository treatises by Emerson Hough and Philip Ashton Rollins, the public may rest assured that the whole truth about cowboys has been about as nearly told as the whole truth has been told about college professors, bankers, congressmen, or any other class of American men.

Nobody who knows him would accuse John Young of being ignorant. He is alert and observant; he has read good books; he is interested in the world about him. However, he has never made any pretensions to being a writer. Hence, although the details of his narrative are given essentially as he supplied them, I have not hesitated to change his arrangement and language and to give his style a pitch in unity with my own. Nor have I hesitated at times to add certain details to his accounts. For instance, he refused to tell what he had done (Chapter VI) at the Mexican ranch-fort occupied by desperate murderers. It was only from George Saunders, who was present on the occasion, that I learned that John Young rode up to the porthole through which his friend had just been killed and shot into it. "John Young would charge hell with a bucket of water," George Saunders commented. Interviews with Mr. Young have supplemented his notes.

In the relation of Mr. Young's own experiences the first person singular has been retained. Consequently the *I* in the body of the book, although it may at times be something of me, represents altogether another Texan from the Texan who, when this necessary explanation is concluded, will not again in the whole book be *I*.

The attempt to collaborate, as though I were a contemporary, with a man who did most of his riding before I was born, necessitates a few personalities. I began my life and grew to maturity on a ranch down the Nueces River in the country through which John Young popped brush. Later I managed a very large ranch in that same country. The names of the old settlers that he tells of have been in my ears since infancy. The practices of open range and brushy thicket that he exemplifies and the temper of a peculiar land that he saw changing from free disorder to mechanical order, from waste to economic efficiency, have all been to me a traditional inheritance. I "speak the same language" that John Young and the people he worked among speak. Furthermore, through reading old newspapers and books and interviewing scores of old timers, I have endeavored to understand minutiae of the range before it was fenced in. Despite rapid and revolutionary changes, the Southwest is still a land of soil traditions, and no man who does not make those traditions a part of himself will write faithfully either of its past or of its present.

Finally, it is with pleasure that I acknowledge the indebtedness of both John Young and myself to our friend, George W. Saunders, of San Antonio, for reading over the unfinished manuscript of the book and offering valuable corrections and suggestions. Also I wish to express my obligations to E. W. Winkler, Librarian of the University of Texas and unexcelled scholar of Texasana, for directing me to many items concerning the land and people to whom a considerable part of this book pertains. Harbert Davenport, of Brownsville, did me the gracious and helpful service of criticizing the chapter on "The Bloody Border." My wife, Bertha McKee Dobie, has given almost every paragraph of the pages that follow the benefit of her incisive criticism. The faults of fact and phrase I must assume as my own.

J. FRANK DOBIE

Austin, Texas
January 1, 1929

A VAQUERO OF THE BRUSH COUNTRY

John Young trading horses, San Antonio, Texas, 1890.

CHAPTER I

THE MAKING OF A VAQUERO

In Southwest Texas, where sixty years ago and more I was "running cattle," cowboys were—and still are—generally referred to as "vaqueros" (often pronounced *bakeros*), "hands," or "cowhands." The word "cowboy" was sometimes used, but not nearly so commonly as now. *Vaquero*—from *vaca* (cow)—was originally applied only to Spanish or Mexican cowboys. But from an early day, Texans, especially those near the border, have used the word without reference to race. Thus in one *corrida,* or outfit, may be found "Mexican vaqueros," "white vaqueros," and "nigger vaqueros."

As for "cowpuncher" and "puncher," I do not recall having heard the terms in the old days, and the use of them, however common in the Northwest, is still limited, among men of the older generation at least, on the ranges of South and West Texas. I remember distinctly the first time I heard the word "cowpuncher" used. It was in the spring of 1879 and I was loading a train of cattle for the Cimarron Cattle Company at Las Animas, Colorado, for Kansas City. We had a man to go in charge of the cattle, but in those days the railroads gave a pass for every car or two of stock. Several boys around Las Animas who had run away from home to taste the Wild West wanted to go back East. They applied to me for passes, which I secured for them as far as Kansas City. When I handed the passes over I gave one of the boys a prodpole with instructions to help our regular man punch up the cattle if they got down in the cars. The boys were a rollicky bunch and they called themselves "cowpunchers," which they literally were, though I doubt if any one of them knew the difference between a jingle-bob and an off-

3

strap. Originally, then, the word "cowpuncher" applied only to the chaperon of a shipment of cattle. The cowpuncher might be the best all around cowman in the country or he might be a sailor who had never saddled a horse. The prodpole was the symbol of his office. Clearly, "cowpuncher" is a misnomer for the cowboy. I have never liked the word. I have done my share of punching cattle on the cars, but even there I was a vaquero.

My father and mother came to Texas from Mississippi in 1849, did their courtship on the way, and were married soon after their arrival at Lockhart in Caldwell County. Father, who was a good carpenter, cut logs and built a house in a grove of live oak trees on Plum Creek just below Lockhart. There in 1856 I was born and christened John Duncan Young, being named after my maternal grandfather. Sixty-seven years later Emerson Hough in his novel on trail driving, *North of 36*, made Lockhart famous, and the heroine of that novel, Taisie Lockhart, lived in just such a house as I was born in.

Our life was nomadic. When I was two years old—though I recall nothing of the matter—my parents and grandparents moved out into the San Saba country and settled at Richland Springs. There, with the aid of a few other settlers, they built a combination stockade and cabin that came to be called Fort Duncan. We lived in this fort, and in it also during the Indian raids our few neighbors sought protection.

Father and Grandfather were both horse men and in settling on the San Saba their purpose was to raise horses. The country they picked is generally conceded to be the best horse range in Texas. There the curly mesquite grass, which cures like hay for winter, and mesquite beans keep horses fat the year round and as strong as corn would make them. The rocks of the San Saba hills give horses good hoofs and train them to be sure-footed. Water there is plentiful and as fresh and healthful as any in the world. The Comanches knew all these things long before the white men heard of the San Saba, and they fought longer and harder to hold the San Saba territory than for any other ground of the Southwest. There for generations they had caught mustangs, and they were not long in finding out that the settlers at Richland Springs kept good horses.

For two years Grandfather and Father held out against the Indians, most of the time afoot. Then Father said that he would not live where he had to walk and we all moved back to Plum Creek. Here Mother and we children remained during the Civil War. After the War, Father became a Baptist preacher, but he spent more time in riding circuit and in looking after his few cattle than in preaching or reading. He was a thrifty man, and before he died he became a well-to-do merchant.

Grandfather Duncan never forsook horses. He returned to the San Saba and established a horse ranch that he maintained as long as he lived. In my early boyhood he and Grandma used to come down into South Texas once in a while to see us, always riding the best horses in the whole country. I worshiped those horses, and Grandfather used to say to me, "When you are big I'll give you a horse every time you visit us." Considering that we sometimes lived two hundred miles apart and that it took a week to ride the distance between us, the promise was not extravagant. Before I was grown, I began making the visits, and Grandfather always kept his promise. To one of these gift horses belongs something like an adventure—but I am getting ahead of my story.

From my earliest recollections my chief toy was a rope. I wanted nothing better. I roped the horses, milk cows, calves, chickens, cats, dogs, hogs, younger children, and everything else that came within range of my loop. At the same time that I was learning to rope I was learning to ride. When I was seven years old, Father left us to enter the Confederate Army. At parting he gave me a good horse and told me that as I was the oldest boy in the family I must use the horse to keep Mother and the children supplied with milk.

That was the year of one of the big drouths in Texas. During the hard winter our gentle milk cows all "dried up" or died, for we had no feed for them. The only chance to get milk was from the longhorn cows on the range. Out on the ranges thousands of these stood around mud holes and bogged and died;

but the country was all open and there were thousands left. Most of the cows were branded, but anybody was welcome to catch up and milk any cow, provided he did not "knock the calf in the head with a churn dasher"; that is to say, starve it by taking all the milk from it.

I became a vaquero. The horse Father gave me was a *grulla* (mouse colored) dun paint. He was something of a race horse and knew more about handling a cow than some so-called cowboys. He gave me many a fall, but I soon learned to ride with a balance and to sense every move he was going to make. This natural anticipating of a horse's movements is what makes an easy rider. When a bucking horse hits the ground, the buster must know which way he will jump next or else get a fall. Nothing but early experience can give a rider this "sixth sense."

To keep the milk pans full I first had to ride out and find a cow that looked as if she would give more milk than the young calf at her side required. The cows that were the best rustlers were often the wildest. After I picked one out, the problem was to get her and the calf into the corral. I could generally drive her all right, but nine times out of ten when we reached the corral she would be afraid of it and would refuse to go through the gate. Since a cow will follow her calf anywhere, especially if the calf is in trouble, what I usually did was to take down my "toy," rope the calf, drag it into the pen by the horn of the saddle, and tie it to the fence. If the cow did not immediately follow, I put my horse out of sight, hid myself near the open gate, and waited until she got up enough courage to nose her way inside. Then I slammed the gate to behind her.

This would usually scare her half to death and she would want to fight. I'd crawl up on Old Paint again, ride into the pen, and rope her. After a while I'd give the rope a *vuelta* (a turn) around a post, and by taking up the slack when the cow ran would finally get her tied up short. Then to keep her from kicking my head off I'd tie her hind legs together. By this time she would be so mad and worried that she would hardly let down a drop of milk. Nevertheless, I'd rub her and pull her teats to let her know that I was not going to hurt her. Then I'd turn her loose and leave her in the pen until morning, when she would have to be tied and her teats pulled again.

By repeating the operation night and morning I might within a week's time be getting a cupful of milk, and within two weeks' time the cow might be gentle enough to stand without being tied. My sister Sarah, two years older than I, generally helped me milk. None of those old longhorn cows gave much milk. One was just a starter; sometimes it took a dozen to supply our family. But Paint and I asked for nothing better than to hunt and break milk cows.

In addition to keeping the family in milk I had various other chores. I drew water with a windlass out of a hundred foot well and carried it a hundred yards to the house. I rode into the brush and dragged up by the horn of the saddle what firewood we used. On Friday or Friday night I shucked and shelled corn to take next morning to the grist mill seven miles away to be ground into our week's supply of meal. Once the sack fell off the horse and the hogs ate up the meal while I was gone after help. That time we had to borrow meal to last until the next Saturday, for the mill ground but once a week. Aside from milk, our principal fare was corn dodgers and salt bacon.

I remember as well as if it were yesterday the first flour bread that I ever tasted. My grandfather and grandmother came down from San Saba to visit us, riding horseback and camping along the way. They had raised some wheat, and they brought enough biscuits, ready made, to last them over the journey. Old as those biscuits were, I thought them the best thing that I had ever eaten. Sometimes to this day when I am hungry the taste of them comes back to me.

The luxury of flour and sugar on the frontiers gave rise to more than one story often told to children to enforce manners and to warn against backwoodsman ignorance. As one story went, the table of a settler was set for a wedding dinner and the guests were being awaited when a "yahoo from up the creek" stopped by on his way home from the mill to deliver some freshly ground meal. Of course hospitality demanded that he be asked to dinner, though his presence at the wedding "infare" was not desired. The hostess decided to say nothing of the impending sociable, but kindly suggested to the fellow that he sit down and eat at once so that he would not be delayed. He lived a long ride up the creek.

The man made free of the good things on the table and particularly free of a plate of sliced pound cake, which was of a rich, golden color like that of corn bread made from yellow meal—a color, if not a flavor, that he was used to. He deliberately spread each piece of cake with butter before eating it. Biscuits were scarce enough—but cake! The hostess saw the cake dwindling; she wanted to steer the hungry guest off on corn bread, but she judged that she had better be tactful. So she pressed him to have some biscuits.

"No, thank you, ma'am," said he. "You save them there biscuits. This here yaller bread is good enough for me."

And the thoughtful guest continued to eat until he had devoured all the "yaller bread" in sight and had stacked up a graveyard full of chicken bones on the cloth beside his plate.

We had no matches, no stoves, and did all cooking in a fireplace. Many a time I saw my father start a fire by loading his pistol with just enough wadding to hold the powder in place and then firing it off with the muzzle pointed close to a bit of cotton. One of the household observances was to cover the fire up with ashes before going to bed so that there would be a live coal to start the fire with next morning. But sometimes the observance was neglected or the ashes were too thin to keep air away from the coals or else so heavy as to smother them. Then I might have to go to a neighbor's house half a mile away to borrow a chunk of fire.

Carrying a chunk of fire so that it would not go out was something of an art and required expedition. If anybody wanted to "borrow" fire, he generally made his call brief. Hence arose the old saying, once common but now dying out, "You must have come after a chunk (or coal) of fire," in protest to a brief call.

Our lighting system was as simple as our ignition system. Daylight saving was almost universally practiced. When sickness or some other emergency required a light—nobody sat up to read—a fire might be kept going in the fireplace. Of course we generally had candles, but we were saving of them. We made them for ourselves as we made soap, liniments, and other necessities. Every family had its own candle mould. Some cotton would be spun on the spinning wheel to make a string for the wick; the wick would be hung in the center of the mould; then melted beef tallow would be poured around the string. The mould, with the tallow in it, was next set out to cool; in hot weather it was a job to get the tallow hard enough to stand alone. The first kerosene lamp I ever saw was a small tin contrivance. I paid a dollar for it, tied it and a gallon can of kerosene on my saddle, and brought them home to Mother.

About this time we learned that kerosene would "knock ticks." One day while we were branding colts we roped a yearling filly that was covered with ticks. She had not shed her winter hair, and it was particularly long. After we had thrown her, we rubbed her all over with kerosene and then slapped the hot branding iron to her. She instantly broke into a blaze and the two boys holding her down—for she was not tied—let her loose. Literally "like a streak of greased lightning," she broke into the *manada* of mares and colts, and right there we had the wildest run inside a pen that I have ever seen. It was a good thing that the pickets were strong.

Quicker than I can tell it, I picked up my rope, ran out into the middle of the pen, and, as she came down the side fence, threw a *mangana* on her fore-feet and at the same time tossed a half hitch over a post so that when she hit the end of the rope I held it without giving a foot and "busted" her flat. She was still burning, but we smotherd the fire out with dirt. She was so badly scorched that when she finally got well she had white spots all over her. The spots never went away and we always called her "Kerosene."

This incident occurred several years after the close of the Civil War, at which time Father came back to us safe and sound. When I was twelve years old we moved to Refugio Mission on Mission River. Here I went to school a few months, though Mother had already taught me to read, write, and spell. Three years later when some neighboring boys were planning to go off to a private school at Concrete in De Witt County—there were no public schools in Texas at the time—I announced that I wanted to go with them. Father replied that he was not able to send me. But I had three saddle horses and ten head of cattle, and with the money that they brought managed to go to school for ten months. At the end of the time I owed the school fifty dollars.

When I returned home, Billie Colville, a rancher, told me that if I would break seven wild *potros* (young horses) he had, he would let me have my pick of the seven. Just about the time I had got them all gentle and had picked out one to keep, an agent of the Concrete school came along and I turned my horse over to him to pay the fifty dollar debt. Being afoot did not bother me. I could ride other people's horses and get money for riding them.

Two or three incidents connected with the school life at Concrete linger in my mind. W. W. (Bill) Jones, who now owns more cattle, acres, and money than nearly any other cowman in South Texas, was a school fellow. One day "Professor" Covey sent Bill and me to Cuero, twelve miles away, to get a package. Now a trip to Cuero was a rare treat. We drove "Tip," a lazy mule, known to be twenty-five years old, to a buggy that had no top. Old Tip did not mind in the least the switches we cut and wore out on him. However, we happened to know that he did mind the report of a gun. When we got to Cuero, we bought a bottle of whisky, a pocket full of cigars, and as many firecrackers as we had money left to pay for.

Soon after leaving town we took a swig and lit up our cigars. Old Tip did not seem any more anxious to get back home than he had been to leave it. But the first firecracker that exploded under his tail put the energy of a whole *manada* of mustangs into him and from there on until we delivered him to "Professor" Covey he hit the ground only in high places. Every time he began to slow down a firecracker popped between his hind legs and away he would break as if the devil and

Tom Walker were both after him. To make sure that the fire-crackers exploded in a strategic spot we cut siene (rattle pod) switches, split the ends, and inserted the firecrackers in the split. We could direct the end of those switches. The sport was cruel, but I doubt if Bill Jones or I either ever enjoyed another ride more than we enjoyed that one.

Another time some of us school boys were in Cuero when the Taylor-Sutton feudists came into town armed to the hilt. There must have been a hundred men on each side. While we boys watched from behind a log, one side backed the other into some cow pens. Had a shot been fired, hell would have broken loose in Georgia sure enough. The leaders recognized this fact, a flag of truce was raised, and the crowd disbanded. Three days later they were shooting each other again, from ambush.

The Taylor-Sutton feud was the most bloody ever fought in Texas. Both families were extensive operators in cattle, em-ploying numerous cowboys. Their quarrel, begun soon after the close of the Civil War, was over unbranded cattle. In the course of ten years scores of men became involved in it and dozens were killed. The feud ended in 1875.

One of the school boys at Concrete was George W. Saun-ders. As president of the Old Time Trail Drivers' Association and also as the head of an excellent live stock commission house, which does business in Fort Worth and San Antonio, George has received a good deal of publicity. I want to add an item. One time when I was at the Saunders home near Goliad, a gang of us boys were lounging on the front gallery. George was sprawled out on a narrow bench about two feet high and some one dared him to roll off. I don't think that he really intended to roll, but he made the motion and off he did roll. The fall knocked the breath out of him and we boys were shaking him when his brother Jack came up from the spring with a bucket of cold water and dashed it on him. The cold water brought George to right now, but when he found that the only paper collar he had was reduced to pulp, he wanted to fight all of us. The outstanding article in his "Sunday-go-to-meeting" apparel was ruined.

When I left Concrete my formal education was finished. I have always liked to read and have read many books, but what schooling I had was just an episode. The range was my real school. By the time I was twelve I was working with regular cow outfits, hunting and driving cattle over a wide country; by the time I quit school, at sixteen, I could hold my own with the most seasoned vaquero. I had no trouble getting all the horseback work I wanted. My first big experience was helping to put up a trail herd of mossy horns.

THE OMNIPOTENT Rope IN TEXAS

The children cry for it | The boys play with it | The young men live by it | Some old ones die by it

CHAPTER II

THE MOSSY HORNS

IN the spring of 1872 a man came into our part of Refugio County buying steers to drive to one of the northwestern territories. He had a contract with the United States Government to furnish beef for an Indian agency. Neighboring ranchmen agreed to put him up 1200 big steers ranging from five to twelve years old at $10 a head. When a Texas steer gets six or eight years old, his horns become wrinkled and scaly; hence the name *mossy horn*.

To start the work we met at the Woods pens on Chocolate Creek some ten miles north of old St. Mary's, which was on St. Mary's Bay. Robert Driscoll, although among the younger men of the outfit, was unanimously chosen as boss, and no better choice could have been made. He was not only an expert vaquero and a genuine cowman, but also a good manager.

The "crowd'—as a cow outfit was then generally called— contained twenty or twenty-five vaqueros, nearly all of them cattle owners and as live a bunch of real cowmen as ever joined in a cow hunt. In addition to Robert Driscoll, I recall Jerry Driscoll, "Coon" Dunman, Tobe Wood, Billie Colville, Henry Barrow, George Maley, Jim McFaddin, N. R. McDaniel, Lieuen Rogers, Jesse Williams, Robert Morton, Andy Martin, Jack West, Martin Reeves, and Joe Doughty. These names are still familiar in cattle circles of Southwest Texas and they show pretty well to what nationalities Texas cowmen generally belonged. I was the only boy in the outfit. There were two Mexican vaqueros in the crowd, and two negroes. Eli, one of the negroes, was horse wrangler; Zeno, the other, an old French negro, was cook. I remember him best by one incident.

13

At that time baking powder was an unknown ingredient. We bought soda in paper packages, and Zeno had a habit of emptying his soda into a wide-mouthed pickle bottle in order to keep it dry. At the same time, calomel was the universal medicine, and some one had brought along a generous supply of it—in a wide-mouthed pickle bottle. The calomel, like the soda, was kept in the chuck box. One day while making bread, Zeno got the calomel and soda bottles confused. We were a sick lot, for, despite the more than peculiar taste, we ate Zeno's bread.

I should say here that camp cooks were just coming into style. Before, during, and immediately following the Civil War it was the custom of the Texas cowhands that each furnish and prepare his own grub. The great organized round-ups, which originated, it seems, on the open ranges of Northern Texas and which could not well be held in the brushy country of Southwest Texas, were not yet known to us. When we gathered cattle, we said that we were on a "cow hunt," a "cow work," a "work," or a "cow drive," or maybe we said we were out "running cattle." Each man had a tin cup, some coffee, salt, perhaps some sugar, and either meal or a supply of corn bread. The hardness of hardtack is nothing compared to the hardness that a big supply of home-baked bread would sometimes attain before the last of it was consumed. If a cowhand, or a group of hands, ran out of bread, nothing was thought of riding over to some settler's house miles away and asking the woman of the house to cook up a supply of bread. She always did this, apparently gladly, certainly graciously. Sometimes the hands took bacon with them; more often they got their meat from the range, killing an animal whenever meat was required.

But to get back to the mossy horns. "Chousing" them was extremely hazardous. They were all outlaws, *ladinos,* as wild as bucks, cunning, and ready to fight anything that got in front of them. Most of them stayed in the brush all day and came out on the prairies to graze only at night. They knew every thicket in the country and could crawl through the thorns like so many snakes. Many of them had time and again escaped from general works. Among them were wrinkle-necked maverick cows and bulls that had never had a loop tossed over their heads.

The first thicket that we stormed netted us about twenty-five steers that must have been branded before the Civil War, but we did not hold them long. They ran out on a peninsula, from which they took to the water like a bunch of ducks and swam to an island a quarter of a mile away. We let them have the island and went on to hunt for something else.

After a hard day's hunt we headed towards camp with around a hundred head of the wildest and shaggiest bunch of scalawag steers that I have ever seen together. They ran and fought all the way, and out of the hundred we corralled only thirty-seven head. A good portion of these had to be roped and led in. When one of these old steers headed out of the herd for the brush he was ready to hook the liver out of anything that got in front of him. The horns were not for ornament. Oftener than otherwise it did no good to rope such a steer, as he would start fighting as soon as he felt the rope tighten. Then if he was thrown down he was likely to sulk and refuse to get up. A vaquero might twist the tail of such a sulky animal until it broke, might kick and spur the hide off his backbone, might rub sand in his eyes, and still the steer would refuse to budge. If he got too hot, he might die right where he lay. Finally if he did get up, he would be so "on the prod" that nothing could come close enough to touch him with a forty-foot pole. While a hand was fooling with one such steer, a dozen others would get away.

Like the razorback, the longhorn had a long, limber tail. It was well proportioned to his horns and legs. The safest and most effective thing to do when an old steer ran off was to tail him. A thorough tailing usually knocked the breath out of him and so dazed him that he would "be good" the rest of the day. Tailing required, first, a swift horse that could "turn on a dime" and knew his business. It required, secondly, a quick and daring rider who could grab a cow's tail on a dead run, deftly twist it around the horn of his saddle, and then spurt a little to one side and ahead so as to give the cow brute a flat bust. There is a way of tailing an animal so that its neck will pop in two. Old time cowhands with a bad temper, a distorted sense of humor, or a craving for fresh meat sometimes broke an animal's neck in this way "accidentally on purpose." Cattle owners, however, would not stand for neck breaking. Really, with a fast horse and a certain sleight that comes only from practice it is very easy to tail an animal down. Even when "busted" gently—if the word *gently* can ever be applied to such a process—a grown animal is almost sure to be somewhat bruised.

After supper of the first day out, we were all squatting and lying off to one side of the camp fire telling about the steers we had or had not caught, when one of the men began to "rag" me. He said that a steer I had undertaken to tail had turned on me suddenly and chased me back to the herd. The joke produced a laugh and somebody else added that I had sprinkled salt on the steer's tail. I admitted that I had failed to bust a steer but gave as a reason that my horse was not fast enough.

At this Mr. Robert Driscoll asked if I thought I could tail one on Ribbon. I replied that I could. "Eli," he called to the horse wrangler, "catch out Ribbon in the morning for John." Now Ribbon had the reputation of being about the best cow-horse in the country; he was a race horse as well. I lay awake most of the night laughing to myself at the thought of what a surprise I had in store for some of those "old brindles" next day.

When I pranced out on Ribbon I was about the happiest boy in Texas, and when the gate was opened for the steers to come out Ribbon and I were in the lead, both "raring to go." I allowed a big steer to head out from the herd. Then I moved up by his side, leaned over, caught his tail in my right hand, gave it a couple of wraps around the saddle horn, and shot the spurs to Ribbon. We stood that steer on his head, turning him a complete somersault and breaking one of his horns. When he got up with the broken horn dangling along his jaw he turned around several times trying to get away from it; then he walked back to the herd completely cowed. The cheers I got were enough to turn the head of any sixteen-year-old boy.

After this episode Mr. Driscoll decided to keep me mounted on fast horses and to put me in charge of holding the cattle during the day. Of course it has always been the boy's job to stand day-herd, but these cattle demanded something more than a novice and I took my appointment as a high compliment. The two Mexican vaqueros were detailed to help me, and we seldom got restless from any want of action. The cattle were turned out of the pen every morning with all hands helping to hold them. Then after they had quieted down, all the men but the Mexicans and myself rode away after more cattle. Herding those mossy horns at night on their own range would have been wellnigh impossible; herding them at any time of day kept the three of us alert and on the move. After having been handled a few days, most of the beeves would have become reconciled to the herd, but every day new cattle were being thrown in with them, and thus the whole bunch remained in a continual state of excitement.

I had studied cattle until I knew their psychology. Generally, by handling them in a certain way, I could make them graze at ease. I knew how to hold them to make them lie down in the middle of the day. A good cowhand has to be much more than a good roper or rider. He has to understand cow nature; he has to be able to make cattle understand him. The test of a cowman lies in his ability to water a herd of cattle in such a way that all of them will drink freely and fully. An equal test, perhaps, lies in his ability to trail cattle in such a way that they will even while on the trail put on flesh rather than lose it. Unfortunately, the steers we were gathering were of a nature that prevented their putting on flesh while we worked. The majority of them were "as gant as gutted snow birds." When I saw one of them restlessly hooking at every other steer he came close to, I knew that he was trying to inform his fellow prisoners that he was an outlaw without respect for men or horses. Then when I saw him throw up his head as if he were looking for something a long way off, I knew that he was intending to make a break for the thickets. By "hollering" at him I could usually start him to thinking of something else and thus save a run. If he did make the break, I tailed him. With that he usually went back to the herd.

Along about four o'clock in the afternoon the outfit would come in with what they had caught, the two bunches would be thrown together, and we would start for the pens. By the time we got within five or six hundred yards of the gate, the cattle invariably started "milling," which means going in a circle. and the milling kept up while we pushed the mass forward. By holding them at the gate we gradually shoved them through it. Meantime old spoilt steers were dodging out in every direction. If a man ran after one, the gap he left in the ring of horsemen let out other steers; so anything that got out had to be let go for the time.

After the herd was penned, we struck for the escaped individuals. Perhaps we would be able to get a little bunch of them together and drive them back. Often darkness found half the hands a mile or two away, each trying to lead a steer in or else tying him down, to be left tied till morning, when the herd would be driven to him so that he would go into it when turned loose. On more than one occasion we lost at penning time as many cattle as had been gathered during the day. And the contract called for 1200 head. To round up 1200 cattle would have been simple. We were cleaning the country of outlaws.

At the end of the first week we moved camp to the McDaniel Ranch on the Medio Creek four miles above the Mission Refugio. The pens here were in the midst of a wide prairie. A detail of the hands would leave this camp in the evening, ride fifteen or twenty miles, sleep a little while on their leggins and saddles, get up before daybreak, boil coffee, eat a little bread and meat, and then work back towards the pens, seldom halting until evening brought the one square meal of the day. Not one of these hands was fat.

The cattle tried to stampede nearly every night, but we slept all around the pens and at any disturbance jumped up and began singing to quiet them. There were several pens of different sizes, and we always kept the steers crowded so that they would not have room to run and thus hit the fence with enough force to tear it down. It was a common thing for them to kill or cripple one or more of their number in these night panics.

That cow hunt was no place for members of the Humane Society. Nothing in the way of kindness would work on those old mossy horns. One way of subduing them was to shoot them through the horns. If a steer went to fighting, it was a common practice to run by him shooting at the thick part of his horn with a six-shooter. If the horn was hit center, the pain of the jar calmed the steer very promptly and he became manageable. If the pith of the horn was punctured, the soreness kept the steer on his behavior for weeks. Sometimes a glancing shot on the horn caused a bullet to curve and come whistling back towards the man who shot it. Occasionally a misshot killed a steer. Cattle were cheap and it was an advantage to get rid of these outlaws at any price. They spoiled the other cattle. They had to be either shot or driven off.

And thus the cow hunt went on. Horses were crippled or gored daily. By something like a miracle none of us was even badly hurt. After working a few weeks we had 1200 head of steers gathered. We delivered them at the McDaniel pens. The buyer, so we heard, scattered them all the way to Kansas. I doubt if half of them ever crossed Red River. On the cow hunt next spring we found several of them back on the coast making trouble.

Bull-tailing, it may be said in concluding this chapter, was practiced by the first Mexican vaqueros of Texas, and long after the Civil War it was a popular sport among the Mexicans of Southwest Texas. On Sunday, the day devoted to the sport, Mexican riders would congregate at some corral where a number of wild bulls had been penned; often they began their Sabbath exercises by rounding up the wildest bulls they could find and putting them into the pen. A bull at a time would be released from the corral to tear out across the prairie; then, yelling and popping his quirt on his leggins, a vaquero would take after him. The sport was full of hazard, for a bull can turn on a horse very quickly. Cattle owners, as stock became valuable, naturally forbade the tailing of their bulls, and the sport died out. English speaking cowboys never indulged in it to any extent. It may be considered as a precursor of bull-dogging.

CHAPTER III

FOR THEIR HIDES AND TALLOW

My earliest experiences in driving cattle to market were with herds bound for the Gulf ports of Southwest Texas—ports that were of far more importance in the early seventies than they have been at any time since. These drives were comparatively short and the herds were comparatively small. I went with one bunch of cattle to St. Mary's—not even a post office now—and there they were traded off for Florida lumber, the shipmasters taking the cattle on board their sailing vessels.

I made various drives to Rockport, none particularly eventful. I recall that after starting thither with one herd of three hundred big steers we met a man who reported the Rockport market to be glutted. We then drove to the packery on Mission River below Refugio, where the beeves were sold at seven dollars around, payment to be made as soon as a certain ship carrying a cargo of salt beef should return. That was, as the old song went, "the ship that never returned." The owners of the three hundred beeves never received a cent for them.

I helped drive several herds to Indianola, on Matagorda Bay, from where they were shipped by steamer to New Orleans. The "coasters," or "sea lions," as people sometimes called the longhorned cattle of the coast country, could swim like ducks and were as wild. Our route to Indianola was across bayous and along lakes, and the "sea lions" gave us as much trouble in the water as wild cattle ever gave anybody in the brush. Most of my driving to the coast was for Dan Doughty and J. M. Mathis. A wild steer finally hooked Doughty to death in the wharf pens. Mathis had built up an immense export business in cattle from Indianola and Rockport via the Morgan Steamship Line, shipping annually from 40,000 to 50,000 head of cattle, most of them to New Orleans. In the early seventies he formed a partnership with T. M. Coleman and G. W. Fulton, the firm being known as the Coleman, Mathis and Fulton Pasture Company. As will be seen in a chapter later on, I had in time an uncommon bit of business to do for these three big operators.

The driving of herds to coast markets implies a feature of the cattle business that is little known and that needs considerable elucidation. Trail drivers who have written their memoirs, historians, historical novelists, and journalists have all combined to make the public fairly familiar with the way in which the teeming ranges of South Texas found, following the close of the Civil War, an outlet for their cattle at the end of the Chisholm Trail in Kansas. The story of the great cattle trails is an epic chapter in the romance and reality of the cow country's history. In fact, the glamour of this phase of the range business has thrown into shadow another phase that was for years of immense economic importance and that was at its peak as bizarre, fantastic, sordid and dramatic as any business can possibly become.

This business, carried on in the very country where the northern cattle trails had their source, amounted to nothing less than the slaughter of tens of thousands of cattle for their hides and tallow, other tens of thousands for their meat, to be pickled, as well as for their hides and tallow, and still other tens of thousands for their hides alone. There is no possible way of getting at the correct figures, but the total amounted to many hundreds of thousands. The slaughter raged in scores of "hide and tallow factories"—as the packeries were fittingly called— that dotted the coast line from Corpus Christi Bay to Galveston Island. It raged on the prairies and in the thickets from the Rio Grande to the Sabine, where thieves, instead of rounding up cattle to drive away in herds, shot them down as they found them and then carried their hides out on pack horses or in ox carts. Along the coast below San Antonio, ports into which a ship has not entered for fifty years throve with the export of

hides, horns, barrels of tallow, and hogsheads of pickled beef—
and also of tens of thousands of cattle on foot destined for
Cuba and New Orleans. For years the Kansas markets did not
absorb more than half of the cattle being raised in Texas. The
story of the other half has never been told. To understand it, a
review of the situation is necessary.

In 1866, according to unreliable and apparently underesti-
mated figures of the United States Census Bureau,[1] 260,000 head
of cattle went north. The drovers of this year generally set forth
with no definite market in mind; they encountered frenzied
fear of "Texas fever." They met bushwhackers. Some of them
met death. A few of them did well. The results on the whole
were disastrous. Consequently, in 1867 only 35,000 cattle went
north. But that year Abilene established itself as a reliable market
and the magnificent Chisholm Trail became a highway for
Texas cattle. Thereafter it was ribboned with herds. In 1871 more
than 700,000 head of Texas cattle went to Kansas. The market
was naturally over-supplied and vast numbers of the drive had
to be held over on the Kansas and Nebraska prairies. During
the severe winter that followed 250,000 of them froze to death.
Not half so many cattle went up in 1872 as went up the year
before. The cry of the great ranges of the Northwest—just being
cleared of Indians and buffaloes—that was to drain Texas of its
stocker cattle did not boom out until late in the seventies. In
1873 came the great panic. Nearly all the banks in Kansas City,
the financial center of the cattle world, went broke. Beef retailed
in Kansas City at 2½ cents a pound, and the cattlemen of
Southwest Texas were warned that they could save money by
selling their stock at home.

The cowmen gave ear unto the warning. Early in 1874 the
Corpus Christi *Gazette,* speaking for a representative section of
the stock country, said: "The packeries at home, combined with
shipments to New Orleans and Havana, have this past season
absorbed the greater portion of our first class cattle. This will
necessarily reduce the drive to Kansas in the spring to probably

[1] United States Census, 1880 (Agriculture), Vol. III, page 975, tabulates the
number of cattle driven annually from Texas, 1866–1880.

not over 10,000 head from the counties of Nueces, San Patricio, and Live Oak, which in the spring of 1871 furnished over 30,000 head to the Kansas market." The drives from Texas to Kansas in 1874 and 1875 were only 166,000 and 152,000 head respectively.

Six or eight years after the Kansas trails opened there were not so many beef on the breeding grounds of Texas as there were at the close of the War, but there was still an abundance of stock cattle and far from a dearth of steers. The Texans were still in the throes of Reconstruction. Land was without value; cattle were without value; money was as scarce as hen's teeth and infinitely more requisite. Owners were often obliged to sacrifice their stock for almost nothing.

With cattle at such a low price that they sold for the value of their hides and tallow alone, what was locally called the "Skinning War" came to be fought. Instead of stealing cattle and driving them off, rustlers rode out on the range and killed cattle where they found them, removing the hides and leaving the carcasses for buzzards and coyotes. Owners naturally became desperate in defense of their property, and in the end men as well as cattle were killed.

Two factors, aside from the low prices of cattle, were largely responsible for this promiscuous and wholesale skinning. In the first place, the custom of the country was that any man could take a "fallen hide" (a hide off a dead cow) when he found it, no matter what brand the animal bore. The hide was his, just as a maverick was his—if he could catch it. In the second place, with the country all unfenced, cattle in the winter time drifted from the north towards the coast by the thousands. The colder and wetter the northers of winter, the more they drifted. In bad years they banked up along bayous and creeks and milled over the prairies. What grass they did not trample down they grazed off. Then they bogged and died until "in some places a man might have walked for miles without stepping off their carcasses." Those that did not bog down grew thin; then if on the tail of winter a hard spell came, they dotted the whole range with their bones.

The cow people of the lower country came to speak of the

"skinning season" as naturally as they spoke of the "branding season." A settler short on a corn crop could count on a "hide crop." The cow outfits of summer became the "skinning outfits" of winter. In the disastrous "die-up" of 1872–1873, for instance, Jim Miller's outfit on the Nueces skinned 4000 dead cattle. Of course, "die-ups" were dreaded by all cattlemen, but they were welcomed by skinners who had no cattle. Then when cattle did not die fast enough to keep their knives busy such skinners killed them. Thus went on a range skinning business exceeded only in magnitude by the contemporaneous slaughter and skinning of the buffaloes.

Range skinning cannot be considered as a legitimate phase of the coastal marketing of cattle, but the same conditions that gave rise to the "hide and tallow factories" occasioned it, to a large extent, also. Consideration of it belongs in any account of what was doing on the range at the southern end of the cattle trails—and of what many trail drivers did with their time during the winters of the seventies.

Amid such a prodigality of cattle, such a lack of market for cattle, such a desperate need for a market, and such lawless confusion, the hide and tallow factories of the Texas coast sprang up to do a business the like of which no other region of North America has ever seen.

Statistics on the exportation of tallow and hides from the United States show that from 21,000,000 pounds of tallow and $292,000 worth of hides sent out in 1869 the figures soared to 102,000,000 pounds of tallow and $2,560,000 worth of hides in 1874 and that in 1875 the value of hides exported rose to $4,730,000. The rawhide reata, which the vaqueros of Texas and Spanish America had used for generations, was coming into use on ships. Something was stirring in Texas.

The requirements for setting up a packery were exceedingly simple. Any man with a herd of cattle that he could not dispose of otherwise might set up a packery in which to take off their hides and make "salt junk" of their meat. Or he might merely save the tallow along with the hides and throw the carcasses to hogs, buzzards, and coyotes.

Thus, when in the spring of 1867 an Englishman named Williams who had a ranch on the Frio River in Southwest Texas found that nobody wanted his cattle, he went into partnership with a Doctor Hughes living at Indianola on Matagorda Bay. Williams was to furnish the beef and Hughes the capital for setting up and operating a packery, and they were to divide evenly the proceeds. Some barrels of salt, a slaughter shanty, pens, vats, ropes, pulleys, butcher knives, and containers for the meat products were the chief equipment of the packery. By the time Williams could gather up a bunch of his cattle and drive them to the coast, Hughes was ready for business. They made a fine extract of beef that they could hardly give away; they sold prime salt beef at $9 a barrel of 200 pounds and salted tongues at $10 a barrel. The business proved a failure, and within less than a year's time Williams sold out his ranch claim and the remnant of his stock—on credit.

How many such packeries as the Hughes-Williams packery sprang up along the Gulf Coast it would be hard to say. At one time in the early seventies a dozen or more were exporting their products through Rockport, the chief center of the packing business for Texas. Rockport became a rival of Galveston. Perhaps the most noted of the Rockport concerns was that owned by W. S. Hall. During eight years of operation he slaughtered more than 40,000 head of cattle, 11,000 head in his peak year.

These packeries used no ice, and while a considerable amount of meat was salted and pickled—Hall, for instance, marketing a thousand barrels in New Orleans one year—tens of thousands of cattle were killed for their hides alone. The old saying, "stingy enough to skin a flea for his hide and tallow," may well have come into popular usage about this time.

At many of the packeries the cooked meat, after the tallow was rendered out, was either fed to hogs or else dumped into the water. Some parts of the animal, such as the loin, which has no tallow in it, were fed to the hogs raw or given to anybody who would haul them away. At times one could haul off *free* a wagon load of the choicest loin steaks.

Much of the waste of the Rockport factories was thrown into

the bay, where shoals of fish fed on it.They could be seined very easily. On shore near by was a hillock, perhaps five acres square, of discarded carcasses that stank to high heaven. In the fall and winter thousands upon thousands of ducks and geese gorged upon it. Finally some Yankees bought the mountain for a song, made the stuff into fertilizer, and shipped it north.

Unless the figures have been juggled, Rockport and Corpus Christi, a few miles away, to leave out of the account all other Texas ports, sent out nearly 300,000 cow hides in 1872.

The big ranches of Texas at this time were all on the coast line, and nearly every one of them had a hide and tallow factory. Captain Mifflin Kenedy, between Corpus and Brownsville, had a packery in which he slaughtered only his own cattle. Salt lakes in his pasture supplied the salt.

Captain Richard King, who established his great ranch in 1853 and who was for years in partnership with Captain Kennedy, had a rendering establishment even before the Civil War. He "attempted to preserve meat for shipment by infusing brine into veins of cattle immediately after they were slaughtered." The experiment proved unsuccessful, however, and thereafter he had his Mexicans pour the tallow into barrels, hang the hides on fences and cast the meat to some six or seven thousand hogs.

At Fulton, only a few miles above Rockport, Coleman, Mathis and Fulton had an extensive packery. At the mouth of the Colorado River W. B. Grimes, whose Rancho Grande branded 25,000 "calves and mavericks" in 1871, had a hide and tallow factory that consumed from one to three hundred head of cattle a day. According to Charlie Siringo, many of them were strays.

In the same vicinity, at Tres Palacios, the noted "Shanghai" (A. H.) Pierce conducted his establishment. He had a way of buying a mixed stock of cattle, butchering the beeves, and then clearing enough on the hides and tallow to pay for the entire herd, thus retaining the stock cattle as "velvet." Massive framed, bugle-voiced, infinite in wit and anecdote, imperious as well as genial in manner, "Old Shang" was known wherever longhorn cows bellowed. He rode through the country with a negro leading a pack horse loaded with gold and silver. When he reached a camp at which he was to receive cattle, he had the negro dump the money sacks on the ground. Then after the cattle were delivered, maybe a week later, he spread a blanket on the ground and on it counted out the money to pay for them.[2]

But the biggest operators in the coast country, both in range cattle and in the hide and tallow business, were Allen and Poole. Estimates of their holdings in the early seventies vary from 146,000 head of cattle to 300,000 head. Very likely they did not know within 30,000 or 40,000 head how many cattle they actually owned. At their packery on Galveston Island they slaughtered during the winter of 1870–1871 "twenty thousand head of cattle for their hides and tallow alone."

At Houston and at other places in East Texas there were dozens of other packeries. These crude establishments that took their toll of hundreds of thousands of Texas cattle in the late sixties and in the seventies were not without precedent. The Texas colonists, like the Comanches and the Mexicans, knew how to jerk, or dry, beef. A staple article of diet with many of them was *carne asada,* or *tasajo*—"jerky" (from the Spanish word *charqui*), which is still prepared and used on many Texas ranches and which is yet an important article of commerce in Mexico. The Texas colonists brought with them also a knowledge of the art of pickling meat in salt brine.

The pickled beef was sometimes called "mess beef," and as early as 1844 "mess beef" was quoted on the Galveston market at $10 for a barrel of 200 pounds. At the same time dried beef was offered by Galveston stores at ten cents a pound. In 1851 or 1852 Gail Borden, who published the earliest permanent Texas newspaper, and whose name on cans of condensed milk—the process of making which he patented—has become familiar to millions, had an establishment at Galveston for putting up "meat biscuit,"

[2] It is doubtful if Texas ever produced a more picturesque character than Shanghai Pierce. What a pity that we do not have a full length portrait of him! McCoy, J. G., *Historical Sketches of the Cattle Trade* (Kansas City, 1874, pages 142–146), has a very frank and not altogether flattering sketch of him. In *The Cattleman,* Fort Worth, December, 1926, B. R. Grimes records a few impressions of him. The best thing that has been written about him is a single paragraph by George W. Saunders, in Vol. II of *The Trail Drivers of Texas* (San Antonio, 1923, pages 361–363).

a form of canned beef. At Jefferson on Caddo Lake, near the Louisiana line, there was, it seems, another packery in operation before the Civil War.

By 1875 choice beef cattle were too high to kill for their hides and tallow, and naturally the packeries became fewer. Yet some of the slaughter houses continued operating for several years, utilizing old cows, rough stags, cripples, lump-jawed steers, and "scalawag" stuff in general. By 1880, however, the packing industry in Texas had become negligible and was to remain negligible until a quarter of a century later, when the Armours and the Swifts came to Fort Worth. By 1880 the great coastal nursery of cattle was being drained of cattle to stock at soaring prices the plains not only of West Texas but of the Indian Territory, western Kansas, the Platte, the Yellowstone, and all that vast region of the Northwest that became so suddenly a cow country. Cow trails made a network over the Western world, the range was prosperous, and the poor-paying and wasteful but ravenous markets of the Gulf coast were razed to the earth.

CHAPTER IV

THE RAZORBACKS

The hog then known in Texas
Was a self-supporting grazer,
With a nose as long as a walking stick
And a back just like a razor.
—George Jackson, *Sixty Years in Texas*

WITH the establishment of the coast packeries a good, though not steady, demand arose for hogs to eat the vast amount of refuse. Most of the Texas hogs at that time were razorbacks. They ran wild like the longhorns, and the woods were full of them. Every landholder had a claim on the hogs that ranged on his land, though the claim, like that on maverick cattle, was sometimes hard to enforce. A few men made the raising, capturing, and selling of hogs a business, but ranch people generally paid the razorbacks little attention except in winter time, when the animals would be as fat on acorns as they were capable of getting. That was the season for cutting and marking the pigs and, with dogs, ropes, and guns, for catching a year's supply of lard and bacon.

A wild hog hunt was as exciting as the famed boar hunt of Europe. Some dogs were so well trained that two or three of them alone would bring in a small bunch of hogs, but before he could learn his business many a dog lost his life from a boar's tusk. These tusks grew to an enormous length, and many of the old boars were savage to the extreme. In fact, they were, when cornered, the most savage animals of the open range. If crowded by a horseman either with or without dogs, a boar was likely to rush under the horse and gash him very seriously. A boar when frenzied was not to be approached by any man on foot. Perhaps the best sport with wild hogs was to hunt them without dogs, sighting them out on openings in late evening or early morning and roping them before they could take cover.

A detailed account of an early day hog hunt in East Texas has been preserved in *A Hunter's Experiences in the Southern States of America,* by Captain Flack, "late of the Texan Rangers" (London, 1866).

An old hunter [says Captain Flack], towards the close of 1848, was bitten with the California gold-fever, and determined to start across the plains to El Paso, from thence to push his way to "the diggins"; but before he went he sold his cattle and land, and as he had two or three hundred head of half-wild hogs ranging round the bayous and swamps, . . . he determined to invite half-a-dozen hunters to assist him in killing down this stock, which he had decided to convert into pickled pork [and sell].

On the appointed morning, well-mounted and armed with smoothbores, rifles, and Colt's revolvers, we found ourselves starting for the lagoons, amongst the reeds and flags of which the hogs harboured, and where they frequently fell a prey to alligators. Upon reaching the first reed-bed we fired it, and as the flame drove out the hogs, we shot them.

For more than a fortnight we continued this work, each day killing as many of the animals as were fit for the purpose in the forenoon, and afterwards, assisted by seven or eight negroes, we cleaned and salted the pork. Each day, too, the cover became scarcer and scarcer, till at length only one tangled reed-bed was left to be burned, and in this were concealed some of the oldest and fiercest boars.

The old hunter, whose name was Green, warned us that we had better look out for these old fellows; for not only was the ground rotten and fetlock-deep in mud, but the boars were, as he expressed it, "some considerably riled" at the incessant persecution and disturbance to which they had of late been subjected.

As soon as all had taken their stations, a light was applied to the reed-bed, which, fanned by a gentle breeze, soon burnt freely. Here and there, and in a dozen places at once, the tall flags and rushes could be seen shaking, as the hogs retreated before the flames. Gradually, but surely, the tongues of the flame licked up the rough jungle which each moment became more and more contracted.

Occasionally some of the younger and more inexperienced pigs broke from their covert, . . . but the older boars clung sullenly to the reeds and seemed determined to be burnt rather than leave the shelter. Nearer and nearer came the fire; and as the heat of the burning grass [increased] and the crackling of the stout stalks could be more plainly heard, the disturbance in the remaining cover increased. At last, when they could bear it no longer, out rushed the remaining pigs—in number about thirty.

Purvis, an old man of huge frame, was mounted on a small narrow-made pony, which was able, perhaps, to carry its owner's rifle, though not his person. At the time the hogs broke covert Purvis had fixed his eye upon a tremendous boar, and rode to give him the meeting. His rifle-bullet flattened upon the boar's shield (the side-skin [and gristle] over the shoulder and ribs is so called, and in old boars is frequently an inch and a half in thickness), and quick as thought the hog had upset the pony, and cut him from chest to thigh. Then suddenly turning upon Purvis, he would most likely have killed him had not Green perceived his comrade's danger and stopped the boar with a bullet in his brain.

At this moment one of the party broke the back of a half-grown pig, and its squeals soon gathered its fellows to its assistance; they "rallied" around it, their heads fronting outwards and their gleaming tusks clashing together as they churned the froth that flecked their breasts and shoulders.

Riding round them, we brought our rifles and pistols to bear upon their foreheads, and, one after another, they were killed. Although this may appear a senseless slaughter, it was in reality a most useful one to the incoming occupant of the land; for had these, or any of these, wild pigs been left, they would have enticed away the tame stock about to be introduced; but having cleared these useless beasts away, a little attention only was necessary to control their successors and keep them tame.

Sometimes the settlers made traps to catch the hogs. A trap was nothing but a picket pen with a door swung from the top. The door opened inward when pushed against and fell shut as soon as force against it was released. It could not open outward. Many of the hogs were used to trying to get inside the wood-fenced cornfields. Some corn would be sprinkled around the pen up to the gate. The gate was not solid and the hog to be trapped could see a profusion of corn under the gate, or door, and inside the pen. He would nose against the door, the door would open inward, and, head down, he would enter. Hard on his heels would follow another hog. Even if the door swung shut the trapped hogs would be too engaged—for a while—in eating to notice their imprisonment. Any hogs outside would be frantic to join in the feast and would very likely find the door. Thus several hogs might be trapped at once, among them great-tusked outlaw boars.

Occasional settlers along the coast seined fish to feed their hogs, but it is extremely doubtful if fish were ever fed in such a wholesale manner as that described by Theophilus Noel in his singular *Autobiography and Reminiscences* (published in Chicago, 1904). Noel, let it be understood, gave himself the credit for being "the greatest fish liar on earth" but at the same time a dealer in "the most remarkable fish truths" that a man ever heard.

"In my day and time," he says, "I have seen many strange things. . . . I have seen a scow, thirty feet long, fourteen feet wide, and two feet deep, moored in Corpus Christi Bay on a dark night amid a school of mullet, when by the raising of a lantern in the center of the boat and hitting the side with oars, in five minutes the boat would be filled, and in ten minutes be sunk by the mullets jumping into it if the light was not lowered. The boat load of mullet would be oared or pushed to the shore, where the people of Live Oak and adjoining counties (the hog counties of Texas) had driven thousands of hogs to be fattened on the mullet that were thrown out as the high tide receded."

During a period of years it was not necessary for the owners of hogs in some of the upland counties of Southwest Texas to drive their hogs to the fish and packery refuse of the coast in order to fatten them on a meat diet. In the spring of 1869 the Snyder brothers of Georgetown found range hogs in Mason County fat on the flesh of cattle that had been killed for their hides.[1] Sometimes cattle were killed for the hogs without much attention to the hides.

"About 1873," says Colonel Ike Pryor of San Antonio, "I contracted for a thousand dry cows in Mason County. When I went to receive the cows I found that about half of them had calves. I was going to drive the herd up the trail and could not take calves. I told the owner that I had contracted for cows and did not want anything else. He did not want the calves either and he told me to do as I pleased. I put the cattle in a pen, a bunch at a time, and had the calves killed—five hundred of them. The veal was fed to hogs, of which there were great numbers in the country."

Contrary to a rather popular opinion, the hog is not native to America, though the javelina (collared peccary) is. The razorback was the descendant of domesticated hogs that had been imported. Just when these domesticated hogs began to run wild and become as savage as their progenitors, the great boars of Europe and Asia, that have time out of mind been pursued by the most daring huntsmen, will probably never be known. Yet history is not altogether silent on the subject. When De Soto with his six hundred men landed in Florida, 1539, to explore for gold, he brought along "thirteen sows." A year later—marvelous example of reproductivity—the thirteen "had increased to three hundred swine," and an allowance of half a pound of pork daily, with some "boiled herbs," was affording, temporarily, the only food the Spanish fortune seekers had.[2] Not all the sows were killed, however, for after the Spaniards had wandered over the land two more years, the swine herd numbered "seven hundred," which, following De Soto's death, in Arkansas, were sold "at public outcry." "From that time forward," says the chronicle, "most of the people [i.e., survivors of the expedition] owned and raised hogs." A detachment of the exploring party now came on down into Texas, presumably

---

[1] *The Trail Drivers of Texas*, San Antonio, 1923, Vol. II, pp. 475–476.
[2] *The Narrative of the Expedition of Hernando de Soto*, by The Gentleman of Elvas, translated by Buckingham Smith, in *Spanish Explorers in the Southern United States*, edited by Frederick W. Hodge and Theodore H. Lewis, N. Y., 1897, p. 171; see also pp. 235, 252, 253.

bringing some of the hogs with them; when they got back into
Arkansas, in 1543, certain Indians gave them hogs—"the breeding of sows lost there the year before." It seems clear that De
Soto and his men left a seed of hogs in the land; and it is altogether probable that the first razorbacks of the South were
descended therefrom.

It is possible that some of the original Texas razorbacks
were the offspring of the wild pigs that Spaniards saw running
loose about the ruins of La Salle's fort, on Lavaca Bay, in
1689.[3] What prize-winning, pedigreed Duroc boar could trace
his line, or what beribboned Amazonian sow of Berkshire purity
could trace her line, to a De Soto sow or to a La Salle pig?
And some of the old Texas razorbacks may have had blood in
them from both sources! The boast of heraldry. . . .

Whatever their origin, the razorbacks were a hardy and
prolific breed. They throve in malarial marshes; they pushed
far ahead of settlers out into the roughest and most arid regions of the state, sometimes ranging as far as ten miles away
from water. They desired no choicer diet than a mixture of
tunas (prickly pear apples) and rattlesnakes. It is good to know
that a few of the old spotted razorbacks still exist in parts of
Southwest Texas. Until a short time ago they abounded in
the dry and broken Devil's River country. They were hunted
down and killed out of this sparsely settled region because they
are great enemies to lambs and kids, and the Devil's River
now belongs largely to the goat and sheep industry.

Coarsely and variously colored, long-snouted, long-tailed,
long-bodied, long-legged, long-tusked, even long in his squeal,
the razorback of Texas and the South became the theme for
a whole cycle of folk jokes and yarns. Modern pipeliners swear
that their mythological hero, Paul Bunyan, laid his famous line
through Arkansas by driving ahead of him a herd of razorbacks that rooted the ditch for the pipe. The story goes, too,
that in early days an Eastern tenderfoot who had recently ar-

[3] *Historical Documents relating to New Mexico, Nueva Vizcaya, and Approaches
Thereto, to 1773,* edited by Charles Wilson Hackett, Washington, D. C., 1926,
pp. 278–279.

rived in South Texas became very much interested in the native hogs. After learning how the settlers had to scour the country for hours sometimes before catching one of their hogs and then had to carry its dirty carcass for miles before getting home to butcher it, he exclaimed:

"All this must take an awful lot of trouble and time!"

"Yes," replied a settler, "it does take time, but, hell, what's time to a hog—and besides we have lots of fun."

The Tennessee version of the story—as told by the fertile anecdoter, L. L. Click, of Austin—goes better. A mountaineer was holding a razorback shoat in his arms and lifting him up so that he could "graze" on ripe persimmons still hanging on the tree. A stranger came along.

"You may get that hog fat after a while," he said to the mountainer, "but it's going to take you a mighty long time."

"Huh," replied the mountaineer, "what's time to a derned hawg?"

There was a time when Texans and citizens of other Southern states were not a bit ashamed of their respective varieties of razorbacks. One time, so one story goes, a real estate agent was showing a stranger some land in the Trinity River bottoms. The stranger saw what he took to be highwater marks far up on the trunks of the various trees and he called attention to these evidences of overflow.

"Oh, no, no," the agent corrected the prospective buyer, "them's not highwater marks at all. That's jest where our hawgs rubbed their backs. Let me tell you, man, this land grows the tallest hawgs in America."

A. L. Steele, of Lovington, New Mexico, who was born in Grimes County, Texas, 1841, tells another anecdote of the patriotic zeal with which some frontiersmen supported the razorback.

"Right after the close of the Civil War," says Mr. Steele, "I was in Natchez, Mississippi, with a herd of steers, from Navarro County. After we got them sold, Wash Little, who was with me, began to tank up on red-eye and to brag on Texas hogs. A Mississippian began glorifying the Mississippi variety, and in order to prevent a possible killing I had to take Wash across the river and stay all night in Vidalia."

Arkansas had zealous—and logical—advocates also, as a story recorded by Dallas T. Herndon in his *Centennial History of Arkansas* will illustrate. "Some swine breeders from other states brought their best specimens of fine stock—Chester White, Poland China, etc.—to a county fair in Arkansas. The local farmers exhibited their hogs, which still retained many of the points of the true razorback, and, to the surprise of the owners of the thoroughbreds, the native hogs won every prize. After the awards had been made, one of the importers approached one of the judges and said:

" 'We are not offended with your action in giving the prizes to your neighbors, but we feel confident that our hogs are superior in many respects to those you have favored, and just for information I would like to ask upon what points you judges based your decision.'

" 'Well, stranger,' replied the judge, 'there's no doubt that your hogs could be fattened easier and made to weigh more, but the trouble is they can't run fast enough.'

" 'Can't run fast enough?' exclaimed the swine breeder. 'This is the first time I ever heard of speed being a good qualification in a hog. Why should a hog be able to run fast?'

" 'The niggers, sir, the niggers,' replied the judge. 'Your hogs would be all right for meat, but the niggers could steal them too easily. With our hogs they would have more trouble in catching them. Do you get the point?'

"The exhibitor evidently got the point, as the conversation ended and he took his fine hogs back home, having learned a lesson in swine breeding that he had previously overlooked."

It used to be a saying in East Texas that a good hog was a hog that could "outrun a nigger and outfight a bear." Bears and panthers were the worst natural enemies that the hogs had. Coyotes would steal the pigs if they got a chance, but an ordinary sow could hold her own against any kind of wolf, and no coyote dared face a grown razorback. In order to protect their offspring, sows with pigs often ran together, the bunches of pigs sometimes aggregating fifty or sixty head.

The very word "hog-wallow" has produced no end of argument among people of the soil. A large number of them have stubbornly held that the depressions in the black lands of Central Texas were caused by the wallowing of early day razorbacks and thus properly acquired their name, hog-wallows. On the other hand, not a few citizens have held that the hog-wallows came as a result of "the seven years" drouth back in the time of the Spaniards." During that awful drouth, they argue, cracks cleft the ground so wide and deep that, even after the seven years of rain that followed, numerous sinks—improperly called hog-wallows—marked where they had been.

Once famous and still pretty well known was the farmer who kept his hogs from falling through the drouth cracks in the land by tying their tails into knots. Equally noted was the man who sought to prevent his hogs from getting out through chinks in the picket fence by tying their tails together, pair by pair. However, it is said that some of the razorbacks learned to walk backwards, and that while one of a pair snouted forward his mate backed after him, many of the couples thus escaping. The razorback was indeed a "right smart" animal. He liked mustang grapes, and when the grapes were well ripe but not yet dropping, he would reach up as high as he could—which was pretty high—clinch a grape-vine in his jaws, and shake and tug so as to cause the fruit to fall.

Not all of the razorbacks kept their long tails. Many of the settlers while marking the pigs bobbed off their tails. There was a joke explanation of this curtailment also. The explanation was that a razorback in his native element, mud, gathered such a heavy ball on his long tail that it pulled the skin backward from his snout so tightly that he could not close his eyes. The tails just had to be bobbed in order for the razorbacks to get sleep.

Jest as one may, when our beef diet was varied almost exclusively by crackling corn bread and salt pork with beans, the razorback furnished a large portion of our food.

One winter the acorns failed. Hogs in Southwest Texas were plentiful but they were too poor to kill. However, the Middle West had a big crop of corn that year and the demand for hogs to eat it was brisk. If we could not eat our own hogs, we could sell them and buy bacon and lard from somebody else's hogs. A hundred miles to the northeast of Refugio, where I was living, Flatonia, then the terminus of the G. H. and S. A. Railroad, afforded a shipping point. We decided to gather up a bunch of the razorbacks and drive them to Flatonia, either to ship or sell.

We worked for about a month roping and hauling hogs to a large pen and finally got six hundred and fifty together. When we were ready to start, all the neighbors and their dogs were present to help. The country around the pens was an open prairie. The gate was opened and the hogs stampeded out, scattering in every direction. While a man was roping one and dragging him back to the bunch, a dozen others would get away. We lost two hundred head before we got out of sight of the pen. At last, though, with the dogs all around them, the razorbacks bunched together and we started on the trail. They kept together pretty well the rest of the day.

That night we penned them in a corral made of pickets and chinked up all the big cracks. The next day we reached the San Antonio River, where we lost fifty head before we got the herd into the water. Hogs, however, are good swimmers, and, after the leaders started across, the others followed.

We had now got the "critters" away from their accustomed range, and from the San Antonio River on they gave us little trouble. The chuck wagon kept ahead of them, and every now and then the cook would throw out a few ears of corn to encourage them on. We lost a few at the Guadalupe River, which we crossed near the town of Cuero—the meaning of which in English, by the way, is *hide,* or *rawhide.* At Flatonia we sold the razorbacks at $6.50 a head and felt that we had made both a good trade and a good riddance.

Now trailing hogs must have been a pretty old business.

In 1827, for instance, the keeper of a turnpike gate near the Cumberland River certified that 105,517 hogs had during that year been driven through the gate on their way to the South Atlantic states.[4] But no doubt most of these hogs were gentle hogs and were driven by men afoot or by men who rode merely to keep from walking. The cowboy manner of roping, running, herding, and trailing hogs in Southwest Texas was something new in hog history. It was only after they came to Texas that hog drovers learned the cowboy manner of handling hogs.

In the sixties and seventies a pork-packing industry at Alexandria, Missouri, attracted tens of thousands of hogs from as far as one hundred miles away. Some of the droves numbered as high as a thousand hogs each and were days on the road, stringing out for a mile or more. Like the cowboys, the hog drovers developed sing-song chants to quiet their charges. One of the chants ran something like this:

> Hog up, hog up.
> Forty cents a day and no dinner.
> Straw bed and no cover.
> Corn bread and no butter.
> Hog up, hog up.

"When night came the drive would stop at some farmer's house and bed down. Most of the farmers living along the road had some sort of corral which could be used to enclose the herd. If the night was cold and stormy, some of the drovers would have to sit up with the herd and keep the hogs from piling up and smothering."[5]

On November 7, 1848, N. M. Dennis and Joe Dennis, with their wives, seventeen children, one cousin, and one negro slave, left Madison County, Arkansas, for Texas with three two-horse wagons, one ox-wagon, and five hundred head of young hogs. Two boys on foot and the negro drove them. The

[4] *Yearbook*, United States Department of Agriculture, 1908, p. 228.
[5] "Driving Hogs to Mississippi River Markets in Missouri," by Louis R. Grinstead, *Wallace's Farmer*, Oct. 12, 1928, quoted in *Missouri Historical Review*, Vol. XXIII, No. 2, Jan., 1929, pp. 323-326.

weather turned so cold that the negro nearly froze to death and several of the hogs did freeze to death. The hogs lived on what they could root out of the ground along the way and the families lived on the hogs. They ate hog meat and they traded hogs to the Indians and settlers for corn. They had left behind them a crib full of corn for which there was no market, but as they approached Red River they found it impossible to get more than a bushel of corn from any one man. One settler bought eighty of the hogs for $80. The hogs swam Red River and then the Brazos River. On February 7, 1849, exactly three months after leaving Arkansas, the Dennis tribe halted in Milam County and prepared to settle. They had sixty head of the five hundred hogs left. As a member of the tribe recorded long afterwards,[6] hog raising in that part of Texas was about the safest stock business the settlers could engage in. The Indians could not steal hogs as they stole horses, and neighborly cow thieves let them alone.

When the full history of trail driving is finally written it will have to include not only the trailing of longhorn cattle, but the trailing of mustang horses, burros, razorbacks, and turkeys. In a day when there were no fences or railroads every animal as well as every man had to stand on his own legs.

At the very time when hogs were being trailed east from Southwest Texas, burros were being trailed from the same place to Colorado for use in the mines. They, too, ran wild like the hogs, particularly in the country between the Nueces River and the Rio Grande. It was not until about 1923 that the King Ranch succeeded in clearing its range of wild burros.

The raising and driving of domestic turkeys for wholesale market in Texas is a very modern industry, but turkeys were actually trailed—long ago when a mile was still a mile. George Bruffey, Nestor of the Montana ranges, has told[7] how in 1863, while still a hundred and twenty-five miles from Denver, he overtook a man who was driving to that place a drove of 500

[6] Dennis, J. J., *A History of the Life of J. J. Dennis and Reminiscences of Early Days in Texas*, 1903, pp. 1–5.
[7] *Eighty-One Years in the West*, by George A. Bruffey, Butte, Montana, 1925, p. 27.

turkeys that he had bought in Iowa and Missouri. He had two boys to help him, and when the wind was favorable they had an easy time, making as much as twenty-five miles a day. He had a big wagon full of shelled corn. The turkeys foraged on grasshoppers and at night they "roosted all over the wagon and sprawled in the sand." They were always up by daybreak looking for grasshoppers. The owner arrived in Denver with his herd of turkeys intact and he cleared good money.

A more realistic account of turkey trailing comes from that entertaining and informing book, *Arizona Characters,* by Frank C. Lockwood.[8] One of the pioneer ranchmen of Arizona, Henry C. Hooker, was in 1866 prospering with a hardware store in Hangtown (Placerville), California, when a fire destroyed everything he had but about a thousand dollars and a dependent family. Compelled to make a new start, he bought, at $1.50 per bird, 500 turkeys from settlers about Hangtown, and, amid jests and banter, set out to drive them to Carson City, Nevada, which was then booming.

With the aid of one helper and several trained dogs, he headed his strange procession across the mountain tops beyond which lay his Italy. As he was coming down the mountain not far from his destination, he was suddenly confronted by a precipice too steep to descend and all but impossible to skirt. The dogs so pressed and worried the birds, trying to force them to make the descent, that they finally became desperate and took to the air. Said Colonel Hooker: "As I saw them take wing and race away through the air I had the most indescribable feeling of my life. I thought, here is good-bye turkeys! My finances were at the last ebb; these turkeys were my whole earthly possession, and they seemed lost. . . ."

But the case was not as bad as it seemed. In the valley below, Hooker, his helper, and his dogs succeeded in rounding up the aerial squadron and steering it once more towards Carson City and Victory. The turkeys brought five dollars apiece. By this Napoleonic stroke Hooker recouped his fortunes. With the profit that he realized from the sale of his turkeys he laid the foundations of his Arizona fortune and his fame as a stockman.

[8] Los Angeles, California, 1928, pp. 141–143.

CHAPTER V

THE BLOODY BORDER [1]

"How many men have you killed?" a boy in Eagle Pass asked the noted bad man, King Fisher, some time before he was shot to death, with the equally noted Ben Thompson, in the Jack Harris Theatre of San Antonio, 1884. At the time the boy asked the question one might have read a very plain sign that marked a certain fork, near Pendencia Creek, in one of the few roads of Dimmit County—on the border.

The sign read:

THIS IS KING FISHER'S ROAD. TAKE THE OTHER.

"How many men have you killed?"

And the soft answer was, "Seven—just seven."

"Oh," the boy exclaimed in a disappointed tone, "I thought that it must be more than that."

"I don't count Mexicans," explained King Fisher.

He did not count Mexicans, though down in Dimmit County he is popularly credited with having made away with nineteen. Once, for instance, he killed three *pelados* (a contemptuous name used by many border gringos and resented by all Mexicans) on the north side of the Nueces. He had a Mexican who worked with him to cross over horseback and drag the dead men at the end of a rope to the south side. On another occasion he killed a "greaser" across the Rio Grande from Eagle Pass, and he had the same faithful Charon rope the dead body and drag it across to the Texas side. His motive

[1] A bibliography of the sources from which this chapter has been derived will be found in "Appendix A" at the back of the book.

for having dead Mexicans cross the water instead of leaving them in it has not been explained.[2]

"He's killed —— white men and no telling how many Mexicans," is a phrase still to be heard all over the Southwest. The phrase used to be a great deal commoner than it is now. To understand that phrase and to understand the next chapter in this life of a border vaquero, we must go back nearly a hundred years. In Southwest Texas the battle of San Jacinto, which made Texas a republic free from Mexican domination, did not end the warfare between Texans and Mexicans. Rather it marked the beginning of that warfare. Much has been said of the troubles between frontiersmen and Indians, but for fifty years and more the clashes between Texas frontiersmen and Mexicans along, and for 150 miles back from, the Rio Grande were so frequent and bloody that they probably cost ten times as many lives as did the struggle between frontiersmen and Indians in the same territory.

While Texas was a dependency of Mexico, the country between the Nueces River and Rio Grande was a part of the state of Tamaulipas. When Santa Anna, President of Mexico and Commander-in-chief of the Mexican armies, surrendered at San Jacinto, he acknowledged the boundary between the new republic and his own country to be the Rio Grande. The Mexican Congress, however, soon denied the existence of any boundary whatsoever, asserting that Texas was still a part of Mexico. For twelve years, theoretically and by overt acts, Mexico maintained that claim, relinquishing it only at the peace of Guadalupe Hidalgo, 1848, which marked the close of the United States-Mexican War.

Meantime and for years to follow, a wide stretch of territory along the left bank of the Rio Grande was little more than a no man's land. Before the Texas Revolution (1835–1836) Irish immigrants had settled around San Patricio just east of the

<hr/>

[2] The author is not prepared to swear to all the statements here made about King Fisher. Some of them are based on an article by W. A. Bonnet in *Frontier Times*, Bandera, Texas, July, 1926; others are based on oral reminiscences of old frontiersmen. Like Billy the Kid and other celebrities of the kind, King Fisher has become rather legendary.

Nueces River near the coast. During the Revolution they left, and it was years before their territory was resettled. When the Mexican troops withdrew from Texas, many of the Mexican ranchers between the Nueces and the Rio Grande withdrew also, and then Texas cowboys—the name "cowboy" seems to have come into popular use about this time—raided into that territory, driving out wild cattle and horses. Sometimes they crossed the Rio Grande and got more cattle.

The Mexicans could also raid. Early in 1842 Mexican forces swept up into Texas and for a few days occupied Goliad, Refugio, Victoria, and San Antonio. President Sam Houston wrote to the Texas consul at New Orleans that every man immigrating into the new republic from the United States should bring with him "a good rifle or musket, with a cartouch box, or shot pouch and powder horn, with at least one hundred rounds of ammunition, a good knapsack and six months' clothing, and enter service for six months subject to the laws of Texas."

In September of the same year General Woll at the head of a second Mexican army captured San Antonio. Texans pursued him to the Rio Grande, from which place their commander ordered them to turn back. But some three hundred of the men refused to obey orders. The three hundred marched against Mier in Mexico, lost ten men in a battle in which they killed—according to unofficial report—seven hundred Mexicans, and then surrendered. The subsequent treatment of the prisoners became a memory for Texans to add to the undying memories of Goliad and the Alamo.

The concentration of American troops on the Rio Grande that marked the opening of the Mexican War shortly after the entrance of Texas into the Union gave for a while security to the lower country. And among these American troops, it may be noted, Texas volunteers distinguished themselves as rebels to discipline as well as fighters against Mexican armies. When the war was over, the United States promptly became oblivious of Texas border troubles and Mexican raids were resumed, though by bandits rather than by troops. The few American soldiers left on the border were for the most part green recruits furnished with green, unacclimated Missouri horses. They chased Comanches in mule-drawn wagons; they could not tell the difference at sight between a *corrida* of King Ranch vaqueros and a gang of *bandido* cow thieves.

Texas had entered the Union largely because it was bankrupt, financially unable to support a government and police its far-stretched borders. The finances of the state were for a long time almost as meager as had been those of the republic. Nevertheless, when the Federal government failed to afford protection, the state government raised militia and rangers to patrol the frontier. The militia and rangers repeatedly suppressed banditry, then on account of the expense of maintenance were withdrawn. When they withdrew, the bandits from across the Rio Bravo repeatedly returned. Thus there was but one thing for the scattered frontiersmen to do: become their own protectors and law enforcers. It was a rôle that custom brought them to accept as a part of the natural order of things.

Although the Comanches and Apaches raided and killed in Mexico as mercilessly as in Texas, there was a tendency among frontier Texans to place Indians and Mexicans in the same category. The tendency was not without some justification. Thus in 1855 a troop of Texans under Captain J. H. Callahan that had pursued a band of hostile Indians across the Rio Grande found themselves confronted by a combined force of Indians and Mexicans. The Texans in retreating burned Piedras Negras, across the river from Eagle Pass. This Captain Callahan may be regarded as representative of a not uncommon type of frontier Texan—though there were other types. He helped to give the border an inheritance that it has not forgotten. He was "pizen" unadulterated for Indians and Mexican horse thieves. He was a fighter "from who laid the chunk." Shortly before he led the expedition into Mexico he had returned to Texas from accompanying a herd of cattle to California, for which service he was paid $1500, not because he was an unusually good trail boss but because he was regarded as the best Indian fighter in the country. How he dealt with Mexican horse thieves is well described by A. J. Sowell in his illuminating book, *Rangers and Pioneers of Texas.*

One day along in the fifties, as Sowell tells the story, Captain Callahan and some of his men surprised a gang of Mexican horse thieves in a thicket on York's Creek near Seguin. They killed three or four of them, the others getting away through the brush. The next morning while attempting to trail down some of the escaped Mexicans, Callahan's rangers came upon a Mexican who was wounded in the leg. He made signs that he wanted to surrender. Callahan rode near and asked him if he wanted to go to Seguin. The Mexican replied that he did. "All right," said the captain, "get on behind me." The Mexican, having bound his leg with a large silk handkerchief, began hopping towards Callahan's horse to get up. The ranger captain drew his pistol and shot him dead.

"In our day and time," says Sowell, writing in 1884, "this would look cruel and brutal, but those were desperate times, and it was death to all horse thieves when caught; and we too must remember that the Texans had suffered terrible things at the hands of the Mexicans. The Alamo and Goliad were still fresh in their minds, but they never shot Mexican soldiers taken in battle."

Another time some of Callahan's rangers captured two Mexican horse thieves, brought them to Seguin, and turned them over to Captain Callahan for judgment. He immediately ordered them shot, and led the way to some live oak trees out from town. There the two condemned men were given picks and shovels and ordered to dig their own graves. One of the Mexicans was an old man, and he dug away in an unconcerned manner, "taking particular pains" to make a good grave. The other was a young man; he wept, protested his innocence, and was so nervous that he could hardly work. The captain explained to him that there was no convenient jail and that therefore the execution would have to be expedited. Finally, when the graves were finished, Callahan's men drew lots to see who must do the shooting. Some of them did not want to take part in such work.

"At the signal the guns all fired except one. Calvin Turner's missed fire. Both Mexicans fell over at the discharge. The old man was killed dead, but the young one was breathing freely when they came up to where the Mexicans lay.

" 'Turner,' said Callahan, 'being as your gun missed fire, you can finish this fellow.'

"The ranger thus addressed, without a word, primed his rifle and, stepping back a few paces, took a quick aim and fired, the ball striking in the head and killing the Mexican instantly."

As the impending doom of slavery drew nearer, Mexicans in some places plotted with negro slaves to rise against the whites. In 1856 a committee of Colorado County citizens reported thus: "We are satisfied that the lower class of the Mexican population are incendiaries in any country where slaves are held, and should be dealt with accordingly. And, for the benefit of the Mexican population, we should here state that a resolution was passed by the unanimous voice of the county, forever forbidding any Mexican coming within the limits of the county." Matagorda County in a similar way expelled all Mexicans. In Uvalde County some time later Mexicans traveling the public roads were forced to produce passes.

During the fifties and sixties Mexicans were doing a great deal of freighting in Texas. They were hauling in their ox carts, from the coast to San Antonio and from San Antonio to Chihuahua and other points in Mexico, goods to the value of millions of dollars annually. In 1857 the intense feeling against Mexicans took the disgraceful form known as the Cart War. This Cart War was nothing less than an effort on the part of certain Texas ruffians to run Mexican freighters out of business. At Goliad old timers still point out the live oak tree to which some of the ruffians were hanged. As the Mexicans freighted for less than their American competitors, business interests protected them.

It would be a mistake, however, to suppose that clashes between Anglo-Texans and Mexican-Texans were during all these years constant. Mexican land owners who had fled from Texas in 1836 gradually came back and restocked their ranches.

Conditions during the fifties were really improving, though shrewd speculators were scheming to get possession of lands owned by Mexicans and, naturally, local Mexicans were restless. Then came the climax of all border troubles in the person of Juan Nepomuceno Cortina, "the Red Robber of the Rio Grande," the most striking, the most powerful, the most insolent, and the most daring as well as the most elusive Mexican bandit, not even excepting Pancho Villa, that ever wet his horse in the muddy waters of the Rio Bravo. He was born on the Rio Grande, a few miles above Brownsville, and belonged to one of the best border families of Spanish-Mexican days. When he emerged as supreme chieftain over some hundreds of *bandidos,* he was forty years old. In person he was a *huero,* or red-complexioned man, blocky in build, powerful of muscle, a wonderful horseman, so ignorant that he could hardly sign his name, "the expression of his face sinister, sensual, and cruel." His fellow patriots affectionately called him Cheno.

As spy and guerrilla he had served in the Mexican army against Taylor's invading forces; he was later promoted to a lieutenancy, but upon being detected in the act of selling horses belonging to the Mexican government he was dismissed from the service. In 1847 he murdered his employer, a Texan named Somerville. A year or two later he was openly stealing horses and cattle in Texas. The grand jury of Cameron County indicted him for theft and murder, but he played hide-and-seek across the Rio Grande until the case was dropped. Just when he and his family established themselves in Texas is not known. The historian of the Karankawa tribe of Indians, A. S. Gatschet, quotes authority for the statement that in 1858 Cortina and some other rancheros wiped out the last surviving band of the Karankawas, the band having returned to this side of the Rio Grande from their temporary refuge in Mexico. Before this, Juan Cortina's brother had been elected tax assessor of Cameron County and Juan himself had become a power in politics courted by county office-seekers. At times he claimed to be a citizen of Mexico; at other times, a citizen of the United States. His mother had a ranch, the San José, a few miles above Brownsville on the Texas side. It was in the brush, "an asylum for horse and cattle thieves, robbers, and murderers, for those men whose enemies would not permit them to live on the Mexican side of the river or who dared not show themselves in the thickly settled part of the state."

In the spring of 1859 Cortina was indicted anew for horse theft—and his real career began. For a while after the indictment he retired to the brushy safety of the Rancho San José; then he began appearing in Brownsville, always armed, always with friends around him. One July day when he was in Brownsville he saw a deputy sheriff haling to jail in no very gentle manner a Mexican who had been his, Cortina's, servant. He ordered the deputy to desist. The deputy did not desist. Thereupon Cortina shot him in the shoulder, put the rescued prisoner up behind him on his own horse, and rode across the river to Matamoros—where the populace at once acclaimed him as the defender of Mexican rights. The sheriff of Cameron County tried to arrest him, but failed. Cortina swore revenge against the sheriff and against all other men who had shown or should show sympathy against him.

A short while before daybreak on the morning of September 28, 1859, the citizens of Brownsville were awakened by cries of *"Viva Cortina! Viva Mexico! Maten los gringoes!"* (Kill the Americans!) There were hardly forty Americans in the town, though the total population probably amounted to 2000; all American troops had been withdrawn. The Mexicans killed five citizens, turned a dozen *pelado* culprits out of jail, and established themselves in the deserted garrison of Fort Brown. Thus Cortina began his reign of terror over the whole lower Rio Grande country. For more than fifteen years thereafter he plundered and murdered.

The year 1859 found in command of the Department of Texas one of various bull-headed and minus-brained United States Army officers that have bungled affairs on the Texas borders, General D. E. Twiggs. In March of that year he declared: "There is not, nor ever has been, any danger of the Mexicans crossing on [to] our side of the river to plunder or disturb its inhabitants, and the outcry on that river for troops is solely to have an expenditure of the public money." He had already ordered Fort Brown (Brownsville), Ringgold Barracks (Rio Grande City), and Fort McIntosh (Eagle Pass) abandoned; he was expecting to patrol the road between San Antonio and Eagle Pass, most of it infested by Comanches, with a few companies of infantry! Fortunately, early in March, 1860, he was relieved from command in Texas by Colonel Robert E. Lee, but a year later the Civil War broke out and then for four years the Texas border was a matter that concerned nobody but the people on it.

Cortina remained in possession of Fort Brown only a few days. Then he retired to his mother's ranch, which he set about fortifying, meanwhile beginning the issue of a series of proclamations in the tone of a righteous liberator. "Our purpose has been," he said, "to punish the infamous villainy of our enemies. They have banded together . . . to pursue and rob us for no other reason except that we are by birth Mexicans. . . . An organized society of Mexicans in the state of Texas will untiringly devote itself to the extermination of their tyrants until its philanthropic purpose of bettering the condition of the unfortunate Mexicans who reside here shall have been attained."

As soon as Cortina got out of sight, the citizens of Brownsville organized a guard. Their cries for help were frantic. The governor of Texas sent Captain W. G. Tobin and Captain John S. Ford ("Old Rip") with rangers to clear the country. At the same time General Twiggs, although declaring the reports concerning Cortina to be "mostly false," dispatched Major S. P. Heintzelman, with about one hundred and fifty troops, to occupy Fort Brown and patrol the border. Heintzelman proved to have horse sense—a rare quality for a United States officer in Texas.

Combining forces, the soldiers and rangers dislodged Cortina from the San José and then for months chased him up and down and over the Rio Grande. By June of 1860, according to Heintzelman's report, fifteen Americans and eighty friendly Mexicans had been killed, while Cortina had lost one hundred and fifty-one men. Before he was driven across the Rio Grande Cortina sacked Rio Grande City. "The whole country from Brownsville to Rio Grande City, 120 miles, and back to the Arroyo Colorado," concluded the report, "has been laid waste, the citizens driven out, their horses and cattle driven across the Rio Grande into Mexico, and there sold, a cow with a calf by her side for a dollar." Many of the Mexican ranch houses that Cortina left because they belonged to his friends were burned by the Texans.

During the time of the Civil War Cortina became a brigadier general in the Mexican army. The United States government forces on the lower Rio Grande made an alliance with him, and one of the commanders, so it is claimed by Ford, promised him a brigadiership in the Union army if he would take Brownsville from the Confederates. That was one brigadiership that he failed to win. He declared against Maximilian, who had become emperor of Mexico, and took possession of Matamoros. When Maximilian was captured and executed in 1867, Cortina naturally stood in the good graces of the incoming regime. He became so powerful that he "made and unmade governors." Partly owing to the cotton trade, no doubt, the border had been "astonishingly quiet" during most of the time of the Civil War, but in 1868 the Cortinistas began depredating on Texas property with an energy and ferocity and in a wholesale manner that had no precedent.

In the early seventies conditions became intolerable. The United States military forces, some of them negroes, were too busy reconstructing Texas citizens to do much towards quelling depredations on the lives and property of those citizens. The state government, under Davis, was a disgrace. However, in 1874, Davis was forcibly ousted, and the next year Captain L. H. McNelly got busy with his famous company of rangers. In defiance of United States orders he crossed the Rio Grande and administered a sound thrashing to the Cortinistas at Cortina's noted ranch of Las Cuevas. In 1876 Don Porfirio Diaz, President of Mexico, took General Cortina prisoner and thereafter kept him under surveillance in Mexico City until sometime along in the nineties, when the "Red Robber" died.

So much for the military side of Cortina's career. The story of his banditry is much more interesting and much more important. At times he had hundreds of bandits operating under him. He notified thieves in Mexico that he would hang them for stealing in that country but that there was plenty for them to steal in Texas. His agreement was to take care of them in Mexico if they would take care of themselves in Texas. All of Texas between the Rio Grande and the Nueces, he time and again announced, belonged to Mexico—and him. One condition only he placed on thieves operating over the territory that he claimed: they must pay him a percentage of their loot. Occasionally he ordered a few of the bandits hanged, not because they were bandits but because they were raiding independently and failing to give him "the royal fifth." His men called the cattle they stole "Nanita's cattle," meaning that these cattle belonged to them by right of inheritance.

And Nanita had plenty of cattle. Following the close of the Civil War, the noted "Rip" Ford was acting as guide to United States troops on the border, and in 1867 he estimated that of stray cattle alone there were 200,000 head in "The Sands" (a great range north and west of Brownsville), many of the strays bearing brands of cowmen living on the northern banks of the Colorado River.

Between the Nueces River—once called "the dead line of sheriffs"—and the Rio Grande lies a tract of land 300 miles long and from one to two hundred miles wide. The assessment rolls of 1870 showed ownership of 299,193 cattle and 73,593 horses in this region. Live Oak and McMullen counties made no tax returns. Tens of thousands of mustangs and thousands of mavericks were claimed by nobody. In all probability the number of cattle and horses actually grazing in the territory totaled well up towards a million. The ranch homes were in some places grouped together for protection; in other places they were solitary. Over much of the territory one might ride for twenty, forty, or fifty miles without seeing a house. Eighty per cent of the inhabitants were Mexicans. The sheriffs of some of the counties were in their graves. There were a few rangers, a few soldiers. The Stock Raisers' Association of Western Texas, the first organization of its kind in America, was in a very loose way seeking to protect cattlemen in the branding of stock, in the sale of beef cattle, and against thieves. Against organized bands of invaders, here today and yonder tomorrow, it could do little. The country was exclusively a stock country.

The plunder was wholesale, immense. How many cattle Cortina came to own will never be known. He stocked the Canela, the Soldadito, the Caritas, the Palito Blanco and other ranches on his side of the river with Texas stock. He made contracts for delivering cattle to be shipped to Cuba from Bagdad, a Mexican port near the mouth of the Rio Grande through which Confederate cotton was exported in enormous quantities after the Confederacy had been effectually blockaded elsewhere. Joseph E. Dwyer, on July 5, 1875, in a communication to General E. O. C. Ord, commanding the Department of Texas, told of Cortina's having delivered 3500 head of cattle to a Spaniard at Bagdad, "more than two-thirds of them Texas cattle."

As the raiding progressed, some of the ranchmen of the lower country gathered together what they could of their herds and set out towards the interior of the state. But the arm of the Red Robber was long. In 1867 his men were raiding as far inland as the San Antonio River. According to W. S. Hall, a stockman of the territory that Cortina claimed and owner of one of the coast packeries, the Mexicans stole 7000 cattle from him, all within a short period of time. He followed the cattle across the river and found them, some of them at least, but the requirements of the Mexican officials were such that it would have cost him more to get them back into Texas than they were worth. So he just let them go.

W. D. Thomas, Texan, saw a captain of the Mexican army driving a herd of 400 stolen cattle along a road on the Mexican side of the river. The captain said: "The gringos are raising cows for me." Generally there were more than enough *bandidos* to handle any herd they gathered up. One herd of only 500 head of cattle being driven out of Texas had 80 armed men accompanying it.

In 1872 the United States government sent a commission of three men to investigate conditions on the border and to take evidence bearing on claims of American citizens for stock stolen in 1859–1860 and during the years following the close of the Civil War. The commission made a very careful and painstaking investigation, took the sworn statements of hundreds of citizens, both English and Spanish speaking, and in the end filed a report, dated at Washington, D. C., December 10, 1872, that is a most astounding document. In 1873 the commissioners came back to Texas and heard additional testimony. They went over the ground from Brownsville to Eagle Pass. "The cattle thieves are today," they reported, June 30, 1873, "far more active than last year."

Figures may be as deceptive as the generalized adjectives often substituted for them. One of the time-worn jokes of the range is on the man who put in his claim to the government for 5000 cattle and their increase, 500 horses and their increase, and 50 *mules and their increase.* Some newspaper satirist figurged out that a flock of 160 goats would if unmolested increase to 2,500,000 goats in ten years' time, and that thus a man who had lost even ten goats ten years ago was entitled to a handsome remuneration. This history is not being prepared as a brief to support the heirs of any cowmen in their claims for indemnity against Mexican depredations. Everybody who knows anything knows that there are two sides to the old controversies between some of the Southwest Texas cowmen and the Mexicans. Nevertheless, figures sworn to by scores of Texas citizens before a United States claims commission may reveal a great deal.

Before those remarkable figures are set forth, however, the method of reckoning the number of cattle in any brand on the open range at any given time should be explained. The only cattle that could be closely counted with any regularity were the calves branded each year. But cattle were generally matured before they were sold, and experience showed that for each calf branded there were, under normal conditions, five other cattle on the range in the same brand. Thus, if a man branded 1000 calves, he reckoned his herd at 5000 head, calves not being counted but "throwed in." Of course, when, about the beginning of the eighties, Eastern capitalists and Scotch and English syndicates got to plunging in the cattle business, "book accounts" were often queerly juggled. "Well, boys," said a jovial soul one night during a terrible Wyoming blizzard, addressing himself to some cowmen whose cattle were dying like sheep and who had contracted their stock to a syndicate for delivery—"well, boys, remember the tally books ain't froze up." But to some figures.

In 1866 King and Kenedy, at that time the most extensive operators among cowmen of the lower country, made a count of their holdings: 84,000 cattle and 5400 horses. In 1869 they agreed to dissolve partnership, and for a year with more than 100 vaqueros they gathered and counted stock. The count showed 48,664 cattle and 4400 horses. They estimated that there were 10,000 cattle "on the prairie," as the saying went; that is, cattle ungathered on the range, most of which, incidentally, were in the brush and not at all on the prairie. Thus the total would be brought up to 58,664. During the three years between 1866 and 1869 King and Kenedy had sold off only 1000 beeves and 570 horses. Now cattle during normal seasons increased at the rate of 33⅓ per cent per year, thus doubling the original stock every three years. The years 1866 to 1869 were normal years free from bad drouths or freezes. Therefore, in 1869 the King and Kenedy cattle should have totaled 84,000 times 2, or 168,000 head, less the 1000 head sold, leaving 167,000. But the count showed only 58,664. Now 167,000 minus 58,664 leaves 108,336 cattle short. Where had this stock gone? Across the Rio Grande, claimed King and Kenedy, and their heirs are still pushing the claim. In 1872 the loss of cattle had, according to this method of reckoning, increased to a total of 216,672, and of horses to 5324.

In 1872 it was estimated that the lower country between the Nueces and the Rio Grande had hardly a third as many cattle as it had grazed in 1866, the decrease being due to Mexican raids. In 1875 it was estimated that the ranges immediately adjacent to the Rio Grande had only 10 per cent of what they had grazed ten years before. Justo Lopez, who lived near a popular crossing, swore in 1872 that he had personally seen 60,000 head of stolen cattle driven across the river.

There was hardly a ranch family in Southwest Texas that did not have a claim similar to that of King and Kenedy, the aggregate claims in 1872 being for more than 750,000 head of cattle, this number including not only cattle said to have been carried into Mexico but the potential increase of that number— often four or five times larger. In short, the ranch claimants estimated a total loss of cattle, horses, and other property to the value of $27,859,363.97. Without doubt many of the losses were grossly exaggerated; without doubt millions of the dollars claimed represented bona fide losses. Not one cent has ever been recovered. Lawyers in Washington after more than fifty years are still piddling with the claims.

The wholesale thievery was accomplished with commensurate waste. For instance, out of one herd of 1600 cattle driven for three days without water, 1000 died before the remnant blindly staggered into the waters of the Rio Bravo. The Mexican market became so glutted with stolen stock that beeves worth from $12 to $18 in Texas went at from $2 to $4 in Matamoros and Monterrey. Not long after the close of the Civil War Colonel Ford saw the complete skinned carcasses of bullocks selling across the river for 62½ cents each. Thousands of carcasses with the hides merely stripped off were left to rot in "the big thicket" near Matamoros.

The Mexicans had no packeries. They skinned for the hides alone and let the tallow rot. Sometimes they brought over trains of ox carts and loaded them with hides taken from cattle killed on the Texas range. The hide market was as busy on their side of the river during the Skinning War of the seventies as it was at Rockport or Corpus Christi. And it was well protected. Many civil and military authorities drew their chief income from affording protection. "Shoot the first ———— gringo ———— — — ———— who comes over here and tries to look at a hide," ordered a hide dealer and political power of Matamoros to some of his henchmen.

Let a few representative instances of *bandido* activities out
in the brush indicate much. Cortina's "right bower" was Alberto
Garza, popularly known as "Caballo Blanco." In the spring of
1873 Garza and another lieutenant, Atilano Alvarado, with
sixty men following them, were stealing horses and skinning
cattle in the then unorganized county of Duval. From their
camp out in the chaparral they sent word to the citizens of the
little town of San Diego to bring either enough money to buy
the hides they had collected or else enough men to skin the
hide-peelers. Jasper Clark, James F. Scott, and nine other Texas
cowmen took the dare, assaulted the camp, and routed the
bandits, who left behind them saddles, bridles, and other booty.
Near the camp the Texans found the carcasses of 80 cattle recently killed and skinned; at another place they found 275
carcasses; at still another 366 carcasses. Not a great while afterwards Caballo Blanco and some of his skinners were "settled."

The troubles with Mexicans were at their worst from about
1871 until along in 1875. One issue alone of the Galveston
Daily News, that of May 9, 1873, reported the following items
from the lower country, all pertaining to *bandidos*: The road
between Corpus Christi and the Rio Grande is almost too dangerous to travel. Thieves with about 70 stolen horses have been
seen on the San Fernandez. Twenty-seven desperadoes are operating near Piedras Pintas. A wagon train has been held up
at Lake Trinidad. A Mexican has been found hanging dead to
a tree near Nuecestown.

Along in November of the same year Mexican bandits took
possession of the Santa Rosa ranch belonging to Cornelius Stillman, driving away seventeen of his saddle horses. An officer
named Claus captured two of the bandits and turned them over
to Stillman, who was justice of the peace. Stillman released them.
He knew that if he did not release them he would be killed. In
December a total of thirty-two persons were reported to have
been killed by Mexicans and Indians around Piedras Pintas,
Duval County.

On May 9, 1874, four white men were surprised and bru-
tally murdered at Penascal, sixty miles from Corpus Christi.

Three Mexicans were intercepted, and before they were hanged they said that their band numbered eleven, among them a white man. The citizens of Corpus Christi offered a reward of $100 apiece for the Mexicans not yet captured and a reward of $500 for the white man. Mathew Dunn was active in trailing down the murderers, and like most other borderers he was cautious even in sleep. It was his habit to sleep out in a corn patch near the house. One dark night he went to the house to get a drink of water and, while inside, lighted a kerosene lamp. Immediately two shots flashed at him from the darkness outside. He put out the light and thereafter took a canteen of water with him when he went to bed in the cornfield.

In March, 1875, a well organized band of 150 Mexicans crossed into Texas near Eagle Pass. On this side they separated into four divisions bent on plunder. Three of the divisions were in time intercepted by United States cavalry stationed at San Diego. But the fourth, headed for Corpus Christi, came within a few miles of the town before citizens overwhelmed it. This raid probably marks the climax of the raids of the seventies; the whole country was aroused; there is no telling how many Mexicans bit the dust as a result of it. Two episodes connected with it deserve to be related for the light they throw on the kindly relationship between Texans and good Mexicans even when the border was bloodiest.

As the bandits were marching on Corpus they captured, robbed, and held as prisoners several "white people"; among them was Mrs. E. D. Sidbury, who was driving to town in her carriage. "Black Santos," long a faithful Mexican servant, was her driver. In the carriage was a trunk containing among other things a small box of jewelry worth several hundred dollars. Black Santos knew where the jewelry was. The bandits ordered him to open the trunk and display the contents. One by one he brought the articles up for inspection but as he rummaged about he managed to keep the little box of jewels out of sight. Fortunately the bandits did not make him empty all the goods out at once or fish down with their own hands; and thus Santos saved the *madama's* finery. That he was running no small risk the next incident will illustrate.

When the Mexicans got to the store of Fred Franks near Nuecestown, they were met at the door by an aged Mexican. The chief, or *capitán,* asked him to join the band, but he refused. The *capitán* promised a large share of the booty; the old Mexican refused more vigorously. The *capitán* began to curse and threaten; the old man closed the door. Then the chief of the robbers plunged after him, dragged him out by the neck, and ordered his men to string him up instantly. The hangman's knot had already been tied and the other end of the rope was over a limb of a convenient tree when Fred Franks himself rushed out to the rescue. For some reason he was unarmed, but he knocked one Mexican down and was laying out another when he was seized and put in chains. Then the hanging proceeded, and in a few minutes the old *peon* who had dared to be loyal to his gringo employer was dead.

These incidents are representative, not isolated. It would be a great mistake for one to conclude that all Texans hated and hunted all Mexicans and that there was no harmony between the two peoples as they lived side by side in the border country. There were good Mexicans as well as bad Mexicans. Between many Anglo-Texans and Mexican-Texans strong ties of friendship existed. The majority of Anglo-Texan ranchers along the border depended almost exclusively upon Mexican vaqueros for their labor; and these vaqueros, generally speaking, proved to be as reliable, as loyal, and as trustworthy as the idealized darkies of ante-bellum days. Born hunters, horsemen, and cow hands, they were superb trailers, and at the risk of their lives they often led English speaking men on the trail of marauders that were sometimes kinsmen by birth as well as by nationality.

At the very time when the border troubles were worst Captain Refugio Benavides commanded a company of state troops made up exclusively of Mexican-Texans and devoted exclusively to suppressing Mexican banditry. August Santleben, borderer and outstanding freighter between San Antonio and various cities of Mexico, has in his book, *A Texas Pioneer,* offered concrete evidence of the kindly feeling existing between many Mexicans and Americans. Again, in an unpublished autobiography, Jesse Sumpter, pioneer citizen of Eagle Pass, testifies to the concord existing between good Mexicans and good Americans along the border not only against bad Mexicans but against bad Americans, many of whom were overbearing and cruelly unjust to the *Tejanos* (Texanized Mexicans).

The ranch gallery and camp fire historians of Southwest Texas have a tale of the times that is too good to leave out, however far from the facts it may have wandered. Among the prisoners taken by the Nuecestown raiders was George Reynolds, a prominent ranchman of Nueces and Live Oak counties who had been born in England. He was in his buggy when the *bandidos* took him, and upon releasing him they kept his buggy horses, a very fine span. Now, it was a principle with George Reynolds, sturdy, law-abiding Englishman that he was, not to allow his stock to be stolen. He often said that he would rather pay a thousand dollars to prevent a thief from getting away with a twenty dollar horse than to let him succeed in his thievery. Acting on this principle, he sent one of his most trusted men, a Mexican, to Mexico to trail down and bring back the stolen buggy horses. After being gone a long time, his man came back and reported that he had found the horses but that he could not get them. They were, he said, in the government stables at Mexico City. With this information Reynolds went to Judge Russell in Corpus Christi and got an order on the Mexican government for the buggy team. Reynolds' man carried the order to Mexico City. It was honored—so the story goes. Had it been issued by the president of the United States, it would very probably have been ignored. Most Mexicans still believe that "if Texas would sit still" they could easily whip the rest of the United States. One reason for this belief is that for every Texan killed at least twenty-five Mexicans have paid with their lives. Furthermore, the Texans have never believed that the Rio Grande was a dividing line between them and justice, particularly just punishment.

The number of Mexicans that were killed on Texas soil as

a result of the Nuecestown (or Noakes) raid and other outrages by bad Mexicans—not all of them direct from Mexico—will never be known. Certainly it exceeded the number killed at San Jacinto. Old timers still tell how the raiders took twenty-five new saddles from the Noakes store and how for a month afterwards every Mexican found in the country with a new saddle was killed. "Yonder's a Noakes," some Texan would say upon glimpsing a Mexican riding on new leather, and if the Mexican had any explanation to give he generally had to postpone it for the other world. In the expressive phrase of the *Texian* rangers, a good many saddles were "won." "Uncle Bob" (R. C.) Barfield, a thoroughly reliable man now living in Beeville, Texas, was a familiar of the border during the seventies. Not long after the Nuecestown raid he saw, so he says, many little ranches in the lower country deserted by their Mexican inhabitants; he saw too the remains of various Mexicans hanging from trees. Captain King had built a bridge across the Agua Dulce Creek between his Santa Gertrudis Ranch and Corpus Christi, and this bridge became notable for the number of Mexicans that were there picked off by Texas men. Mexicans were shot on sight and pitched into Clark Lake, into the Oso, into the Agua Dulce.

Walter Billingsley, of San Antonio, is responsible for the following account. One time during these troublous days a group of Texans were riding ten or fifteen miles out from Corpus Christi when they met a well dressed Mexican followed by his *mozo* (servant). The *caballero* had no "pass" and could not satisfactorily establish his identity. The more hot-headed of the Texans began to prepare a rope, but J. N. Garner and another man protested, saying they felt sure the Mexicans were innocent travelers. The crowd voted Garner and the other protestant down, however, and the two rode away. A few days after the Mexicans were hanged, it was learned that the *caballero* was a merchant of Laredo and a good citizen of the state.

The friendly Dubose family at Rancho Saco had two Mexican brothers named Doroteo and Benito working for them. Doroteo had been in service a long time and was much trusted;

the children loved him. Benito had come from Mexico only a few months previously. Some ranchmen suspected the brothers of being implicated with Mexican cow thieves and arrested them. The night after the arrest Duff Hale and Jim Scott were assigned to guard them. They did not have to stand guard long, however, for a party of vigilantes came and took the prisoners away. A few days later the bodies of Doroteo and Benito, lashed tightly together with a rope and riddled with bullets, were found out in the brush. Nothing had been proved against them.

As a result of the feeling aroused against them, Mexicans from Austin and other regions far interior stampeded for the Rio Grande. As late as 1879 an order was issued by local citizens for all Mexicans to leave the Frio Canyon within three days. There was, yet is, so much exaggeration that often one does not know how far to go in believing what is told concerning those old days of border warfare. Certainly the complete story was never chronicled in the few contemporary newspapers, which carried news neither from nor to a majority of the border settlers.

One voluble pioneer recently declared that in 1876 a Mexican about to be hanged in San Diego confessed to Judge J. O. Luby that he had murdered nineteen men and cut the tongues out of three others. Jolly old Judge Luby, who yet walks the earth, is writing a book about the Rio Grande country; perhaps he will discuss this case. The actions of men are always guided by what they believe to be the facts rather than by the facts themselves. What the border folk have thought and felt and talked, as well as what they have shot, belongs to the record.

There were raiding and counter-raiding, eye for eye and tooth for tooth. Fiery-memoried W. G. Sutherland, patriarchal Irish school-master of Bluntzer, avers that Mustang Gray crossed with a dozen men to Mier, rounded up a *partida* of Cortina bandits, herded them back to Texas, penned them, ear-marked the whole bunch, branded two of the wildest, then let down the bars and advised the now no longer mavericks to swim the Rio Bravo back to their own range and forever afterwards to keep water between them and Texas soil. The only trouble with this story is that Mustang Gray had been dead several years before Cortina started raiding. However, before Cortina arose Mustang Gray had dealt raw-handed enough to inspire a whole cycle of such tales, and a brave old ballad that celebrates his prowess was sung for a generation on the Texas frontiers and up the cattle trails.

All up and down the Rio Grande the undeclared war between Mexicans and Texans went on, but below Del Rio—because the country above Del Rio was not settled until later—the warfare was fiercest. In 1872 the alcalde of Villa Nueva, Coahuila, across from the Kinney County line, had men employed to steal cattle in Texas and drive them over to him. One morning eighteen Texas range men surrounded the town. All the Mexicans fled or tried to flee except the alcalde, who took refuge in his adobe house, from which he opened fire. One of the Texas boys besieging the Mexicans was John Pulliam. He was riding a hard-mouthed mule, and that mule carried Pulliam, in spite of desperate sawing on the reins, right up to the window of the alcalde's house. The rider was hit in the head by a bullet that killed him instantly. That night he was buried out in the brush, on the Texas side, by Jack Potter, "the Fighting Parson," one of the characters of the frontier.

Six years later "Fighting Jack Potter," while traveling alone over the country, camped near the place where he had helped bury John Pulliam. In the night he heard somebody after the hobbled ponies. He jumped out of bed, grabbing his gun and his shoes, and ran towards the horses. He saw a man and shot at him. It was just one of the Mexican thieves that were constantly on the prowl.

Along in 1877 some Mexican raiders waited on the alcalde of Camargo, across the river from Rio Grande City, and asked: "Is it possible that you are going to deliver us to the Americans?"

The indignant reply was: "Do you suppose I consider you jerked beef to be handed over to the gringos and chewed up. Go back *where you belong* and attend to your business."

Where they belonged and what their business was may be

deduced from the fact that some months afterwards some of them were arrested on this side, examined before a judge at Rio Grande City, and imprisoned. Immediately a band of their compatriots slipped over, shot the judge, and opened the jail. The rangers went down, secured the cooperation of Mexican authorities, who were by now becoming more cordial towards Americans, and after some activity not recorded in the ranger reports kept in the adjutant-general's office at Austin, peace reigned.

A good many of the borderers were "no slouches" themselves when it came to rustling cattle, and some of them got fair exchange from the Mexican ranges for "Nanita's cattle" that Cortina's men drove out of Texas. Particularly was this true towards the close of the seventies and along in the eighties when the Texans got the upper hand. However, a state of almost continual civil war had depleted herds in northeastern Mexico, and the loud complaints of Mexican *rancheros* that their cattle were being consumed by certain hide and tallow factories on the Texas coast must be considerably discounted.

Instead of raiding into Mexico directly, the Texans, such as were engaged in handling Mexican cattle, more commonly secured them from Mexican cow thieves. It is said, with how much truth cannot be asserted, that King Fisher killed near Espantosa Lake, in Dimmit County, eight Mexicans who had just delivered to him a herd of "wet" cattle and with whom he had quarreled over the price. King Fisher had a definitive way of settling quarrels. Another time, so another story goes, King Fisher paid Mexican smugglers their price—and then waylaid them as they were returning to the Rio Grande and recovered the money from their bodies.

It is doubtful if Texans ever raided quite so much into Mexico from the Texas line as they did from Arizona. Here, according to William M. Breakenridge, an old time Arizona sheriff and author of *Helldorado,* the raiding and smuggling was very heavy. The raiders, or rustlers, he says "were nearly all Texas cowboys whose feeling towards the Mexicans was so bitter that they had no compunction about stealing from them or shooting them and robbing them whenever they got an opportunity. One of their men did a thriving commission business acting as the banker and disposing of the stolen stock. . . . They confined their crimes to stealing stock and robbing Mexican smugglers who were bringing Mexican silver across the line to buy goods with. They generally killed the smugglers."

When troubles were at their worst on the Texas border, however, comparatively few cattle or horses were being brought over from Mexico. The border country was simply too sparsely settled to admit of either organized reprisals or organized resistance. A band of Mexican outlaws could cross over, ride a hundred miles inland, kill, round up a herd of cattle or horses, and be back in Mexico before their trail was found. In testimony before the Claims Commission of 1872 Captain McNelly summed up the situation thus:

Many of them (the border citizens) have not nerve enough to take an active, decided stand, either by giving information or by personal assistance. Still, a number of them have done it since I have been out there, and some eight or ten, probably twelve, have been killed on that account. It has been the history of these border counties that when any man, Mexican or American, has made himself prominent in hunting those raiders down, or in organizing parties to pursue them when they are carrying off cattle, he has been either forced to move from the ranch and come into town or he has been killed. . . . While the resident Mexican population who have any property are in sympathy with our people, there is a large floating population who have come over from the other side . . . and who are the spies and informers of the raiders.

An instance of intimidation is given by Colonel Ford:

The Federal Court in Brownsville appointed a grand jury to investigate. But when a Mexican appeared before them and told them in plain terms that should he tell what he knew his life would pay the forfeit, he was excused from swearing. . . . A Mexican who had taken the oath of allegiance to the United States was spotted. What chance had he but to remain silent?

Of course some ranchmen of power were bold in their defense. Captain King and Captain Kenedy both kept private rangers scouting over their territory. At headquarters of the King Ranch a lookout was frequently posted on top of the warehouse to scan the surrounding country. Captain King, who had been more than once ambushed, traveled with armed outriders as guards. Some of the old Spanish ranch houses of the country were veritable forts.

To make border troubles worse, outlaws from other states and better controlled parts of Texas sought refuge along the Rio Grande. Frequently they acted in collusion with the Mexican bandits. Much of the trouble can be summed up in one word—Reconstruction. But about the middle of the seventies the tide began to turn against chaos. Diaz had come to power in Mexico. He stood for law, as he interpreted law. His idea of inspiring respect for law was to "'dobe-wall" the lawless—stand them up against an adobe wall and shoot them. For the time it was a good idea. It was carried out with remarkable effectiveness by General Ramon Treviño (1841-1891), governor of Nuevo Leon. He, perhaps more than any other one man below the Rio Grande, was responsible for quelling the *bandidos*. Nevertheless, for a while the brisk campaign for law and order in Mexico was hard on Texas. Like all hunted things, the *bandidos* sought refuge. Their best refuge from the *rurales* behind them seemed to be the left bank of the Rio Bravo.

The only way to deal with this bandit element was to deal with them relentlessly. Taking a lesson from the Texas rangers, United States troops began following marauding bands of Indians and Mexicans not only to the Rio Grande but into Mexico. General McKenzie made his first sally into Mexico, after Kickapoo Indians, in 1873. In 1877 Colonel Shafter and Lieutenant Bullis both followed raiders into Mexico. Even though the raiders followed might be altogether Indians, it was a well known fact that they were selling stolen stock to Mexican sympathizers.

The decisive act against Mexican banditry had come, however, before the army's sympathies were fully enlisted. On June

12, 1875, McNelly's rangers met on the old Palo Alto battlefield a gang of Mexican cattle thieves in the very act of thieving. The rangers at once "naturalized" thirteen of them, took the bodies to Brownsville, and laid them out on the plaza. Whoever claimed the bodies could have them, McNelly announced. Claimants appeared for but one body. Among the dead was a white man named Jack Ellis. This swift, summary action of the rangers did not put an end to murderous raiding, but it turned the balance against the murderers and raiders and it gave the people on this side of the Rio Grande a chance to lift up their heads and act more independently.

About this time minute companies, concerning one of which several details will presently be given, were getting organized. Out in Duval County Hines Clark captained a company of revengeful law bringers; to the east in Live Oak County, Henderson Williams, Jim Ussery, and Sebastian Beall were responsible for a company; down the Nueces River Martin Culver commanded; to the northeast of Culver's territory Buck Pettus had a kind of private corps; on the coast below Victoria Jim McFadden led his men. In almost every settlement of Southwest Texas some stockman headed a movement against lawless Mexicans and against lawlessness in general.

"And no telling how many Mexicans," as a result of this uprising of the inflamed citizenry, bit the dust. Rocky times, rocky times in Texas.

CHAPTER VI

IF NOT LAW—THEN ORDER

WHILE Cortina's bandits were driving "Nanita's cattle" across the Rio Grande to Matamoros and selling them for one-fifth of what their legitimate owners could have sold them for in Texas; while the strains of "Mustang Gray" were soothing longhorned steers on lonely bed grounds for a thousand miles up the Chisholm Trail; while the murders at Penascal were yet fresh talk over half of Texas and Mathew Dunn was sleeping in the corn patch, a canteen of water by his side and no light about him; while the thickets of Southwest Texas from Goliad to Devil's River were hiding white men as shy of civilization as the native javelina hogs—but not in the least gun shy—there occurred in Refugio County a deed so horrible that the whole country was aroused against Mexicans as it had not been aroused for a generation.

The date was June 8, 1874. I was not yet eighteen years old. At that time my family was living near the old Refugio Mission in Refugio County. Some time along in the morning a rider brought word that the Swift family, our neighbors, had been murdered the night before by Mexicans. What I saw when I arrived at the Swift ranch shortly thereafter changed me from a simple-hearted country boy to a hard-nerved man boiling for revenge. There on the ground just outside the house were the bodies of Thad Swift and his wife cut to pieces. The details are too revolting to describe.

In that day and time there were no banks. All of the money in use was gold and silver, and whoever had any usually kept it in a trunk under the bed or perhaps in a sock or sack somewhere about the house. Swift was a sheepman and he had been to St. Mary's the day before and sold his wool, bringing the money, about $700, back home with him. For this money he had been murdered, evidently by Mexicans who were working for him. The morning after the crime not a Mexican was on the place. The house had been ransacked, and all the money, together with a few pieces of jewelry belonging to Mrs. Swift, was gone.

Within a short time after I reached the Swift home a number of men had gathered. Despite the lack of telephones and telegraph, important news spread nearly as rapidly—by the "grapevine telegraph"—in those days as it does now; within thirty-six hours riders from seventy-five miles away had come to join the posses. But we did not wait thirty-six hours to act. Jephtha Williams, sheriff of the county, made a talk to the men, saying that the murderous Mexicans were no doubt on their way to Mexico and that by hard riding we might catch them before they reached the Rio Grande. A strong posse at once set out.

I did not go with this posse. I had another trail to follow. However, before taking it up I advised with Sheriff Williams. I told him that a bad Mexican named Marcelo Moyer, who lived thirty-five miles to the north in Goliad County, near the Saunders and Cyrus Lucas ranches, had been at the Swift ranch the day before and that I believed him guilty of the murder.

"Go get him," was all that Williams said.

Late that afternoon two other young men and I set out. We rode all night, stopping at every ranch house along the route to inquire concerning passers. Several persons had during the day seen Moyer making tracks for his hang-out, and had noticed that he was carrying a large Bowie knife in a scabbard on his saddle. During the night nine men joined us; so when just at sunrise we rode up to the Moyer house there were twelve of us.

The house was made of split logs, the logs set in the ground endwise. Nobody had ever noticed before that there were portholes in some of the logs; the portholes, diamond shaped, showed plainly now. They had, as a matter of fact, been cut into the logs when the house was built and then daubed up with adobe mud against the day of battle. The day of battle was at hand. The house had a cellar also. It was a regular fort.

As our horses clattered up on the hard-baked ground in front of the house, a voice in Spanish asked what we wanted— "*Qué quieren?*" I replied that we were hunting down murderers of the Swift family, and I ordered the door opened. We had thrown all caution to the winds. The door did not open, and Dan Holland rode up to a porthole in order to peer inside. A bullet struck him squarely in the chin, breaking his neck. He was my friend. I rode up close enough to thrust my six-shooter inside the same hole and emptied its contents within the house. We afterwards found out that one shot had somehow filled a Mexican's face with splinters from a log. The fight was on.

Meantime more men were gathering and we drew out some distance, keeping the house surrounded. We youngsters wanted to charge it and end the business, but older heads held us back. About eleven o'clock Phil Fulcrod, sheriff of Goliad County, George Saunders, and nine other men arrived from Goliad. They had ridden twelve miles in one hour and their horses were totally exhausted. About the time they arrived somebody saw old man Moyer down in the field. A man drew his Winchester down on him and was about to fire when George Saunders interfered. Then old Moyer surrendered. Two or three hours later the Mexicans in the house, under promise of protection, also surrendered to Sheriff Fulcrod. By now more than a hundred Americans were around the house.

Antonio Moyer was placed on a horse, Marcelo Moyer and his father were placed in a hack, and thus the three prisoners, guarded by Fulcrod and eight or ten deputies, were started for Goliad. A lot of us, however, did not propose to put off a punishment that we knew the Mexicans deserved. The guard and prisoners had gone only about three miles when we surrounded them. The guard offered practically no interference, and in the mêlée that followed Marcelo was shot dead. Old Moyer was wounded and down on the ground. A maddened ranch boy rode his plunging horse over him, at the same time emptying his six-shooter at him, without effect. Another man dismounted and cut the Mexican's throat with a butcher knife. Antonio Moyer, who, it will be remembered, was on a horse, made an attempt to run but had his arm shot off and was soon dispatched. In the wild shooting George Saunders' horse was wounded with a bullet.

While this trouble with the Moyers was going on, a scouting party of citizens caught two Mexicans that were known to have been at the Swift place the evening preceding the murder. They were put in jail, but within a short time a mob took them out, carried them to the pens back of the Swift house, and hanged them from a pole that was fixed over a gate. The house was no longer inhabited, and the bodies swung there, in full view of the public road, for a week before they were cut down.

We were not blood-thirsty men—not consciously at least— though we had a natural masculine craving for action. We were simply frenzied by the outrages that had been committed and were desperate for revenge. The day that we took the Moyers I joined Coon Dunman's Regulators. Dunman belonged to a line of fighters, his father and uncles having come to Texas in the twenties and done their share in gaining Texan independence. During the Civil War Coon Dunman himself had led a band of guerilla fighters in Louisiana. The avowed purpose of the Regulators was to make every Mexican who could not give an account of himself either leave the country or take his chances of kicking at Texas soil with nothing to stand on. We were really a vigilante committee. Soon, however, the Dunman Regulators were absorbed into a company of thirty-six minutemen commanded by Captain Henry Scott.

Scott was a remarkable leader. He had been "raised fighting Indians and Mexicans." When only ten years old he was with his father in an Indian fight near the present town of Brownsville. That was about 1840. His father was killed in this fight and he himself was captured. After the Indians had taken him two hundred and fifty miles into Mexico and had held him a while, he escaped one night, mounted a pony that was picketed near by, and finally got back to the Texas settlements. He served as captain in the Confederate Army. He was a man of sound judgment and strict honor and was a great *hombre* among the Mexicans, who bowed to him and called him Don Enrique. He kept his power over them by the same methods that Don Porfirio Diaz in Mexico kept his power—by an iron hand and relentless strength. He had been a warm friend of Thad Swift's.

As minutemen we furnished our own horses and ourselves, without thought of any sort of pay. We were all active men, and we stood ready to respond to any summons, day or night. Of course we were scattered over a wide region, and, living in the saddle as most of us lived, we were frequently away from home. No matter where we were, however, every man of us kept a horse saddled at night. Sometimes there would be no call for weeks at a time; then some report might send us seventy-five or a hundred miles away at the utmost speed. When word of the Nuecestown raid flew across the country some of us were in the "Pull Tight" (Blanconia) settlement. The news reached us about dark; by daylight we were at Borden's Ferry on the Nueces sixty miles away. These minutemen were never enrolled by the state, but if rangers deserve a pension some of the minutemen deserve it also.

One night a band of Scott's men surrounded a gang of fifteen Mexican horse thieves in a thicket. The attack on them was to be a surprise, and naturally some of the younger men were feeling shaky. Before we scattered to go into the brush, Captain Scott called his men about him and said: "Boys, don't fire too quick. Get as close as you can and aim at the middle of their bodies. Just keep it in mind that Mexicans can't hit you." Within an hour Texas had a dozen fewer horse thieves within its borders. Scott's company remained organized for two or three years, though I was not with them towards the last.

Soon after the Swift murder seventy-five or eighty men from half a dozen counties met one night on the Rosilla Prairie —a noted round-up ground in Refugio and Goliad counties. The object of the meeting was to make preparation for killing every Mexican in old Labardee (Goliad). Sentiment was wild and it seemed that a most horrible slaughter was to be effected, when George Saunders, a very young man, stepped forth to make a speech. George Saunders thinks that the speech he made and the result it had will be credited to him by Saint Peter; nobody will be inclined to disagree with him. His talk was something like this:

"Men, most of you are older than I am and some of you may think that I am impertinent in taking a stand against you. But you are about to do something that will bring you shame and that will put a blot on the history of Texas that can never be erased. We have been forced into desperate measures. Our people have suffered outrages. Yet not one of us, I believe, carries in his heart a desire to murder the innocent. If you go down there to old Labardee and massacre all the Mexicans, you will murder good men and innocent women. Not all Mexicans are bad. You know that. You know that there are Mexican men and Mexican women who are as true and loyal and faithful as anybody ever was. You know that among the bad Mexicans at Labardee there are many good ones. In fact, there are more good ones than bad ones. I am in favor of dealing with the bad ones as they deserve. I will never take part in a wholesale butchery."

Then George Saunders walked out and drew a line on the ground.

"Now," he said, "all of you that are in favor of using judgment and justice and that are against a massacre step on this side of the line."

Every man stepped over the line.

I have already said that Captain Henry Scott was a friend of Thad Swift. He swore that he would bring to justice every Mexican implicated in the Swift murder. Now Juan Flores, one of the leaders in this crime, had escaped to Mexico, where, so we learned, he was boasting of the way he dealt with gringos. Scott sent Frank Boggas into Mexico to negotiate with Cortina for the delivery of Flores. Boggas was gone several weeks. One late evening a few days after he had returned and reported, fifteen of Scott's men struck camp on the east bank of the Rio Grande several miles below Laredo. About midnight we saw a skiff coming over to our side. When it landed, two men with a prisoner between them stepped out. The prisoner was Juan Flores. Then by the light of a little fire Captain Scott counted out five hundred dollars in gold to the Mexican captors. After we had seen them row back across the river we put Flores on a pack horse and started with him for Refugio. On the way we had to pass through several Mexican settlements. Word had somehow got out that Juan Flores, who had become a hero, was being brought back, and there were threats of a rescue.

We delivered Flores to the sheriff of Refugio County. He was tried by a jury of the law and sentenced to be hanged. The hanging was public and just before the trap was sprung he said in his peculiar pronunciation of English: "Goodbye, boys. Don't be bad like I was."

Thus ended the last of the Swift murderers, but, as has already been shown in the preceding chapter, the Swift episode was but one of many episodes of its kind. About this time representatives from various counties met at Mission in Refugio County to consider ways and means of demanding passports from all Mexicans. The country was so big and unorganized, however, and Mexicans were so numerous that nothing ever came of the proposal.

No doubt many Mexicans who did not deserve death met it during these times; this phase of the troubles has been treated of. Nor were the Mexicans the sole victims of reckless and prodigal killing on the part of English speaking Texans. The bare facts of one representative border feud—with some of the names disguised—will illustrate the lack of racial or national distinction in the shedding of blood.[1] Towards the close of the Civil War a cowman by the name of French who ranched on the Leona River, a tributary of the Nueces, killed in a most base and cowardly manner two Mexican cattle buyers who had trusted him so far as to leave a *maleta* of silver dollars in his ranch house while cattle they had contracted for were being gathered.

[1] For a full account of the feud the reader is referred to Williams, R. H., *With the Border Ruffians*, New York, 1907, pp. 383–392.

A Mexican vaquero who witnessed the murders escaped and spread the news. Asa Mitchell and other vigilantes in San Antonio learned of the murders and captured French and hanged him on a china tree that grew in front of the house of Padre Sanchez on Alamo Plaza in San Antonio. The good padre had the tree cut down; the Civil War ended; and the two sons of French, Jim and Dick, who had been in the Confederate Army, came home.

They swore to "get" every one of the men who had had anything to do with the hanging of their father. First they stole into camp before daylight one morning and shot a man named Simons and another named Bishop before those unfortunate law bringers could roll out of their pallets. The next morning they were at the McConnel ranch miles up the Leona, and when old man McConnel walked to the door of his house in the dawning he fell dead across the threshold with two bullets through his head. The French brothers went inside, had breakfast, and then set off for the Hay ranch, a day's ride across the prairie. On the way over they met Hay. He ran; his horse stumbled; and while he was on the ground beside his fallen horse, the brothers shot him dead.

Victim number five was a man named Stokes. He lived near the court house of Atascosa County. When Jim and Dick French arrived in the vicinity of his home, they found that Stokes and his son had left three weeks before with a bunch of cattle for Eagle Pass. They knew that he would be coming back soon; so they rode leisurely down the road towards Eagle Pass. A day's ride out they came upon the two Stokes men nooning it under some live oak trees beside a water hole. They got down, passed the time of day, watered their horses, ate dinner, and then, while everybody was saddling up, acted. Jim French shot the Stokes boy dead. Dick French fumbled his pistol, and the elder Stokes, whose Winchester and six-shooter both were on his saddle, ran. A bullet through the leg brought him to the ground and he was yanked back to the tree that shaded the body of his dead son and hanged.

The French boys were literally blood mad. They turned

now and rode back to Atascosa Court House in search of Jake Peat. They found him in a saloon and beat him to the trigger—the only one of their seven victims who had had a chance for his life.

Asa Mitchell, chief of the San Antonio vigilantes, was built for the stern times he took part in. Although he put up the first tanyard among the Texas colonists, was prominent in defense against Indians and Mexicans, and later took the lead in organizing the first negro Sunday School in San Antonio, he is oftener remembered for an unconscious but significant gesture he made one hot night at a prayer meeting in San Antonio. While praying fervently he reached into his coat pocket to get a bandana to wipe his face and yanked out instead—a tidy rope. In the other pocket of his coat was a Bible. He was not a hypocrite.

Rocky times in Texas, rocky times.

As the bad Mexicans were thinned out, their places, for a while, seemed to be more than refilled by bad white men. In 1877 State Adjutant General Steele issued a booklet of 227 pages giving the names and description of some 5000 men "wanted in Texas." A large number of the 5000 had been in Southwest Texas for years, keeping in the brush along the border. Nearly all of them were single men and not one in twenty was a bona fide Texan, though they all added to the reputation that Texas was enjoying abroad. They were without money; they did not want to work; they had to live. Their recourse was gambling and thieving. Wherever there was a chance to prey on society they went. At a fair in the little town of Gonzales, for instance, between a hundred and a hundred and fifty gamblers, for the most part transients, were counted in one room.[2]

The outlaws were generally well organized and thus had the unorganized citizenry so completely cowed that a desperado might openly murder or steal without fear of arrest. The majority of them were horse thieves, and these gangs of horse thieves had well linked and well swiveled chains that reached all the way from far down in Mexico to the Red and Missis-

[2] Galveston *Daily News,* Oct. 16, 1873.

sippi rivers and points beyond. Many of them had friends and protectors among the isolated ranchers. The code of these ranchers—however some of them may have failed to live up to it—forbade stealing from a neighbor, but it generally permitted trading in "wet" horses—horses stolen in Mexico and smuggled across the Rio Grande. Now, a man who was making profit out of stolen horses was likely to protect the men who stole the horses. Again, many border ranchers who did not deal in "wet" stock remained neutral towards the outlaws in order to buy immunity from their depredations.

According to the Galveston *News* of February 27, 1878, there were in Texas at that date 750 warrants out against horse thieves alone and perhaps that many more horse thieves in jails over the state, while yet hundreds of other thieves unnamed and unknown roamed at large. One student of the times estimated that at least 100,000 head of horses had been stolen in Texas during the preceding three years. If a horse thief was caught red-handed by the owner of the stolen horses, he was likely to be hanged on the spot.

Under such conditions various counties of Southwest Texas in the early and middle seventies found themselves without a sheriff and without an applicant for the sheriff's office. One such county was Bee. During Rockport's boom days, while that town was expecting a deep water harbor and a railroad to Mexico, my family had moved thither. The railroad did not materialize and the water got shallow instead of deep. Good residence and business houses could be bought for what the nails in them had cost. Many deserters of the village could not sell, even for the price of the nails, the property they were leaving.

Father simply tore our house down, put the lumber on a big wagon, to which were hitched six yoke of oxen, handed me the prodpole, and told me to gee, haw, and hike for Beeville, seat of Bee County, sixty miles inland. He had bought a small tract of land on the Aransas Creek not far from town. While we were rebuilding the house, putting a picket fence around a hundred-acre pasture, and digging by hand a hundred-foot well, Captain D. A. T. Walton, a gallant Confederate veteran, was reluctantly accepting the office of sheriff of Bee County. The Swift murderers had all been run down. I was craving further action. Captain Walton was craving somebody who wanted to act. He made me his first deputy. I was nineteen and feeling my oats.

Two of the bad men hanging about the town were John Dwyer and Ed Singleton. One afternoon after they had spent a full morning in drinking they set out from Beeville in a buggy with the expressed purpose of going to Rockport to purchase whiskey for setting up a saloon in Dog Town, Mc-Mullen County. Before they left, Dwyer had displayed a large amount of money that he was carrying on his person. About sundown somebody came in from the direction of Rockport with the word that Dwyer's dead body was lying beside the road a few miles away. The body had been rifled. We caught Singleton in Indianola, where he was about to go aboard a ship, Dwyer's money in his possession.

Singleton had no defense. Court met shortly after his capture, and he was sentenced to be hanged. He appealed his case, and while decision of the higher court was pending I had charge of the jail in which he was lodged. It was just a lumber shack and had to be guarded day and night, for Singleton, like nearly all other outlaws of the time, had friends—and desperate friends at that who would not mind risking their lives to liberate him. The district judge advised Sheriff Walton to take the prisoner to Galveston for safe-keeping.

The best route to Galveston at that time was by stage for something over a hundred miles to Flatonia, the terminus of the G. H. and S. A. Railroad, and thence by rail. If we set out openly for Flatonia we felt sure that Singleton's friends would attempt a rescue. So one night another deputy sheriff and I put Singleton on a horse and rode with him into a thicket on the Aransas Creek, where we chained him to a tree. The next day Captain Walton reported that we had gone to Galveston, and he had plenty of fun watching the antics of Singleton's friends when they failed to pick up our trail. For sixteen days our meals

were brought to us there in the brush. Then I rode into Beeville and answered questions about the trip to Galveston. That
night Captain Walton and I left for Flatonia with Singleton.
Until we reached the railroad he was in joyous spirits; he was
really expecting to be rescued at any moment, but when we
got on the train and I snapped a handcuff on his right hand
with the other end on my left hand, he wilted.

After considerable delay the case was affirmed and Singleton was brought back to Beeville to hang. He remained hard,
cool, and hopeful to the end, for his was to be the first legal
hanging of a white man in the country for a long time and he
could not believe that his followers would allow any such pro-
cedure. Meantime I had resigned as deputy sheriff and Sheriff
Walton was so expectant of a jail delivery that he got a half
dozen rangers to guard the prisoner. While they guarded,
Singleton wrote a letter to his mother saying that he would
never be hanged in public "before a gaping multitude of fools,
especially Bee County fools." Finally he made out a most peculiar will, to which the press gave wide publicity. In it he bequeathed his skin to the district attorney, J. J. Swan, who had
prosecuted him, directing that it be stretched over a drumhead
and that the drum be beaten, to the tune of "Old Mollie Hare,"
in front of the courthouse every year on the anniversary of his
hanging "as a warning to evil doers." The remainder of his
anatomy he bequeathed to the doctors, "in the cause of science."
On the eve of his hanging he played seven-up the night through
with the rangers. He was hanged April 27, 1877.

There was plenty for sheriffs to do. For instance, one of
Walton's deputies named Clark undertook to arrest a hard
case at Papalote, which is in Bee County. After an exchange
of several shots the outlaw's gang rescued him from the officer.
A few nights later Clark went out to the well in his yard to
draw a bucket of water. While he was drawing the water somebody shot at him at such close range that his clothes were set
on fire, though he was not touched. A little later Tim Hart,
an old settler, left his home on the Papalote with a sack containing $1800, which he intended taking to Beeville. He never

arrived at his destination and until this day has not been seen dead or alive.

Captain Walton remained sheriff of Bee County for twenty years, and probably there was not during his time a better respected or a better feared sheriff in Texas. Despite the fact that he gave me plenty to do, I quit him in the spring of 1876 to go up the trail to Kansas. I shall tell about that trip in the next chapter. When I got back in the fall, I again became a deputy under him, but I wanted to be a ranger. The chance soon came.

Live Oak County, just west of Beeville, was at this time very sparsely settled and very much given over to the outlaw element. The following news item taken from the Galveston *Civilian* of March 6, 1873, will illustrate the free and easy manners of some of the citizens around Oakville, the county seat.

On Thursday last, in the town of Oakville, Thomas Shern, and Charles Jones, alias Charles Fox, attacked J. T. Pierce in his own house, and the parties exchanged some twenty-five shots, doing no further damage than splintering the gallery posts, breaking glass windows and looking glasses, alarming the women and children, and stopping proceedings for a time in court. The sheriff, his deputies, the jury, and the bystanders were required to arrest the belligerents, who were then fined by the Judge $100 each and sentenced to three days' imprisonment in jail, for contempt of court. The grand jury found true bills against some of them. One of them, Tom Shern, broke guard and made his escape. The guard followed Tom, firing as they went, for a distance of several miles, and with what result is not known, only that they did not get his body.

According to Clabe Robinson, who now lives at Beeville and who is compiling a history of Live Oak County, more than forty men were killed in or near Oakville during the ten years following the Civil War. Oakville had a population of perhaps a hundred people; its population has not grown much since. "During the decade of these murders," says Mr. Robinson, "exactly two men were arrested for serious offenses and put in the Oakville jail. These two were strangers in Oakville and were charged with an offense in another county. While they were in jail a party of men shot through the window and killed them." Several oak trees in front of the old jail afterwards became noted for the private hangings to which they lent their limbs. Contrary to a popular superstition, the limbs did not decay; they are still strong and sound and some of the old residents take pleasure in detailing the stories of the hangings.

But times were about to change. In the summer of 1876 Captain J. H. McNelly, just back from laying out thirteen dead bandits on the plaza at Brownsville, took up headquarters for his company at Oakville. That fall he sent word to Sheriff Walton that he wanted a man who knew the brush. Walton knew that I was a brush popper and that I hankered for ranger service; so he gave me the chance.

When I got to Oakville I found Captain McNelly sick. Lee Hall—"Red" Hall as the boys called him—lieutenant of the company, took me in charge. That night the ranger boys told me that in order to enlist I must be twenty-one years old and that Captain McNelly would not enlist a man who drank. The drinking proposition did not bother me, but the age limit did. I was only twenty. The upshot of the matter was that I would not misrepresent my age and was, therefore, signed up not as a ranger but as guide at regular ranger wages—forty dollars a month. In addition to paying the forty dollars, the state furnished a carbine to each ranger, ammunition, and rations for himself and mount. The ranger furnished his own mount, his own six-shooter, and his own clothing. So far as there was any uniformity of dress, it was the result of custom and not of official regulations. Most of the rangers wore the boots and hats appropriate to cowboys. Most of them had been cowboys.

Hunting outlaw men in the brush along the Nueces and Frio rivers was like hunting outlaw cattle. They were here today and there tomorrow. They could hear a twig break as far as a buck deer could hear it. It was their habit to hide out in the brush in bands ranging from four or five to a dozen or twenty in number and to keep a representative watching the rangers. If the rangers got wind of such a camp and went to it, they were likely to find only the ashes of a fire over which stolen beef had been roasted and around which cards had been played. Or if the rangers made a surprise, there would generally be more dead men than prisoners. A camp like this was usually surrounded at night and attacked about daylight, when the scattering would take place. It was a common belief in those days that every Texas ranger had a peculiarly vigilant guardian angel. The hardest old ranger frequently kept a soft spot for his guardian angel. I can vouch for mine.

About the first duty assigned to me as guide was the picking of a route through some thickets in San Patricio County— thickets that I had "choused" many a maverick through. Just before this Sheriff Ed Garner of that county had been murdered while he was at church, and Captain McNelly was determined to round up the gang responsible for the murder. It took some time to rope the cut-throats all in, but we got most of them.

To detail our various scouts would be tedious. As the rangers had but one horse apiece, they generally took a good rest after each campaign. It was these periods of rest, with nothing to do but set rat dens on fire and practice shooting at the rats as they came out, that turned me from the ranger service. Early in the spring of '77 the wanderlust was surging in me strong, and again I was on the trail for Kansas.

I have always been proud that I was associated even for a brief while with the McNelly rangers. It was a remarkable company and McNelly was a remarkable man. He was dying of tuberculosis when I entered his employ and on September 4, 1877, a few months after my resignation, he died. Before he was a ranger he had made a notable record in the Confederate Army. His successor in command of the ranger company was Jesse Lee Hall, and Hall was one of the outstanding men of the frontier. Among other good deeds, he broke up the astounding Taylor-Sutton feud. While he was making Southwest Texas a safe and prosperous place for honest people to live in, the state treasury ran short on funds and it was given out that Hall's company would be disbanded; but the citizens were so appreciative of the work being done and were so anxious for it to continue that they held a meeting at Goliad and subscribed funds for maintaining Hall's rangers until the next legislature should convene. Most of the money was subscribed by cowmen; when it was used up and still the state had made no provision for paying the rangers, the cattlemen of Nueces County raised other funds.[3]

Unless one keeps in mind such cooperation as this, one is likely to overestimate the number of thieves and outlaws in the country and overlook the upright citizens, who owned the country and who made it what it later became. The doings of the desperado element were so widely bruited that many a young man came to Texas with the idea that he must be "bad" in order to be in style. This feeling is illustrated by a story that went the rounds of the press in the late seventies. One day, according to the story, a walking arsenal fresh from the East made his presence known in Austin by getting as drunk as a fiddler's clerk and announcing that he was out to kill "a man wearing a plug hat." Ben Thompson was at that time doing nearly as much to make Austin famous as Jim Ferguson has done since. He was a bad man from Bitter Creek. Somebody told him of the stranger's appetite. Ben Thompson was an accommodating sort of fellow. As he walked into the saloon wearing a plug hat, the walking arsenal shrieked with delight.

"You're the fellow I been looking for," he yelled. "I'm bound to kill a man with a plug hat on."

"Oh, you wouldn't kill a poor dude like me, would you?" whined Thompson.

"Yes, I would," yelped the amateur, reaching for his gun.

His reach exceeded his grasp. However, the two bullets that bored into him did not touch his vitals and he got well—a wiser man.

But to get back to the rangers. In 1880 Hall resigned from the service to become manager of the Dull ranch in La Salle and McMullen counties. And here as his guest came a young

[3] Galveston *Daily News*, June 1, June 13, and August 2, 1877.

man who was to make the chaparral, the outlaw, the ranger, the Mexican sheep herder, the cowboy troubadour, the drouth, and other features of Southwest Texas familiar to the whole world. The young man was Sydney Porter, better known as O. Henry. "Red" Hall was his teacher. Really, McNelly's old company seems to have had more literary associations than any other ranger company Texas has ever had. In it was Horace Rowe, poet. Above all, in it was N. A. Jennings, subsequently a newspaper man and author of *A Texas Ranger*, a book vivid in detail, rushing in action, and pulsing with life. It was published in New York in 1899, but for some mysterious reason was never widely circulated. Copies are now almost unprocurable, but some day the book will no doubt be revived. It is too good to be lost to circulation.

CHAPTER VII

UP THE CHISHOLM TRAIL

For a quarter of a century—as long as trail driving lasted—it was the ambition of every ranch boy in Texas to go up the trail to Kansas. It was also the ambition of thousands of boys in Massachusetts and elsewhere, and many of them obeyed Horace Greeley's advice in order to realize the ambition. I might have gone sooner than I did, but I had been having plenty of action—and action, even though off the trail, seemed to keep me satisfied. In the spring of 1876 I took the first chance that came my way for a trip to Kansas.

The herd belonged to a man named J. W. Simpson, who accompanied it as trail boss. It consisted of 2800 head of mixed cattle. We left San Patricio County in March and drove to Abilene, where the cattle were sold; then we delivered them on the Platte River. I was just a hand, furnishing my own horses and drawing two dollars a day.

It did not take many days to accustom men and cattle alike to the routine of the trail. By daylight every morning the cattle would be up and grazing away from their bed grounds, headed north, and all hands except the last guard would have eaten breakfast. Then, while the last guard ate, the rest of us would begin stringing the cattle out. By the time we had them in good traveling formation the men left behind would be up with us and in their places. All day it was "walk along, little dogies," halting only to graze and water. The cattle began putting on flesh at once. At night the outfit was divided into three guards. Normally this arrangement left several hours for sleep, but if the weather was bad or threatened to be bad the boss usually had us all on herd. He said we could "sleep all next winter."

To see one of his men sleeping or taking it easy actually seemed to hurt that man Simpson. Sometimes he ordered every man on herd when two could have held the cattle. Three of us hands furnished our own mounts, and every time something was to be done that required using up extra horseflesh, one of the three stood a good chance of receiving an order. Still, there was no open rupture between boss and men.

Different trail outfits had different methods of handling the saddle horses at night. With some outfits a *remudero,* or wrangler—"night-hawk," he was often called—herded the horses; other outfits had no night-herder for the horses but simply hobbled them. But no matter how the horses were handled, horse thieves were likely to make away with some of them on a dark night. If they were herded, a thief could slip in among them and drift a few out; if they were hobbled, a thief could catch what he wanted, cut the hobbles, and drive or lead them away. A night wrangler meant an extra man on the payroll; we had no night wrangler. So every evening each man had to hobble his string of horses.

One evening a week or so after we had left home, while we were hobbling our mounts before eating supper, two likely looking young men rode up to camp. Naturally they received an invitation to 'light, unsaddle, and eat. They were mighty accommodating and helped us finish hobbling, but they did not unsaddle. They said they had a long way to go and would have to be making tracks as soon as they had a bite to eat. A little after good dark they pulled out.

When the remuda was rounded up next morning, six horses were missing; luckily for some of us, all six were Simpson's. We were confident that the two young men had stolen them, and Jack Walton and I wanted to trail them down. Simpson, however, said that he could not spare us from the herd; he said it would be cheaper to buy more horses than to delay with hunting down horse thieves. Those six horses were the worst loss we suffered at one time, but all the way up we were bothered by thieves. Once a fellow made the mistake of taking a horse that belonged to me. I followed and brought the horse back. One of the tricks of these trail jackals was to hide horses in the brush at night and then for a neat price offer next morning to find them. Another trick was to ride up to a herd when bad brush or a bad river was just ahead and ask for a job. After working with an outfit a day or two and getting on to the way affairs were run, the disguised thieves might pick out two or three of the best horses at night and skip. By the time daylight revealed their thievery, they could be thirty or forty miles away. They knew that a big trail herd could not dally. Plenty of men that tried to work the trail drivers in such ways were caught and hanged or shot. Horse thieves were worse in the Indian Territory than anywhere else.

Most of the tricks of the trail, however, were harmless and good natured—like the one once played by Tommie Newton at Doan's Crossing on Red River. Tommie loved a joke. None of his hands had ever been up the trail before; so they did not know what Red River looked like. Ten miles away from the crossing Tommie rode on ahead to scout. He found that the water was very low and he saw that some long, dry bars of sand in the river were very white. Turning back, he halted his chuck wagon on an elevation of ground in full view of the river but too far away to permit accurate observation. All that could be seen was the winding channel and the glistening white sand, which, with the sun shining on it, looked like water. Tommie told the boys that the river was on a rampage, but that he was going to string the cattle out and put them over, and that they had better strip for action.

"When we hit the bank," he said, "there'll be no time for taking off clothes and six-shooters. You had better shuck now and put your stuff in the wagon. I'll go ahead with the wagon and cross it on a ferry boat above that bend."

The boys shucked off everything but their hats, undershirts, and drawers. Instructing them to graze the cattle an hour longer and then come on, Tommie took the wagon ahead. Of course he forded without trouble, at a point invisible to the boys. Then he sent the cook on to make camp two or three miles beyond. What Tommie's cowboys said when they approached the white sands and while they drove on in their undershirt-tails can be better imagined than printed.

Practical jokes like that were always being played on the trail. The Indians in the territory were, when not positively dangerous, a great nuisance on account of their demands for beef, which they called "wohaw." To prevent the Indians from stampeding their herds or causing other trouble, the trail men generally paid tribute. It was customary for every trail boss to put into his herd any animal that he recognized as having been lost by drivers in front of him. Experienced cowmen knew the majority of brands to be found on the trail all the way from the Rio Grande to the Arkansas. Animals picked up in this way were either delivered to their owners in Kansas or were sold and the money later delivered—though, of course, tens of thousands of cattle were driven off and sold illegitimately.

Anyway, one time up in the Indian Territory Bill Jackman picked up a big steer that he recognized as belonging to Ike Pryor, who was a couple of days' drive ahead. He was taking the animal along with perfectly honest intentions when one day a puff-paunched Osage Indian with a gang of warriors and squaws behind him rode up to the herd and asked for the chief. Jackman was pointed out. Then the Indian gravely handed over a folded slip of paper. It read as follows:

"To the trail bosses: This is a good Indian. I know him personally. Give him beef and you will have no trouble getting through his country. Ike Pryor."

Jackman handed the letter back to the Indian, rode into the herd, cut out Ike Pryor's fine beef, and told Uncle Sam's children to take it. As they chased the animal off, some of them shooting at it, they yelled "wohaw, wohaw," but "he-haw, he-haw" was what Bill Jackman's crowd said when they saw Colonel Pryor in Dodge City—though he was just plain Ike at that time, not yet having been commissioned by the prickly pear-flatterers of Southwest Texas.

When our herd trailed into the prairie dog country of the Indian Nation we were amid an unfailing source of amusement and pleasure. As South Texas boys, several of us had never seen prairie dogs before, and even those among us who had seen them were glad of their society. They were good company. We listened to their chatter along the trail; we talked back to them; we shot at them. When there were rocks within reach, we chunked at them. Occasionally a cowboy would get one of the little creatures cut off from the town of holes and then a merry chase would follow. In after years I was to live much among prairie dogs, but I have never wearied of their company. I shall be sorry, indeed, when the United States government, which has done much to destroy the natural life of America, has poisoned off all the prairie dogs. As Burns expressed himself towards the mouse, so I have always felt towards the prairie dog, even if he is a great destroyer of grass:

> I doubt na, whiles, but thou may thieve:
> What then? poor beastie, thou maun live!
> A daimen icker in a thrave
> [An occasional ear in a shock of corn]
> 'S a sma' request;
> I'll get a blesing wi' the lave [rest],
> And never miss 't!

Had the animals been called prairie squirrels instead of prairie dogs, they would probably have been killed off long ago for their meat. Their diet, like that of squirrels, is strictly vegetable, and their flesh is clean. Only their name has been against them as a game animal. Some years ago two enterprising young men in West Texas made good money shipping prairie dog carcasses, cleaned and refrigerated, to northern markets, where they were sold as squirrels—until food authorities discovered the trick that was being played. Then the business went under. I should like to know how the myth ever got started that rattlesnakes and prairie dogs live in harmony. Rattlesnakes go into the holes to eat the young dogs, but as soon as the old dogs discover such an intruder they set up a very excited chatter and dozens of them together begin kicking dirt in the hole that the snake has entered.

It was "a whoop and a yea and a-driving the dogies," and the herd snailed on "to the camp fire far away." With clear days and fair nights and the grass high and fresh all about us, with prairie dogs talking in their friendly way and deer and antelopes and turkeys hardly ever out of sight, with the scene ever changing, and with nothing to listen to but the silence— or the sounds—of nature, trail life was wonderfully pleasant. I do not know anything more wholesome and satisfying than seeing cattle come in on their bed ground at night so full and contented that they grunt when they lie down. If a stranger happened into camp, the news he had to tell was regarded as a boon.

After supper the boys not on herd would tell yarns, sing songs, wrestle, and act generally like a bunch of kids, which mostly we were. Like many of the outfits, ours had a fiddle, and while some artist in spurs "made it talk," we often put the end gate of the chuck wagon on the ground and then took turns dancing jigs upon it. Or maybe some lad would take the fiddle out to the herd with him and "agitate the catgut" to the tune of "Billy in the Low Ground," "Dinah Had a Wooden Leg," "Hell Among the Yearlin's," "Old Rosen the Bow," "Cotton-Eyed Joe," "Saddle Ole Pike," "Sally Gooden," "The Devil's Dream," or some other such favorite. Many a night I have led Lake Porter's horse around the herd while he made the longhorns snore to music.

Some people say that the reason cowboys sang to the cattle was to prevent their being frightened by any sudden or irregular noise. There is something in that, but I am sure that the music of the fiddle was appreciated by some of the old time longhorns—whatever may be the taste of modern whitefaces. One lazy old brindle steer that always stayed in the drag by day and slept on the south edge of the herd at night seemed particularly fond of "One Evening in May"—a waltz tune. More than once Lake Porter and I stopped to see him wriggle his ears and kind of blow in an appreciative manner. Pleasant it was on a warm, clear night to circle slowly around a herd of cattle that were bedded down quiet and breathing deep and out there to catch the strains of song or fiddle coming from camp, where the fire was like a dim star. But it was pleasanter to be in camp and, while just catching now and then a note from singer or fiddler on herd, to be dropping off to sleep. As long as a cowboy heard music he knew that all was well.

One of the subjects that cowboys on the trail frequently discussed at night was the stars. The stars were our timepieces. Only one man in our particular outfit started out from San Patricio with a watch, and he got it so full of water when we crossed the Brazos that it quit running. The Mexican vaqueros out in Arizona call the Great Dipper *el Reloj de los Yaquis* (the Clock of the Yaquis)—presumably because the Yaqui Indians depend upon it. And *el Reloj de los Yaquis* was our clock—more clearly and beautifully illumined than the dial of any hour plate that ever looked down from cathedral or state-hall tower. We could not hear its chimes as it revolved around the North Star, but in clear weather we changed guards according to its position as accurately as the Moslems of the East bow at sunset to the muezzin's call to prayer. As the Dipper swings completely around the North Star every twenty-four hours, the boys on first guard noted carefully the position of the "pointers," or "hands" (Alpha and Beta) in their relation to the pole star, and when these "hands" had marked off a third of the night, a man went to camp and awakened the next guard.

However, the Dipper sometimes gets down too low behind the horizon to be observed. Then other stars—unless cloudiness prevented any observation at all—must be relied upon. A man used to watching the rising and setting of the stars can gauge the hour of night by them as easily as he can gauge the hour of day by the position of the sun. One of the common stories of the range was of the nigger cowpuncher, "from over East of Victoria," who was told by a certain cowboy to watch the North Star and when it set to call him to go on guard. The poor nigger was on the first relief. About daybreak he rode into camp, where the cowboy had already got up after his long night's sleep and was drinking coffee. "Massa Tom," the nigger said, "I dun watch dat stah all night and he nevah move one bit."

Perhaps it was interest in the stars as timepieces that led us to other celestial interests. Anyway, we frequently took pleasure in pointing out to each other not only the Seven Sisters, Job's Coffin, Jacob's Ladder, the Great Hunter, the Big Bear, and other commonly known constellations, but our own fancied configurations. One group of stars we called the Texas Star. The Milky Way—called also the Milkmaid's Path and familiar to vaqueros from the border country as *El Camino de San Pedru* (St. Peter's Road)—offered unlimited possibilities for the fancy. In herding at night the men rode around the cattle in opposite directions, half of them clockwise and half of them counter-clockwise. If the cattle were quiet, two cowboys meeting each other on their rounds would frequently stop for a talk.

"John," said Jack Walton to me one night when we met, each of us throwing a leg over the saddle horn, for our night horses were gentle, "I've got the purtiest girl in Jericho figgered out in that Milkmaid's Path. Let me show her to you."

He showed me the best he could, but I must confess that I saw a herd of cattle with the riders in place and the remuda behind more plainly than I saw the girl. I remember hearing an argument in camp one night over the question as to whether the person burning brush in the moon was a man or a woman. Well, we might differ on some of the heavenly aspects, but the star that we all, particularly all of us on the last guard, agreed was most interesting and beautiful was the Morning Star, the rising of which directed the horse wrangler to bring in the horses and the cook to start wrestling with his pots.

Many of the older and more experienced range men could by means of *la Epacta* compute the phases of the moon for weeks ahead. They got their method from the Mexicans; it was nothing less than a crude and popular usage of the means employed by astronomers for calculating the epact. Almanacs were not always plentiful and it was worth something for a frontiersman to know when the light of the moon would come with Indian horse thieves; it was worth something to know whether the moon would be full or waning when a herd was to be taken through the Wichita Mountains, where the Indians often gave trouble; and at a time when a great many people planted their potatoes, weaned their children, and castrated their colts by the moon's phases or the signs of the zodiac, certainly an ability to predict the moon was valued. Friendly Dubose, from Nueces County, a pioneer among pioneers and a great man to take horses up the trail, was noted for his accuracy in forecasting the phases of the moon by means *la Epacta*.

Now, I have heard it stated by good and honest trail drivers that when there were no watches and when the clouds prevented observation of the moon and stars, then the guard on herd always ran over time and thus called the next relief late rather than early. I cannot claim that I and the men I herded with were always so generous. On a dark night with no maid in the Milky Way to watch or no Star of Bethlehem—we had such a star—to trace in its rising, the hours sometimes got very, very long and somebody was almost sure to get "shorted" on the guess as to the time. Frequently it was the last guard that stood the longest watch.

Aside from watching the heavens and depending on his own instinct as to time, the cowboy on herd had one other possible source of time measurement—his night horse, or, as he sometimes called this important animal, his "nightmare." The night horse was generally the surest footed, the clearest sighted, and the most intelligent horse that a cowboy had in his string. He was ridden only on herd at night, and while his work was frequently easy it was, again, likely to be exceedingly hard. In every remuda there were certain horses known to be night horses no matter what cowboy might have them assigned to his mount. Thus, as may be readily seen, the night horse was oftener than not a seasoned animal of wide experience. If so, he was likely to know within a few minutes when it was time for his rider to quit "circling them longhorn cattle" and head for the wagon. If he knew, he tried to convey his knowledge by pulling on the bits and shaking his head. Of course some night horses would get anxious to quit before their time was up, but a man soon learned how far he could depend on his night horse's actions.

Asa Jones, of El Paso, who has traded cattle and ridden horses in nearly every county between the Mississippi River and the Grand Canyon, often recalls a night horse branded CID and called Sid that he used to ride up on the Plains. When the time came to change guard, according to Asa, old Sid might, by main strength and awkwardness, be persuaded to make two or three more rounds of the herd. Then in spite of hell and high water he headed for the chuck wagon. However, if the rider there got down, threw the reins over Sid's head, and waited a minute, he could then remount and go back to the herd. Sid always knew when his time was up.

I find that I have been dwelling long on the pleasanter aspects of trail life. Perhaps memory is too much of a softener; yet even at the time I lived it I loved the life as much as I love it now in memory. Hearing old-timers prate about their "sacrifices" and trying to make martyrs out of themselves has always disgusted me. I and the other happy-go-lucky cowboys of the frontier that I knew made no unusual sacrifices for the sake of posterity. I am glad that I was not born later into a more mechanically comfortable and a softer cushioned age. We, like all men of all ages, were pretty much creatures of circumstance. That circumstance sometimes brought out in us endurance and fidelity almost heroic, modesty shall not prevent my admitting; but if we had not grown up with the soil between our toes, the wind in our faces, the starlight in our eyes, and a peculiar and strict code of ethics in our consciousness, perhaps we might not have been able to meet the tests that were applied.

> On stormy nights when wild northwesters rave,
> How proud a thing to fight with wind and wave!
> The dripping sailor on the reeling mast
> Exults to bear, and scorns to wish it past.

Not alone was it his breed that made the American cowboy

stick to herd and horse until only death could drag him loose; it was his occupation.

"We had a negro cowboy named George," says an old time Plains cowman,[1] "who was not very well clad because he liked to pike at monte too well to buy clothes. We all had colds and coughs till it was like a bunch of Texas pot hounds baying a 'possum when we tried to sleep. One bitter night I was near George on herd and tried to get him to go to the chuck wagon and turn his horse loose, but he was too game for that. His teeth were chattering as he said to me, 'I can stand it if the rest of you all can.' Presently I saw him lean over his saddle horn, coughing, and he looked like he was losing his breath. By the time I got to him he was off his horse, as dead as a mackerel and as stiff as a poker. He had simply frozen to death sitting on that horse. We placed his body in the chuck wagon on his bed and drove to the Palo Duro and on the highest hill we could find we planted the poor black boy, rolled in his blankets. The ground was sandy; so we could dig a grave deep enough that the coyotes would not claw into it."

The worst night that I spent on this first trip up the trail, or that I have ever spent with cattle anywhere, was on the Solomon River north of Abilene. Within two or three miles of our camp there must have been a dozen other herds, all of them waiting for their owners to give the word to deliver. When we unrolled our beds down on the ground that night under the open sky, it was clear, though there was a kind of clammy stillness in the air that indicated a low barometer. When about eleven o'clock one of the men on guard came in to call the second relief, he said that the cattle were restless and that a storm was coming.

"All hands to the herd," were the orders.

Sometimes when cattle stampede they stampede from a reclining position—one jump to their feet and the second jump to hell. But ours were up milling about, clacking their horns, getting ready to run an hour before they broke. The lightning had begun to play and the rumbling thunder off in the distance

[1] Mack McAvoy, in *The Cattleman*, June, 1927, p. 21.

was getting nearer and nearer. They started just as a flash of lightning made the whole world a blinding, blue white. It came from right over our heads and by the time the clap of thunder reached us the cattle were gone, the roar of their running mixed with the roar of the sky. No description of the stampede of a big herd of cattle at night under a Kansas storm can convey the reality of it.

Three or four of the boys riding like drunk Indians got in ahead of the leaders and swerved them back. Then the herd began to mill, running in a circle, the cattle in the center of the circle climbing over each other. Constant flashes of lightning gave us glimpses of them. Balls of fire were playing on the tips of the long horns and on the tips of our horses' ears. Snakes of fire ran over the back of the cattle and darted along the manes of our mounts. Everybody was yelling, but some of the boys instead of yelling in a way to quiet the cattle, long and low and trembly, were yelling in a way to make the cattle more excited. A little distance off to the right of us I heard more yelling and rumbling, and I knew that one of the neighboring herds had stampeded also. The wind was not yet blowing much, and the seething mass of cattle gave out waves of heat that were almost scorching. The rattle of horns and hoofs and hocks was terriffic. With every fresh clap of thunder every animal not too tightly wedged in the mass seemed to jump straight up, and the impact that followed jarred the ground. I knew that we were not going to quiet those cattle down that night.

Before long a sheet of water began pouring down, and the lead cattle broke through our line. Some of us had our slickers on and some had slickers in their hands waving them and slapping them at the cattle in an attempt to hold them back. We might as well have slapped them at the devils of the storm overhead. The cowboys of that day generally believed that heat and steel attracted electricity. Fighting a stampede is hot work. Less daring cowboys who wore slickers took them off so as to let their bodies cool and thus lessen the attraction for lightning. Many a pair of steel spurs and many a six-shooter were cast upon the prairie under Kansas lightning. In no time our cattle had run into the neighboring herd and the two herds were blending and splitting. The herd no longer had a defined point. It was every man for what he could see. Maybe three men would get cut off with a little bunch of fifty cattle and maybe one man would be "hanging and wrestling" with a thousand head. In the pitchy darkness the ground all looked alike and the lightning blinded more than it illuminated. If a man rode over a bluff, into a prairie dog hole or a gully, or if he kept on level ground, no matter. He "hung" with the cattle, waiting for daylight to come—or until he broke his own neck or perhaps only a horse's leg. Every gully and sink was full of water; the soft places in the ground were boggy, the hard places were slippery. How any man could keep going for hours in such country under such conditions without a serious accident seems almost miraculous. If a man's horse fell, the rider instinctively clung to the reins; then if the horse could get up, it was mount and go on.

At daylight some of the cattle, absolutely crazy with fear, were still running. Two of us—the other man a stranger to me —had got cut off with a bunch of five or six hundred head, mostly big steers, and as soon as we could see, I knew we must be eight or ten miles from camp. I have heard of big steers running as far as twenty-five miles. If we thought that bunch of longhorns we were with would come to their senses with daylight, we were fooled. It looked as if they were going to run us as well as themselves to death. Had I had my six-shooter I should most assuredly have shot the leaders. As it was, I rode up under their blowing nostrils and finally, by flashing my slicker down on the ground in front of them, made them dodge back and to one side. The crazy steers following close behind piled up three deep on the animals that had checked. The result was a few more broken horns and legs—and the run was over. Such means were employed only in extreme cases.

As we headed back in the general direction of our herding grounds, I saw that we had four or five brands represented among the cattle. There were other bunches in sight, some with men after them, some loose. Every herd in the country had run; between ten and twelve thousand cattle were mixed up. It took us five days to get them together and separated into the original herds. Then they ran again, and half of the cutting out and shaping up was to do over.

It kept raining and storming. Good horses were ruined for life. All the horses were ridden down. There was no such thing as lying down in a dry bed for a few hours of unbroken sleep. The cow chips, our principal fuel, were all wet and half the time we could not get enough hot food and coffee. In such times a cowboy swore that he'd never go up the trail again, that he "wouldn't chouse cattle for no damn man." But, so far as I know, no cowboy ever quit while his life was hardest and his duties were most exacting. I never even heard one express the intention of quitting instantly. A certain sense of loyalty to his herd, an ingrained code of fidelity to his trust, kept him rubbing tobacco juice in his eyes to stay awake and risking his life after some wild, crazy brute of a gaunt, ten-dollar cow. If in the midst of such gruelling and desperate work there was plenty of "belly-aching," there was plenty of cheer.

No insurance company would in those days insure the life of a cowboy; nor is insurance for cowboys obtainable even now except on payment of a very heavy premium, about three times that required of miners, who lead a life dangerous enough. Prairie fires, swollen rivers, stampedes, storms, freezing blizzards, man-killing horses, fighting cattle, holes for horses to step into and trees for them to run against, desperate men and savage Indians to lie in wait for him, a rope that might betray him constantly in his hand—all these perils and more were a part of the cowboy's daily lot. Wherever he rode, alone or in a cow crowd, death was reaching for his bridle reins. Let three significant items culled from newspapers of fifty years ago illustrate the varied perils to which he was subject.

Frio County: A few days ago, near the Frio, the body of a man was found on the prairie, with the head completely severed from the body. Near the body was found a horse, with a rawhide lariat fastened to the saddle, the other end of the lariat being attached to the horns of a steer. This lariat, for a distance of three or four feet, was freshly stained with blood. The supposition is that in lassoing the steer the rider accidentally got his lariat wound around his own neck and was then dragged about by the steer and horse until his head was completely torn from the body.

Wilson County: Mr. Taylor Crain, a well-known stockman, was running his horse in attempting to corral a wild bunch of horses, when his horse fell, the horn of the saddle striking Mr. Crain on the breast. Death followed on Saturday.

Callahan County: One week ago last Sunday Mr. Frank Shelly, a promising young man and a resident of this county, while at a round-up at Simpson's rancho, on Clear Fork of the Brazos, in Taylor County, about thirty miles from here, allowed his horse to run over a yearling, throwing Mr. Shelly on his head and shoulders, which probably broke his neck, as he became unconscious, in which condition he remained until his death on Monday at 1 o'clock.

If when he got to town, after long months out in the brush, on the lone prairie, or on the long, long trail, the cowboy "cut loose" and had "a little fun," he can hardly be blamed. He was a healthy animal. He was full of vinegar and pride. He was anything but a gun-toting, swaggering murderer ready to shoot the daylights out of the first man he met. He came generally from venturesome ancestors, the makers of frontier homes. Among the cowboys, true enough, there were "bad" men, vicious men; but the great majority of them were honest and truthful and were against outlawry and viciousness. They were hard and diligent workers, and men who work hard out in the open generally lead straight lives.

After the great stampedes on Solomon River we pointed our herd north by west for the River Platte. The cattle were "spoiled" now and they gave us lots of trouble, but none of their runs was at all comparable to the one I have described. We were glad when, after a long swim, we counted them out to Simpson's buyer on the north bank of the Platte and turned our horses for the ride of more than a thousand miles to South Texas. Simpson sold most of his horses and I sold two of mine. We kept plenty to carry us home.

When we got down as far as Belton I turned west to pay my grandparents on the San Saba a visit. I have already told of Grandfather's offer to give me a horse every time I paid him a visit. On this visit he gave me Payaso (Clown), so named on account of his mottled face. He was gentle and about six years old—just old enough to have good sense.

Payaso proved to be the best and most faithful horse that I have ever ridden. He was an all around horse, equally good on the road and in the brush. His training on the rocky hills of the San Saba had made him a sure-footed mountain horse. He never stumbled. In time he became such a good cutting horse that I could ride him into a herd, show him the animal that I wanted to cut out, then remove the bridle and let him act alone. Without further direction he would take the animal right out, no matter how rapidly it dodged. He was as good for roping as he was for cutting. Sometimes I actually felt ashamed of myself in his company—he knew so much. Indeed he was a kind of equine genius in the business of handling cattle. I loved him. I never struck him or more than barely touched spurs to his sides. He learned to come to my call or whistle. He was very fond of sugar, which I often gave him, but feeding him sugar and corn never impaired his wonderful foraging abilities. When we stopped alone somewhere out on the range to spend the night, I had no fear of his leaving me.

CHAPTER VIII

BRINGING IN THE STRAYS

WHEN I quit the rangers in the spring of '77, I quit with the intention of making another trip up the trail. As will be recalled, I had gone up with Simpson's herd the spring preceding. This time I engaged to go with One-Armed Jim Reed, of Goliad. Reed had lost an arm in the Civil War, thus earning his sobriquet, and he was one of the best known characters in the cattle kingdom. An Alabamian by birth, he had come to Texas at an early date, had shipped cattle by boat from old Powderhorn (Indianola), had driven them to Mexico, had trailed them through Louisiana swamps, and then after the northern trails opened had become one of the big drivers. He had heard the owl hoot in all sorts of places and he liked to talk of what he had seen and heard. With his one hand he could outbrand most other men with two hands, and he was regarded as the best poker player that ever hit a cow town. At the time I began working for him he had quit doing much work on horseback except cutting, for he was too busy trading, receiving, and delivering cattle to work on the range; but he knew what was in every herd that he owned. He would help shape up and start off his herds from South Texas, then go by rail to Kansas, and when his trail bosses reported there they would find One-Armed Jim present with eye open to appraise every cow.

With our herd were Reed's sons, Paul and Jim—and also his famous race horse, Rover. Rover was the favorite race horse of Southwest Texas and his owner really seemed to think more of him than of all his other possessions combined. One time when I was at the Reed ranch in Goliad County, Rover took the colic and went to rolling over and over on the ground. Old

One-Armed Jim got out in the pen with the horse and rolled on the ground in sympathy. We boys laughed at his antics—we couldn't help laughing—and he chunked us all out of the pen. He was sure that Rover was going to die, but Rover got all right and Reed went on lending him to his friends, as usual, to match races, always appearing himself if possible to see the victory. The year that he took Rover to Kansas he won some big stakes around Dodge City.

Now, before I started to work for Jim Reed I had considered another job. When we got about a hundred miles up the trail, I decided to turn back and take it. It was a job peculiar to the times and conditions, and in order that people of the fenced-in world of the present day may understand it, some explanation is necessary.

From the beginning of the cattle business in Texas, the code of the open range required that every cowman should brand not only his own calves but all other calves that he rounded up. Of course these "outside" calves were supposed to be branded in accordance with the brands on their respective mothers. So long as only cattle owners branded cattle and so long as all cattle owners were fair with each other, every stockman gained the natural increase of his cattle, no matter how far off his cows might scatter.

This system was working very well in Texas before the Civil War. Then came four years during which the range industry, like every other industry in the South, went without direction. At the end of the War there were more cattle in Texas than there had been at the opening of the War. A majority of them were in Southwest Texas. As soon as the ranchmen got back from the War they began branding their cattle and trying to get them again under control. Many of the best men who had helped to keep order on the range before the War broke out never returned. Widows and orphans could not ride out and struggle against the confusion. By 1867 the more fortunate and enterprising of the cattle owners had to a limited extent regained control over their property, but a new market that was destined to revolutionize the cattle industry was being established to the north and a new element was riding the range. Prominent among this new element were cattle thieves.

The branding and selling of estrayed cattle became a complicated business in which thieves were proficient. The cowmen developed a custom of paying four bits apiece for all calves branded away from the home range. Some men made a living by this "outside" branding. But there was nothing but honor to prevent such a man's putting his own brand on a big calf—and maybe claiming the four bit fee besides. Honor is not a universal quality. If the unbranded animal was over a year old and not following a branded cow—if it was a maverick—then, according to custom, it belonged to the man on whose range it was found; however, a great deal of the range was claimed in a very loose way, some of it had no claimants at all, and even under the most favorable circumstances no ranchman could keep more than a general watch over his acreage. Given an inch, it is human nature to take a mile. Some cowmen proposed a law against branding any animal except within an enclosure; such a law if enforced, would have prevented promiscuous branding, but on the whole it was regarded as impracticable. All any man needed in order to start a brand of his own was "a rope, nerve, and a running iron." The struggle for existence on a fierce frontier developed nerve; ropes and running irons were cheap. So calves were branded legitimately and illegitimately, and so cow thieves were developed.

Now, even if all his cattle that strayed off were kept in his brand and if their increase also were branded correctly, how was a ranchman to sell them and derive profit from them? He might take part in the works and roundups for many miles in every direction, but still he could not hope to bring home and to deliver to some buyer everything that was out. It became the custom for every cowman when selling off his own cattle to sell also any other stock of a like class that he found on his range. Custom fixed his fee as agent at a dollar a head for all such cattle that he delivered. It was fifty times easier to bring home the money for a steer that had strayed fifty miles

BRINGING IN THE STRAYS

away than it was to bring the steer home. Before he could leave any country with a herd, a buyer was required by law to have a bill of sale describing the brands, class, and number of cattle in his herd. An authorized county inspector was supposed to see that the bill of sale was correct and to keep a duplicate of it.

Furthermore, the inspector was required to turn this record over to the county clerk, who recorded it in a well-bound book called "The Stock Record Book." This book was open for inspection at all times.[1] Stockmen from far and near came to look at it, or sent representatives to look at it. It told plainly if any cattle had been sold in the brand or brands claimed by any cowman; how many cattle had been sold; and at what price they had been sold. If the price was not given, the classification of the stock was given, prices each year for the several classes of stock—cows, yearlings, beeves, etc.—being standard. The book also told who had sold the cattle and who had bought them. After consulting it the cowman, or his representative, knew from whom to collect. The number of brands in the country, considering the population, was astonishingly large. Thus, in the Stock Record Book of Atascosa County for 1875 the description of 1700 head of cattle delivered by James Lowe to Ellison and Dewees, May 8, occupies twenty-four folio pages and notes several hundred brands.

A description of a delivery of cattle under the system that has just been explained may be clarifying. It is taken from a sketch written by T. W. Carmichael in *The Cattleman* (Fort Worth, Texas, June, 1919).

On March 3, 1873 [says Mr. Carmichael], I left San Antonio as a cowboy with the Carmichael and Wadkins outfit to go to the range at Bandera, eighty miles to the northwest. We took the cash, all gold 20's, in specie belts, to pay for the steers. For two weeks I carried a belt around me containing $2500. . . . That was one time I got awfully tired of too much money. There were no banks on the range and paper money was counterfeit.

When we arrived at Bandera we found 5000 cattle rounded up by a ranchman from whom we were to make our "cut out." We

[1] For typical entries in one such stock book see "Appendix B."

cut 800 aged steers, none under four years old, and paid $11.25 a head for them. Each steer was run out singly close by the brand inspector, who sat on his horse and called the brand on each steer, which was placed on record by his clerk, who also sat on his horse. There was no room around for a man on foot. This ranchman sold that day more cattle belonging to other brands than he sold of his own brand. The inspector kept the records and the cattlemen settled with one another by these records. Doubtless men received pay for cattle they had never seen, the steers when calves having been branded for them by other cowmen. Some of these cattle were a hundred miles from the home ranches of their owners.

The great weakness of the open range system of selling lay in the fact that plenty of men in the country who were selling other people's cattle—and having them inspected too—were irresponsible. When the owners whom they had voluntarily represented sought them in order to collect, they very often could not be found. Sometimes if found, they could not be collected from. Furthermore, vast numbers of cattle were being secretly driven out of the counties without inspection or with bogus bills-of-sale. A few inspectors operated in a manner to favor cow thieves.

So, alongside the system of inspection and recording, grew up a custom whereby stockmen exchanged brands with each other and represented each other by power of attorney. One reputable cowman might have power of attorney from a dozen or two dozen other cowmen living off in other counties. They in turn represented him on their ranges. Such cooperation did much towards preventing irresponsible men from selling everything they could round up. It really "converted" a good many cow thieves. Eventually it led to the organization of what is now known as the Texas and Southwestern Cattle Raisers' Association—the most powerful organization of cowmen in the world. Order on the range, however, was a long time in arriving.

In addition to having their sales recorded in the county stock books, most cowmen kept accounts of their own and were ready to exchange tally books (called also "beef books") with other cowmen and to settle at any time. "Stock meetings," or "cattle settlements," were held about once a year in each county, and were widely attended. For instance, at a meeting in Goliad County several representatives from Atascosa County would be present. Every cowman knew hundreds of brands, and for most of the cattle that he had sold he knew with whom to settle. But generally he had sold some cattle in brands unknown to him. He would seek at these meetings to find the owner. Thus at the meeting in Goliad County Doc Burris might announce: "Here's $15 for a beef branded Seven Two Bar that I sold last spring. Who claims the money?"

Then a man from Atascosa County, C. C. Fountain perhaps, might speak up and say: "That brand was bought out last winter by Jim Lowe, of Dog Town. I'm representing him."

The money, less one dollar charged for selling and delivering the animal, would at once be turned over to Fountain.

As men engaging in the cattle business became more numerous and as, in consequence, the brands to be reckoned with became more numerous also, naturally it became more difficult to settle for all stray cattle sold. Sometimes the stock meetings lasted several days. They might be held in town or they might be held out on the range. If out on the range, one or more of the big cowmen would furnish chuck wagons, cook, and grub that was free to all who came. The meetings were frequently occasions for social pleasures as well as for business. Poker, horse racing, and conversation were the chief amusements. Bags of gold and silver were handled around camp as carelessly as so many bags of corn.

The development of such a system speaks eloquently for the honesty of the pioneer cowmen. But, as has already been said, there were men not honest to take advantage of it. The law of population requires that a man shall run in order to keep from being run over. The history of all America is the history of increasing population. In Southwest Texas affairs got to the point that many cowmen considered it necessary to steal in order to keep from being stolen out. However, there were many fine exceptions; for example, the Pettus men, of Goliad

County, would not brand an animal unless they were sure it was their own and they consistently ate their own beef.

Nevertheless, the distinction between "mine and thine" tended to become so loose that perhaps the majority of ranch people followed the custom of killing only other people's cattle for beef. One of the old jokes of the range was of the man who had never tasted his own beef except in the camp of a neighbor. Free beef meant waste beef. Most range men ate but two meals a day, breakfast and supper. Their life was nomadic, bedding here tonight and yonder tomorrow night. Some of them thought nothing of "beefing" a heifer every evening, roasting a great "bait" of it over the coals for supper, eating some more of it with the morning coffee, and then leaving the remainder, perhaps three-quarters of the animal, together with the hide, for the buzzards and coyotes. During eight months of the year the blow-flies were so bad that meat could not be kept except in a jerked condition, and the men were too busy riding—and often too averse to any kind of dismounted activity—to cut the meat into strips and dry it. In 1874 a cowman at a meeting of the Stock Raisers' Association of Western Texas (a very loose organization), held in Pleasanton, complained that each year enough choice beef—generally fat calves, yearlings, and heifers—was thrown away on the prairies of Texas to supply the largest city in the state.[2]

In short, so long as the range was unfenced—particularly the brushy range of Southwest Texas in contradistinction to the range of the open plains—no owner of land or cattle could control his own property. Without fences, no man could keep his own cattle on his own range, to brand and sell the increase; no man could breed up a herd, for all the scrub bulls in the country were free to mingle with his stock; no man could afford to feed his cattle during drouths, for any feed put out would be largely consumed by cattle not his own; nor under such conditions was there much incentive for a cowman to spend money in digging wells, building tanks and making other improvements on the great commons. Had all men been equally enterprising and had

[2] *Western Stock Journal*, Pleasanton, Texas, 1874.

all men been honest and cooperative, then the continuance of open range methods even in a brush country might have been successful; but the world of human beings has to be considered as it is.

Here are two advertisements of 1877 from two representative cowmen on the Nueces that tell more as to the inability of owners to control their own stock than many pages of exposition could tell.

All honest, good, industrious, poor men with families, are welcome to kill an occasional calf of mine for food, provided they do not waste the meat, and all my honest neighbors are welcome to skin and sell the hides of my dead animals, but living animals must be untouched. The killing for food, skinning or selling must not be kept secret. John Timon.[3]

The scarcity of cattle and the persistency upon the part of stockmen to sell everything they can find in the cow line compels me to inform them that I want none of my cattle sold for less than $12—or abide the consequences. Wiley Rix.[4]

Another striking instance of the confusion existing on the open range in southern Texas is found in a complaint published by a man of Medina County.[5] "I had about 1600 head of cattle collected to drive," he says. "I sent for the inspector. He came, but could inspect only part of the herd—on account of my not having certified or personal authority of the owners. Out of the 1600 head I received authority to take only 806 head—had to turn the balance loose."

Many of these cattle turned loose were drift cattle from the north. In Texas, brands are recorded by counties and not by the state, as in New Mexico and some other states. Thus, in Shack-

[3] Oakville *Tribune,* Oakville, Texas, Nov. 7, 1877. What John Timon proposed to do with people not honest who ate, skinned, and sold his cattle, he does not say. Perhaps it was fortunate that the brush prevented his seeing too far out over the range. Timon was a San Patricio County man, but his cattle were scattered so badly that he advertised in adjoining counties. Jim Ursery of Live Oak County, who ran the Heart H brand, advertised in the same way.
[4] Oakville *Tribune,* Oakville, Texas, Oct. 1, 1877. Again the threat of helplessness.
[5] *Western Stock Journal,* Pleasanton, Texas, June 23, 1874.

elford County, one man only could record the Buzzard Rail
brand, belonging to Judge Terry Lynch, but no law prevented
a certain man from recording as his own the Buzzard Rail in
Medina County, far to the south, where some of Lynch's cattle
drifted. The brands on cattle, the cooperation of honest cowmen, the laws of the state, and the vigilance of inspectors were
all by hook and crook circumvented. True, many cowmen on
account of cheap grass, the general rise in the prices of land and
cattle, and their own extraordinary energy and sagacity, amassed
fortunes; but in view of the confused conditions on the open
range it seems almost a wonder that any cowman prospered.[6]

A. H. Huffmeyer, of San Antonio, an old time cowboy and
trail man, tells an illuminating story on himself. During the
era of free grass and free cattle he was living in Frio County,
roping mavericks for another man and dodging thorns to protect his own skin. "In the fall of 1876," he says, "I decided to
work for myself a while. First, I had to select a brand and mark
that no one else ran. After considering a good many combina-
tions, I adopted 7 T 6 on the left side as my brand and smooth
crop of the right ear and under-half crop of the left ear for my
mark. After six weeks of hard riding I had put the stamp of
ownership on 250 head of mavericks. Then one day a friend
asked me if I had recorded my brand and mark with the county
clerk. I replied that I had not and that I did not know a record
was necessary. He warned me that unless I attended to the matter at once somebody might steal the brand from me. The very
next day I went to Frio Town, the county seat. When I told
the clerk what I wanted, he opened his big brand book and
showed me where ——————— ———————— had nearly a month
before entered my brand and mark in his own name. This fellow had a legal claim to all the cattle I had branded; and for
all my hard work I had nothing but a lesson on the disad-
vantages of ignorance."

[6] John Clay, outstanding authority on the cattle business of America, says (*My
Life on the Range*, Chicago, 1924, pp. 180–181): "The gains of the open range
business were swallowed up by losses. From the inception of the open range
business in the West and Northwest, from say 1870 to 1888, it is doubtful if
a single cent was made if you average up the business as a whole."

Certainly during the seventies open range conditions, particularly in the brush country, seemed to be approaching chaos. Chaos demanded order, and the means of order were to be barbed wire—"bob-wire," most people used to call it. If barbed wire had not come, it seems now as if a great part of the brush country would have been denuded not only of cattle but of the cattlemen in their desperate efforts to control either their own or somebody else's stock. The "Big Steal," to be described later on in this book, will enlarge on the desperate lack of order that the open range led to. Barbed wire meant to the cattle industry what Eli Whitney's cotton gin meant to the cotton business.

Of course before barbed wire came there had been earlier moves towards fencing. Men like Shanghai Pierce, Jim Reed, and Monroe Choate had been tangled in the briar and wild rose hedges of Louisiana—and they had little desire to fence their lands in such a manner. At an early day many of the ranches in South Texas had, where timber was available, small horse pastures enclosed by picket fences, sometimes of the stake and rider variety, sometimes of poles (mesquite or oak) laid between parallel lines of upright posts. Where there was rock, some fences were made of it. But all these fences were laborious and expensive to build, and were, furthermore, inadequate for holding in massed stock. The poles soon rotted and the rocks soon became displaced. For years a legislative fight went on over the question as to whether the farmer should fence in his field against stock or whether the stockman should fence in the stock from the fields. Before barbed wire came the stockmen held the power.

The first pasture fences were on the coast. Here a few men by running a line of fence across the necks of peninsulas secured protection against the thousands of drift cattle that came each winter. A mile or two of fence might thus cut off several thousand acres. The result was to make the drift heavier on the man outside and back of the fence; his demand for fencing increased. About 1870 people began using, to a limited extent, planks from Florida to build fences. In 1872 Captain Mifflin Kenedy enclosed with smooth, or "slick," wire the first big pasture in Texas; the next year Captain Richard King fenced a big pasture. Both of these men used a great deal of lumber also.

In November, 1874, J. F. Glidden of De Kalb, Illinois, patented his revolutionizing product. To manufacture the product he formed a partnership with I. L. Ellwood, also of De Kalb. Then Glidden and Ellwood engaged Henry B. Sanborn, together with a man named Warner, to "sell" barbed wire to the public. Sanborn reached Texas in 1875. At first he met violent prejudice against his ware. Shanghai Pierce, for instance, king of cattle kings on the coast, voiced popular sentiment when he declared that cattle and horses would cut themselves to pieces on the barbs and all die of screw worms. The story of the fight against screw worms on the ranges of low altitude has never been told; it is a gruesome story. Sanborn, however, sold some of the wire to merchants in North Texas. Coleman, Mathis and Fulton, who had already fenced in an immense pasture with smooth wire, bought a carload of it. By 1880 fencing was the order of the day—and in many places wire-cutting was the disorder, sharp but shortlived.[7]

My new job was with Coleman, Mathis and Fulton. Their range was east of the Nueces River and up from the coast for many miles. Despite their fencing activities, thousands of their cattle were yet outside and thousands of them had drifted or been driven across the Nueces into the wild and bloodily contested country between the Nueces and the Rio Grande. Bill Malone and D. C. Rachal, big cowmen also, were joint employers. These men turned over to me a hundred saddle horses, ten Mexican vaqueros, and one white boy, and told me to bring their cows home. As usual I furnished my own mounts—and Payaso, of course, was among them.

What a country to cover! What a range to work in! In the "Big Thicket" thirty miles up the Nueces from Corpus Christi

[7] The whole story of Sanborn's introduction of barbed wire is told in *The Cattle Industry of Texas and Adjacent Territory*, by James Cox, St. Louis, 1895, pp. 500–503. Other men arose to contest with Glidden the honor of having invented barbed wire, but the evidence favors Glidden.

it was estimated that there were 2000 head of maverick cattle.[8]
Sam P. Fusselman's hands were shooting them with repeating
rifles. Among them were hundreds of branded cattle as wild as
the mavericks.

I took up headquarters at Rancho Saco, the old John Scott
ranch, near the present village of Bluntzer, Nueces County, on
the west side of the Nueces River. Not far from the ranch was
a typical settlement, called also Rancho Saco, made up of six
or eight American families, who had congregated for protection,
and perhaps twice as many Mexican families. The settlers all
ran cattle and most of them considered it a proof of intelligence
that they owned no land but used either state land or the unfenced range of some man who had been "fool enough to sink
his money in real estate." The homes of these settlers were, with
two or three exceptions, shanties; not one of them was provided
with a hydrant. Some of the settlers had little patches of corn;
all of them were contemptuous of farmers and were violently
opposed to farm immigration. But the Rancho Saco people
were not the cow thieves.

According to arrangements, I was to catch not only cattle
belonging to Coleman, Mathis and Fulton and to Rachal and
Malone, but also any that I found belonging to other ranchers
east of the Nueces. These other owners gave me a dollar a head
for whatever stock of theirs I recovered. This was the customary
price for bringing in strays. Bringing in strays on a commission
basis was a regular business. Jim and Neville Dobie of Live Oak
County, for instance, once took an outfit away down in the
Sands to bring back at a dollar around cattle that had got away
from Live Oak County ranchers; another time Jim Dobie, with
Wildcat Jones and some other men, took a herd of stolen cattle
away from some hard characters that had them rounded up in
the brush of McMullen County and brought them back for delivery to the Live Oak County owners.

If my business had been merely to gather cattle in the
straight brands of the owners whom I represented, the work
would have been comparatively simple; but in the first place I

[8] See Galveston *Daily News,* "Wild Cattle," March 14, 1878.

had perhaps two hundred brands to scour for. Coleman, Mathis and Fulton alone owned more than a hundred brands that they had bought out, range delivery. Some of these brands were on a few dozen cattle only, while now and then one of the brands was borne by many hundreds of cattle. This was the era in which little owners felt compelled to sell their brands out to the big operators. There was so much drifting and driving, so much working and stealing that a little man could not possibly cover the broad area over which his cattle were being scattered.

Coleman, Mathis and Fulton at times had buyers out scouring the country for cattle, many of which were slaughtered at their packery. One of the most active of these buyers was Friendly Dubose of Rancho Saco. He used to ride with a morral of gold tied to the horn of his saddle and was generally accompanied by a Mexican vaquero with another morral of gold. One of the important brands belonging to Coleman, Mathis and Fulton was the T H C, made thus, $\mathcal{H}$, which they had bought from Tom O'Connor for $30,000. O'Connor for some reason doubted his ability to negotiate a trade with the company, and he offered Jerry and Bob Driscoll either $5000 or 5000 acres of land to make the trade. The Driscolls took the land—and were secretly laughed at by some people.

In addition to looking out for a very large number of brands, I had to inspect closely for burnt brands—brands that cow thieves had mutilated. Every burnt animal that I found belonging to one of the men I represented I rebranded in his brand.

The brand mutilations were of two kinds. First, the brand burners might "run," or change, the original brand into another device. For instance, at a later time brand burners ran my Y brand into an O X, thus $\mathcal{O}\mathcal{X}$. Secondly, thieves might, with a flatiron, blot out—blotch—the original brand into a solid burn and then run their own brand on the animal in another place. As the long and large company brand of Coleman, Mathis and Fulton, C M F, $\mathcal{CMF}$, was very difficult to run into something else, the rustlers with a hot smoothing iron would obliterate the old brand and at the same time remark the animal's ears. Of course, the great blotched scar would show that the animal had been stolen, but the identity of the original owner would, presumably, be undecipherable. However, with the light just right on the blotch I could generally make out the old device, a scar under a scar. Practice in brand reading enabled one in the same way to detect the old part of a brand that had been changed into something else. Even when the old brand had been carefully traced over with a hot iron in order to make it blend with the new part of the brand, it usually remained visible to the practiced eye. Some corner or curve in the old device was likely to prove stubborn for blending into the new device; the efforts of the thieves on such brands would show in heavy, ragged burns. However, many brand burners used a good deal of ingenuity in making up brands that would envelop certain brands they had elected to tamper with. A stamp iron makes a neat, sharp outline that is difficult to burn into something else; but a great many calves were branded on the range with running irons, and the devices made with running irons were often crude and irregular, just as hand-printed letters are more crude and irregular than those printed in type. The brands made with running irons were best suited for burning out.

It was against the law for anybody to mutilate any brand, even his own. The law further required that every brand should be recorded in the county of its origin. A man who had blotted out a brand and put another in its place was naturally chary of putting this new brand on record. He simply ran it, trusting to get the cattle out of the country at the first opportunity. Such an unrecorded brand was called a "slow brand." I found west of the Nueces hundreds of cattle branded $\overline{\text{BD}}$. This brand was not recorded in any of the lower counties, but it was known to belong to a man whose name I shall not call.

Every time we gathered up a bunch of cattle we found a lot of burnt animals among them. Payaso here got his training as a cutting horse. For a while I put a good-sized herd across the Nueces once every two weeks. When we were working down on the Arroyo Colorado, about fifty miles from Corpus, I found some stout picket pens that thieves had been using to brand their stolen stuff in. I burned those pens to the ground.

Naturally my activities were being watched by some of the rustlers. I received several messages saying that they intended hanging me to a mesquite limb; frequently one or more of them would be present at the very time I was rebranding the stolen stock. But it has always been my observation that few men will fight to kill when in the wrong. I knew that I was in the right and went ahead—while the talk went on.

One time I was moving my outfit over to the Santa Rosa to begin working that country. On this particular occasion I was riding along behind the remuda, the unarmed Mexican vaqueros scattered out ahead of me. Presently I saw six horsemen, riding two abreast, coming from the direction in which we were going. Just as the last pair passed me I heard one of them say, "There's that damn fellow now."

Somehow this tickled me, and turning in my saddle, I replied, "Yes, here he is."

We rode on our respective ways. I had recognized some of the men as brand burners. I had a Winchester in a scabbard on my saddle and I had a six-shooter on my hip, and out of the tail of my eye I watched the crew until they were swallowed up in the brush.

By the time I got back to Rancho Saco two weeks later I had forgotten the episode, but one of the ranch boys reminded me of it by asking if I had seen anything of six men the day I left the ranch. I told him that I had seen them. Then he said that they had come to the ranch not long after I left, inquiring for me. They asked what kind of horse I was riding. The boys told them that I was riding Payaso—he was getting to be well known. Before the men left Rancho Saco one of them told a Mexican that they had come to hang me for the way I was driving cattle out of the country and that they wished they had recognized me when they passed me. The facts were that they had recognized me and that their nerve had failed them. They knew that

I had recognized them too; my laughing in their faces had had its effect.

My work took me among various Mexican rancheros, and I want to say here that I found them strictly honest. When we found our cattle among theirs they would tell us frankly that the cattle were not theirs, but at the same time they requested proof of our right to them. This proof was readily given. They were a long-suffering people. Many of them had been intimidated, much against their will, into harboring bandits from Mexico, and outfits on this side were constantly stirring up their stock.

Generally they raised more horses than cattle, some of the rancheros possessing more than a thousand horses each, and the way they handled these horses was truly remarkable. The stock horses were divided into *manadas* of one stallion and about twenty-five mares each, and every *manada* was in a different color, one of sorrels, one of duns, one of blacks, one of browns, one of *grullas* (mouse colored), one of *moros* (blues), one of paints (black and white or bay and white), and so on. A big green prairie dotted with these variously colored *manadas* was a beautiful sight. To keep thousands of wild horses matched up in such a precise way cost a world of time and patience and could have been accomplished only where labor was very cheap. In order to form a *manada* that would stay together a ranchero would cut out a bunch of mares or fillies of the requisite color and place a stallion with them; then for weeks he would keep a vaquero loose-herding that *manada* by day, penning them at night. In time the stallion would establish a jealous claim over the mares and would alone, without any herder, keep them together. Of course the stallions, meeting at waterings and on the grazing grounds, would often fight each other and steal each other's mares. Riders had to be out constantly keeping the bunches in order.

I carried a large cowwhip, and one day while working on the Mexican range I popped it without let at the running cattle. Several *manadas* took fright and mixed with each other and the cattle. In no time the color scheme was destroyed and not a *manada* in the round-up maintained its identity. The old don who owned them, while he had been courteous to me, was very much put out. He could not have been blamed had he "got on the prod," for he had no end of trouble rematching his colors. I helped him all that I could, and before I left his range he was in a good humor again.

I shall never forget the mosquitoes of Rancho Saco. I had been used to mosquitoes all my life, but I never suffered from them so much as I suffered that summer at Rancho Saco. I am told that mosquitoes are not so bad on the coast country as they used to be. I hope that they are not. Many a night I have heard the bell on our remuda mare going *cling, cling, cling* for hours at a time while the horses ran from and fought the mosquitoes. If the night was calm and the Gulf breeze afforded no relief against the insects, animals were simply maddened by the torture. Cattle would bunch up on the prairie and crowd together as a means of relief. The warmth and effluvium of their massed bodies seemed to drive away mosquitoes. We cowboys possessed no mosquito bars, and often we put our beds down in the middle of a pen with cattle all around us so as to get rid of the pests. A run of the cattle might have been disastrous to us but we were ready to take any chance in order to escape mosquito bites. Sometimes we kept a fire going all night and by sleeping in the smoke got relief.

One day I had been gathering cattle on the west side of the Agua Dulce and was camped by a deep and boggy hole of water on that creek when a messenger rode up with a letter from Palo Alto. He also brought two bottles of beer that the Meuly boys, who owned the store at that place, had sent gratis. Just as I was taking the bottles, Lee Rabb appeared on the east bank of the Agua Dulce, his outfit having been working on that side opposite mine. The creek was too boggy for him to cross; so I called to him to toss over his rope and let me tie something on the end of it. I put one of the bottles of beer on the rope and he dragged it to his side. There was a mutual "Here's how," and then he rode away, waving me *adios* with the empty bottle, which he pitched into a clump of prickly pear.

That was the last time, perhaps, that a white man saw Lee

Rabb alive. That night he corralled his herd at the Petronilla
and went to a Mexican *baile*. He was sitting inside the Mexican
house drinking coffee with a *senorita* and talking to her when
his *caporal* (straw boss), jealous and drunk, pointed a gun
through the window at Lee's back and shot him dead. The
murderer then caught the best horse that Lee had and pulled
for the Rio Grande—that line for which so many men on both
sides of it have strained—that line which has for so many men
meant life or death. Lee Rabb's murderer crossed it and thus
saved his life and won reputation on the other side for being a
hero. He had killed a gringo. I did not hear of the trouble until
several days later and then it was impossible for me to leave my
outfit and go in pursuit of the murderer, but I wanted to go.
Many did go. The murder stirred up feeling that was already
intense.

The guilty Mexican was never caught, but his deed made it
hard on some other Mexicans. Just how badly the Mexicans of
the country were scared can be illustrated by a story that a yellow negro named Albert, whom the Rabbs had raised, was
responsible for. Albert told the Mexicans that Mrs. Rabb, Lee's
mother, had offered fifty dollars for every pair of Mexican ears
brought to her. Albert used to go on and picture a great string
of the ears that Mrs. Rabb was accumulating. She had them
hung up in her house, he said, as a kind of "charm." Incidentally, Mrs. Rabb's famous Bow and Arrow brand is among
the thirty-six representative Texas brands that decorate the
walls of Garrison Hall on the University of Texas campus.

For more than fifty miles outward from the Nueces River
my vaqueros and I scoured the country. We caught and turned
back thousands of cattle. One trip with a herd across the
Nueces came near being my last. It was a dry time and there
was no indication that the river would have much water in it,
but when we struck it, some distance below San Patricio, we
found it full from a head rise. The cattle were thirsty and the
leaders plunged in to drink. Directly they were in swimming
water with the swing and drag cattle pushing them on from
the rear. Fortunately the lead cattle did not try to turn back,

and thus cause a mill, which in deep water is always fatal; they headed straight across. Now, for a long distance out from the river and all up and down it on the east side, the brush grew very thick. Our cattle were as "snaky" as so many jack rabbits. If they got a chance to scatter into that brush they would certainly get away from us, and we had to deliver this particular bunch at the Coleman, Mathis and Fulton headquarters.

Before going into deep water I generally undressed, or at least removed my heavy leggins, boots, spurs, and six-shooter. But there was no time here to take off anything. "Come on, *muchachos,*" I yelled, and spurred my horse into the water. He was afraid of it and turned back. The white boy with me and a Mexican who was an excellent swimmer then took the lead and I managed to make my horse follow.

When we were in mid-current a piece of driftwood floated under the nose of the Mexican's horse, causing him to scare and wheel back. Immediately horse and rider both sank out of sight. The current was fearfully swift and there was a strong undertow. In a moment, however, the Mexican and his horse bobbed up—right at my horse's head and a little below. My horse tried to shy, wheeled halfway around, and went under. I was not caught altogether off guard, and when I saw that the horse was going down I put one foot in the saddle and jumped as far ahead as I could, pointing up-stream. On account of the uncontrollable disposition of my horse I had not removed the bridle before putting him into swimming water; a moment after I left him he got one of his feet tangled in the reins, and while he drowned he turned over and over in the water, fairly making it boil. Meanwhile the Mexican had got scared and quit his horse also. Despite the fact that he was an expert swimmer he seemed unable to keep up and going. Presently he went down not to reappear. Powerless to help, I had to watch both him and my horse drown.

My boots, leggins, spurs, six-shooter, and ducking coat seemed to weigh tons. I could not use my legs at all but did manage to keep paddling with my hands. I shall always believe that my Guardian Angel held me up by the coat collar and helped me get to the bank. That was about the hardest struggle I ever had in water, and I have tussled with every stream between the Rio Grande and the Platte.

The white boy who swam ahead of me was just fifteen years old. His name was Archie Parr, now of Duval County. For many years he has been state senator from the Twenty-seventh District, the district nearest to Mexico. On the senate floor Archie once boasted that he carries every vote of this district in his vest pocket, and he always delivers those votes. Well, we held the herd, and the next day we found the body of the drowned Mexican far down stream and also the drowned horse, his foot still tangled in the bridle reins.

One of the seven hundred wonders of the world has always been to me the recklessness in water of cowboys who could not swim at all. A yarn told by O. E. Brewster, ramrod of the Cherokee Strip Cowpunchers' Association of Oklahoma, illustrates the recklessness admirably.

"A man named Murchison," says Brewster, "was boss of our outfit, and working with it was a younger brother of his, Joe Murchison. Joe always carried two six-shooters, a rifle in a scabbard, a dirk, and wore, of course, the usual leggins, boots, and spurs that went to make up a peeler's rig. He could not swim a lick, but when we had to cross a swimming stream he always refused to take off a single pound of his hardware and he made fun of anybody who did lighten up. Most of the hands would pull off the heavy parts of their equipment and tie them to the saddle horn.

"Once when we got to the Cimarron it was up big swimming. Joe plunged in, spurs, leggins, 'hog-legs,' and all. His horse made it out into the deepest water and then sank. Joe went under with him and neither reappeared. We scattered downstream, throwing in ropes, chunks of drift, everything we could find, hoping that Joe would bob up and grab something. About two hundred feet below our crossing place the water was shallower and some willows leaned over into the stream. After a while Joe's head appeared under the willows and he reached up and pulled himself out. He swore that he had walked on the bottom of the river bed out of the deep water.

" 'Well, I guess you'll pull off some of that luggin' the next time you go into deep water,' somebody said.

" 'Hell, no,' Joe replied. 'I can't swim and if I hadn't had all this weight on I'd never in the world been able to keep myself down to the bottom so that I could walk out. Weight's what saved my life.' "

Guardian angels, guardian angels—even when a cowboy was laughing at the devil and swearing he did not give a damn.

CHAPTER IX

DODGING COMANCHES AND HUNTING WATER

I HAVE already spoken of a visit to the San Saba on my way home from a trip up the Chisholm Trail. I have spoken too of a present received from Grandfather Duncan at this time— Payaso. Now, immediately after coming into possession of Payaso I made, for private reasons, a considerable *pasear* into the Devil's River country to the south and west. A part of the time on this *pasear* I had with me a Seminole Indian. This Indian showed me some water holes that very few people then knew anything about.

Some fifty miles, as the crow flies, above its entrance into the Rio Grande, Devil's River widens into a long water hole called Beaver Lake. This is the uppermost dependable water on the stream; above it Devil's River is a dry canyon that twists northward for a hundred miles or more. Riding straight north from Beaver Lake one had to go eighty-five miles, crossing a high divide on the way, before coming to the next permanent watering, the Concho. The head draws of Devil's River are dry and gravelly, and even after a rain one can ride for miles down them without finding any water at all. The side canyons are so large and washed that a man not acquainted with the country will follow one thinking it to be the main course of drainage only to find in the end that he has been led out upon a barren, rocky hillside. The few water holes, those shown me by the Seminole, are generally difficult of access and are on the inside draws. Until along in the eighties few range men knew about them. When I learned of their location I did not know that within a year's time I should be piloting a herd of cattle across this drouthy region.

After gathering strayed and stolen cattle west of the Nueces, for Coleman, Mathis and Fulton and other ranchmen, all through the summer of 1877, we got the range fairly clean and so quit. Along in the fall I rode up into San Saba County to pay my grandparents a visit. A short time after my arrival I received a message from Moore and West, well known cowmen, saying that they had bought 2500 head of two-year-old steers near Eagle Pass and were going to locate them on the Colorado River north of Fort Concho (now San Angelo). I had told Mr. Moore of my scouting through the Devil's River country and of the water holes. His cattle would have to pass through this country; he wanted me to pilot them. In his message he said that the herd was already on the trail; that it would go to Fort Clark, fifty miles north of Eagle Pass; thence ninety miles northwest, by way of San Felipe Springs (Del Rio), to Fort Hudson on Devil's River; and thence twenty-five miles on north to Beaver Lake (near the present wide place in the road called Juno, Val Verde County). The dry stretch of eighty-five miles from Beaver Lake to the Concho was worrying him. It was across this stretch that he wanted me to act as guide. I could meet the herd at Beaver Lake, where it would rest a day or two before attempting the desert. If I did not meet it, it would go on anyhow—"but please come if possible."

The message had been delayed in getting to me. I judged that if I was to reach the herd at Beaver Lake I had better be making tracks. When I told Grandfather Duncan and two or three other pioneers of the proposition, they shook their heads and said, "Full of the moon." The Comanches were being subdued, but they were still up to their old habit of raiding down upon the Llano every full moon. Their recent murdering of Isaac Kountz and Sam Spear was the talk of the country. My route would necessarily take me across ground that they were accustomed to passing over on their raids. The moon was gibbous. I struck out, riding Payaso.

The first night I spent in Llano. I heard there that a few people had got together at the junction of the North and South forks of the Llano River and had named their settlement

Junction City. I planned to follow up the Llano until I found this settlement, to proceed thence on out to the headwaters of the North Fork, and then to pass over the divide to Beaver Lake.

When I left Llano town the roosters were still crowing. Late in the afternoon I watered my horse and was ungirthing him when something whispered, "Don't do it." So I merely took the bridle off and left the saddle on him while he grazed out on a picket rope and I ate a cold snack. My intention was to ride on a little farther before camping for the night. After eating, I stretched out on the grass, my mind utterly idle. All at once I noticed Payaso raise his head and point his ears towards a piece of open ground covered with high grass. "It's either a wolf or an Indian," I said to myself, and looked too.

I saw what I took to be a wolf walking slowly through the high grass. I could just see the top of his back. For want of anything else to do I watched him until he disappeared behind a tree. I kept watching for him to pass the tree and was gazing rather intently when I saw him peep from around the trunk. Such action was not exactly characteristic of a wolf and my curiosity was aroused. In my pocket I carried a small, single-barreled spy-glass. It was hard to focus but it would magnify. Without moving my position I took the spy-glass out and focused it on the tree, which was fully two hundred fifty yards away. What I saw was not the face of a wolf but the face of an Indian. He had seen my horse and was trying to locate me. For some cause my hat began to move on my head. I did not know how many other Indians might be around me, and though my trigger finger itched, I considered it best not to shoot. I began to pull in on the stake rope. When Payaso was almost over me, I raised myself up quickly, yet cautiously, so as not to make him jump, made a *bosal* around his nose with a half-hitch of the rope—for I had no time to bridle him— jumped into the saddle, and was gone. One of the best ways to deal with an Indian was to ride away from him on a good horse.

For several miles I kept my course, at a good speed; then

I made a right angle, so as to throw any pursuer off the track, and in a nice grassy plot of ground pretty well surrounded by timber I dismounted for the night. I staked Payaso out where he could eat his fill, spread my saddle blanket down for a bed, and, with my saddle for a pillow, was soon fast asleep. I do not know how long I had been asleep when I felt a sudden pull of the blanket from under me that almost threw me on my head. I had gone to sleep with my six-shooter still buckled on, and as I struggled to my feet I grabbed for it; but what I saw pulling the blanket was not an Indian but a cow. She must at some time have been a gentle milk cow belonging to some settler. A saddle blanket is saturated with salt from the horse's sweat. Cattle in the Llano country have always required salt. This cow had scented the salt in my blanket and she had come to get it. She had about half of it in her mouth and had evidently been chewing on it for some time when I awoke. I suppose I had moved in my sleep and scared her, causing her to jump back; she had nevertheless kept a firm mouth hold on the salty blanket. I dropped my gun and right there that old cow and I had a real tussle to determine which of us should have the blanket. I won out and slept on the disputed property the remainder of the night. However, it took me some time to get back to sleep after the scare.

About three o'clock in the afternoon next day I came to the ranch owned by Tobe Joy, one of the characters of Kimble County. He appeared to be very glad to see me, and when I asked if there was a road from his place to Junction City, he replied that there was but that the Indians seemed to be using it that day. He said that they had passed his ranch that morning going towards Junction and that he thought my best plan would be to remain where I was until next morning, when he would go with me. I thanked him, told him that I was in a hurry, and went on.

When I got to a ranch on Johnson Fork owned by Jerry Roberts, I found him and some other men roping horses in a corral and cutting arrows out of them. The Indians had passed his ranch that morning, Roberts said, with some stolen horses and had got some of his. Roberts and the other men had followed them, attacked them, and recaptured all the stolen horses together with two Indian ponies. The Indians upon being pushed closely had dismounted and taken to some low cedar brush. One of the Indian horses captured was covered with blood. When the Comanches were hard pressed they had a way of shooting arrows into horses they were driving so as to make them travel faster. I helped throw some of the wounded horses down and remove the arrows. Roberts insisted that I stay all night, but I told him that I was due in Junction City and rode on.

It was dark when I rode into the "city," but all the inhabitants had their eyes "peeled." They had heard of the Indian raid and they were expecting trouble. Their horses were under guard in a strong corral. I put mine in with them and took my turn at standing guard.

When daylight came I got my first clear view of the new town. It had been established among some trees that were well known for supplying convenient limbs on which to hang horse thieves. About half a dozen log cabins were in sight. One of the cabins was later enlarged and made into a hotel. The owner advertised it as "the only second class hotel in America," and in order to induce patronage further advertised that if any of his guests wanted to go fishing he would go with them. At the time I visited Junction, Kimble County was one of the hardest places in Texas. Abundant water, convenient brush—mesquite, cedar, and pecan trees—fish for the cost of a hook, game, and maverick cattle on every hand—all had combined to make it an ideal hiding-out and living place for outlaws. Many criminals who had been routed out of the Nueces and Rio Grande country had repaired thither. A few months before I got there the rangers had literally rounded up the whole country, and cut the bad men out of the round-up—only to find that there were not enough good men left to act as a jury to try the bad ones.[1] Naturally a good many of the desperadoes had escaped the rangers' hunt. In addition to being infested

[1] For a vivid account of Kimble County outlawry read Chapter VII of James B. Gillett's *Six Years with the Texas Rangers*, Yale Press.

with criminals, the country was still a remount range for the horse-thieving Comanches. Really, I thought for a while that the people were going to forcibly prevent my riding on west. When I told them that I had to get to Beaver Lake, they said the Indians would take that very route on the way to the Pecos, their rendezvous grounds.

Nevertheless, I was willing to take my chances. I had great trust in my Guardian Angel, and, as it turned out, the trust was well founded. I failed to see a single Indian sign, and at Beaver Lake I found the herd ready to move. None of the cowboys with it had seen any Indians either. The weather had turned showery, and, as we soon found, a big rain had fallen towards the north. The Indians, knowing about this rain and the water put out by it, had crossed the divide above my route.

The rain was a God-send. Even if I had been able to locate enough water in the hidden holes for the cattle, the rough trailing past them would have worn the hoofs off most of those young steers. Any way that one could take it, except following a rain, those eighty-five miles between Beaver Lake and the Concho were a nightmare for men with cattle. I pointed the herd for the Johnson Water Hole on Johnson's Run, near which I was years later to help establish the pretty little town of Ozona. We took our time driving, found plenty of water, lingered a day on the fine grass and abundant water of the Concho, then without mishap arrived at our destination on the Colorado.

In just about a month's time from the day I left Grandfather's ranch at Richland Springs I was back. I had made the whole trip without carrying a thing with me except my six-shooter and Winchester, a slicker, a little coffee, and some hard baked bread—made from the John Duncan wheat that I shall always remember as having given me my first taste of biscuits. Of course I had got provisions at various places and had eaten with the cow outfit as long as I was with them. Also, I had ridden extra horses out of Moore and West's remuda. Payaso was still fresh and alert. In a few days I rode him on down into the lower country to get some of that sleep that all cowboys were supposed to catch up on in the winter months, to help drive a few small bunches of cattle to coast packeries and ports, and to run horse races. A longer and more exciting trip than any I had yet made was to begin with next spring's grass.

CHAPTER X

ESTABLISHING A RANCH ON THE PLAINS

JIM HALL, a relative of mine, and some of the Duncans owned a controlling interest in the Cimarron Cattle Company. Their range was on the Dry Cimarron, in the southeastern corner of Colorado and over into New Mexico and Oklahoma. In the spring of 1878 they claimed a herd of 15,000 cattle on this range and they were anxious to establish a ranch in the Panhandle of Texas. I was offered an opportunity to join in on this new ranch proposition; so I put what small funds I could rake up into the enterprise and took the job of driving a herd of cows to the Plains and locating the ranch.

It must have been along in May when we set out from Refugio. Our herd was made up of 1300 young cows and about 50 bulls, all branded with a newly devised brand, the Spur, made thus: ━┏ . That was the year it rained; it rained behind us, it rained ahead of us, and it rained on us. Every stream we crossed was swimming. The San Antonio River at Stribbling Crossing in Goliad County was bank full; so was the Coleto. We camped on it, just south of Yorktown; and here while some of the boys were practicing with their six-shooters, Buck Spradlin let his gun go off before it was out of the holster. The bullet entered the fleshy part of his thigh and did not hurt him nearly so badly as it scared him. We swam the Guadalupe River at Gonzales and then followed on up Plum Creek to Lockhart. When we got near the log cabin in which I was born I turned aside to look at it.

Beyond Round Rock, soon to be made famous by the death of Sam Bass, we struck the Western Trail. A few nights later a sudden rain called us all to the herd. At the time I went to bed the sky was so clear and the weather was so promising that I had removed my trousers, thinking to get a few hours of peaceful sleep. I awoke and began dressing in such a hurry that I got my trousers on wrong side in front. Before I could get them changed and my slicker on I was drenching wet. A half dozen times that night I rode into gullies of swimming water. The cattle scattered so that it was noon before we got them together; a count, however, showed that we had not lost a single cow. The worst feature of the rain and the run, to me, was that I had a high fever. I had remained chilled for hours. Some of the boys located a country doctor; he gave me calomel and stayed around camp for three days while I recovered.

The one man in our outfit that I recall most often and most vividly was Sam, the negro cook. He always had a cheerful word or a cheerful song, and he seemed to have an affection for every one of us. When we camped in the vicinity of brush every cowboy before coming in would rope a chunk of wood and snake it up to the chuck wagon. That wood always made Sam grinning happy whether he needed it or not. He was about thirty-five years old, as black as a crow, and weighed around 225 pounds. As he had been raised on a ranch, he was a good rider, and frequently one of the boys would get him to "top off" (ride first) a bad horse. One day a cowboy remarked that Sam was too big and strong for a man but not big enough for a horse. At that Sam said *he was a horse* and that he would give a dollar to any man in the outfit who could ride him without spurs. That evening we camped in a sandy place and Sam announced that he was ready to play horse if any man thought he could ride. It was agreed that I should win the first dollar. Sam stripped stark naked, wearing only a bandana around his neck for the rider to hold on to. I really did not have much confidence in my ability to stay on him, for as a boy I had often been thrown by buck negroes who took me on their backs. Nevertheless I pulled off my boots and mounted. Sam started out by jumping straight ahead until he judged I had accommodated myself to that "rhythm"; then he suddenly stopped short and whirled back. I kept straight on, landing on my head.

After that every fellow in the crowd had to show off his ability at riding a bucking negro and every one of them tumbled.

When we started out from South Texas Sam had a banjo, but one night someone accidentally stepped on it and demolished it. However, we had chipped in and bought a fiddle at Yorktown, and whenever he got a chance Sam would pick "Green corn, green corn, bring along the demijohn," on his fiddle. Among other selections he had a kind of chant called "Dog" that the boys often called on him to give. The words, evidently not of negro origin, ran thus:

There was a man who had a dog, a bobtailed ornery cuss,
And this here dog got this here man in many an ugly muss.

The man was on his muscle, and the dog was on his bite;
To touch that bobtail son-of-a-gun you were sure to start a fight.

There was a woman who had a cat that fit a fifteen pounds;
The other cats got up and slid when this here cat came 'round.

The man and dog came along one day by where this woman did dwell;
The cat he growled fe-ro-cious-ly and made for the dog like—rip.

The man he cussed and ripped and swore and picked up a big brickbat;
He swore he'd be damned eternally if he didn't kill that cat.

The woman she said she'd be darned if he did and picked up a big shotgun;
She whaled away and shot him in the back with birdshot number one.

They carried him home on a cellar door and the doctors healed him up;
He's never since been known to tackle a cat or own a terrier pup.

Some folks may turn up their nose at this, but I don't give a darn for that,
For it goes to show that a man may tackle the wrong old Thomas cat.

The most memorable fact of our whole trip of six hundred

miles from Refugio County on the coast to the head of Pease River far up on the Plains was Fort Griffin, located in Shackelford County on the west bank of the Clear Fork of the Brazos. It was understood that the Cimarron Cattle Company would have money there for me to pay off hands and buy a three months' stock of provisions for the ranch I was going to establish beyond; but when we arrived, there was no money in the mail. As Fort Griffin was on the edge of the settlements and as there was neither mail nor provisions to be had west of it, nothing remained to do but wait until I could hear from headquarters. In the course of a few days I received the money. Meantime we held our cattle across the river some distance below the town, half of the boys taking turn with the herd while the other half took in the sights.

And in 1878 there were sights in Fort Griffin. Established eleven years before as an outpost against Indians, it became soon after the battle of Adobe Walls, June 27, 1874, headquarters for thousands of butchers engaged in annihilating the "southern herd" of American bison and also for cowmen and cowboys engaged in establishing ranches on the vast ranges that the slaughter of the buffalo and the attendant subjugation of the Indians were leaving vacant. I had seen Hell's Half Acre in Fort Worth, but here was Hell's Half Hundred Acres. It was beyond all odds the worst hole that I have ever been in. The population at this time was perhaps five thousand people, most of them soldiers, gamblers, cow thieves, horse thieves, murderers, wild women, buffalo hunters, altogether the most mongrel and the hardest-looking crew that it was possible to assemble. The fort proper and a big store were up on a hill. The sights were down under the hill in "the Flats," where every house was either a saloon, a gambling den, or a dance hall, generally all three combined. No man who valued his life would go here unarmed or step out alone into the darkness. If about daylight he walked down to the river he might see a man hanging from one of the cottonwood trees with a placard on his back saying, "Horse Thief No. 8"—or whatever the latest number was.[1]

[1] See West Texas Historical Association *Year Book*, Abilene, Texas, Vol. II, p. 6.

All drinks were two-bits apiece and cigars were the same price. One saloon, the Adobe, popularly called the Bee Hive, had on its front a painted sign representing two hives overhung by branches of flowering honeysuckle and innumerable bees entering and emerging from the hives. Beneath was this verse:

Within this hive we're all alive,
Good whiskey makes us funny;
So if you're dry come up and try
The flavor of our honey.

Everybody seemed to be dry. It was no uncommon sight to see lousy Tonkawa Indian bucks, brutish thugs who called themselves buffalo hunters, and hideously featured wrecks of women all together in the most beastly state of intoxication. The gambling dens ran day and night but were in full blast from midnight on. Keno, poker, monte, chuck-luck, rouge et noir, roulette, faro, casino—every kind of game that the professional gambler might ask for or the tenderfoot be fleeced by was there.

Excepting a comparatively few transient cowboys, some of whom occasionally considered it their duty to shoot out the lights, about the only native or even thoroughly adopted Texans in this town of the Texas frontier were the Tonkawa Indians. Despite the fact that their warriors had given aid to rangers and troops in fighting hostile Indians and despite the fact that the warriors were excellent scouts, the Tonkawas on the whole were the most beggarly, the most degraded, and the most contemptible human beings imaginable. They soon found our camp and hung around it like so many buzzards. Sam threatened to quit cooking unless I detailed a man to help keep them away. They would steal anything, from a dirty dishrag to a sack of flour, that they could lay their hands on.

But the thug element of Fort Griffin was the buffalo hunters—not, generally speaking, the men who had engaged in that business for years and were units in regular skinning crews, but tramp hunters who had drifted out to prey alike on man and beast. They were from Wyoming, from Colorado, from Arkansas and Missouri, from tough Kansas, from everywhere. Some of them had hidden on the Rio Grande until the rangers broke up their gangs there. Many of them were afoot looking to get away and ready to kill a man for a horse or five dollars. There were still some buffaloes scattered over the Plains, but the great slaughter, which reached its climax in 1876 and '77, was over. Estimates of the number of hides brought into Fort Griffin in 1877 vary from 100,000 to 200,000. Before I arrived the price had gone down to sixty cents apiece; wagon trains were carrying them to Fort Worth, but acres of ground were still covered with them.

According to Edgar Rye, a newspaper editor of Fort Griffin and Albany, whose book *The Quirt and Spur* is pretty much a history of Fort Griffin, the traffic in hides at that place between 1875 and 1879 was far greater than the business with ranchers and trail outfits. In the warehouse of one store alone were thirty tons of lead and five tons of powder to supply buffalo hunters.

I talked with cowboys and buffalo hunters who made no bones about charging various bosses with having murdered members of their skinning crews in order to get out of paying them. At that time I had never heard or seen the range ballad called "The Buffalo Hunters," which John A. Lomax in his *Cowboy Songs* has since popularized; but I have no doubt that the song is based on fact. It tells how "a man by the name of Crego" hired the composer of the song to go out on Pease River to "the range of the buffalo." After describing the miseries of the life the skinners led, it concludes thus:

The season being over, old Crego he did say
The crowd had been extravagant, was in debt to him that day;
We coaxed him and we begged him and still it was no go—
We left old Crego's bones to bleach on the range of the buffalo.

The breakup of an industry always leaves men desperate. Many of the buffalo hunters were making for the Indian Territory, the happy hunting grounds for desperadoes; others were making for the Black Hills. Numbers of them were turning into cow thieves. In fact, the majority of the cow thieves that were for some years to depredate upon the ranches of the Plains were recruited from the so-called buffalo hunters. This statement is, I know, at variance with the testimony of some of the old timers; yet it is supported by evidence other than my own. Frank Canton of Oklahoma, for many years inspector for the Texas and Southwestern Cattle Raisers' Association, now dead, has left this testimony: "After the buffalo hunters had killed off all the buffaloes, they went over to the Comanche Agency at Fort Sill and traded their rifles and ammunition to the Indians for ponies. Then they came back to Texas, lay around the government posts for a while, and soon commenced to steal cattle." [2]

I cannot express myself too strongly against the class of men who called themselves buffalo hunters, though again it must be understood that many of the regular skinners were fair men. This opinion has been shared by other observers. Not always were the men who called themselves buffalo hunters truly such, say Root and Connelley.[3] "Scattered here and there over the plains and mountains were bands of desperadoes . . . ostensibly hunting buffalo and other animals for their hides; but really it was plain that their object was to steal stock, rob the express coaches and passengers, and at times murder was resorted to in carrying out their hellish designs." When Mrs. Adair, wife of the John Adair who was to become known all over the West through his partnership with Charles Goodnight, crossed the Plains in 1874, she recorded this impression of the buffalo hunters: "Many of these men are the roughs of the frontier, criminals flying from justice, notorious ruffians and murderers, and the settlers are more afraid of them than of the Indians." [4]

Just before we got ready to leave Fort Griffin three men who were heavily armed and who announced themselves as

2 *The Cattleman*, Fort Worth, Texas, May, 1923, p. 23.
3 *The Overland Stage to California*, Topeka, Kansas, 1901, pp. 99–100.
4 Adair, Cornelia, *My Diary, Bath, England*, 1918, pp. 96–97.

cattle inspectors came out to the herd and demanded my bill of sale. I showed it to them. Then they inspected the cattle and advised me that I was entitled to a certificate showing that I had a clean herd. They said that their charges for inspection were twenty-five cents per animal and that the certificate for my herd of 1300 cows would therefore cost me $325. I asked the spokesman of the inspectors if that was the penalty for driving a clean herd past Fort Griffin. I also asked for his authority to collect the money. He replied that he did not have to show me papers of authority and that, if I did not pay, the soldiers of the post would take charge of the herd until I produced the money. I told him to bring on the soldiers. At this the men hummed and hawed and consulted; then one of them confided that they would compromise on the payment of one hundred dollars. I knew that they were dead beats. I did not pay a cent and had no trouble getting the herd away.

On the trail again, we were as happy as a bunch of free niggers until we reached the Salt Fork of the Brazos. At the place where we struck it the water was about three hundred yards wide, muddy and ugly. When I rode over to pick out a crossing I found the water hardly deep enough to swim a horse, but waves were rolling on the surface, and hidden bars of quicksand threatened every step. I decided to put the cattle across in small bunches. Out of every bunch we took over, several bogged so that they had to be roped and dragged out. One cowboy's horse bogged and drowned. When the last cow was across we threw the herd into a grassy bend of the river and left them alone while all hands turned to cross the saddle horses and the chuck wagon.

The wagon held what was to be our food supply for three months and we could not afford to take chances on having it turn over. After the remuda was headed right, two cowboys took charge of it while the rest of us tied our ropes on the wagon, so as to help guide and pull it if necessary, and started across. All went well until we reached the opposite bank. Then one of the lead work horses bogged and fell. Before we could get him up, the wagon had settled fast into the mud and quick-

sand. We all had to get down into the water and scratch the
wheels loose. At last, however, we pulled out on dry land, as
wet, stiff, and tired as it was possible to be.

"Where are the cattle?" somebody asked.

We had been so busy that we had not thought of them,
considering them safe. At the question we all instinctively
turned our eyes up and down the north bank. Then somebody
uttered some words that would not look well in print. The
cattle had all recrossed to the south side and, well scattered out,
were quietly grazing. Why they had recrossed the river I do
not know. Certainly they had gone "agin nature." Facts are
stubborn things.

I never believed in keeping a river between herd and camp.
It was too late to try to bring the cattle over again. We simply
turned around and took the remuda and the wagon over to the
cattle. By the time we pulled out on the south bank it was dark
and rain was falling. We rounded up the herd, but they would
not bed down. They walked and milled all night long, never
attempting to run but never still. It took all hands to hold them.

Of course the river rose from the rain; but the weather
"faired off" next morning, and we were not a bit sorry to
mark time for a couple of days while the water went down.
We got across without much trouble and went on towards the
Wichita. It was bank full, and, knowing that it would soon
run down, for we were near the head of it, I decided to lie over
a day. While we were there something occurred that fixes the
date exactly, July 29, 1878.

Along in the afternoon while the cattle grazed over the
prairie and we boys were all sitting in the shade on the bank,
some of us half asleep and nobody paying any attention to the
sky, we were suddenly startled by a wild yell from Sam. When
we looked towards him we saw him coming in a dead run. That
Indians were after him no one doubted. In ten seconds every
man was on his horse, gun out, running to meet the frightened
cook.

"Lawdy, Lawdy, the world's coming to an end. Looky at
the sun." This was his greeting.

We looked at the sun. It was passing into eclipse and soon the darkness was such that stars became visible. No newspaper had prepared us for the phenomenon, and Sam was not the only person on the outskirts of civilization to be frightened. We cowboys had sense enough to know what an eclipse was, but I afterwards heard of many frontier folk who had been scared.

We trailed on across Paradise Valley, which was dotted with antelopes. We were bound for somewhere on the upper reaches of Pease River. We struck a rough broken country over which no wagon had ever before rolled; but by digging down banks and pulling with ropes attached to our saddle horns we got the wagon up the steep places. Finally we crossed the last divide between the Gulf of Mexico and Pease River.

The whole world lay before us to choose our range from. All a man had to do at that time to establish his claim in the Panhandle was to strike camp in unappropriated territory and say that he wanted all the territory between certain bounds. His rights were respected. After scouting around several days and getting an idea of the country, I piloted the chuck wagon to a cottonwood motte beside a spring that drained into Pease River. Our journey was at an end. The Spur Ranch was established. Nothing remained to do but locate the cattle and "dig in" for winter.

Less than two years before there had not been a ranch in the Panhandle of Texas. Then in the winter of '76 Charles Goodnight had driven 10,000 head of buffaloes out of the broad and grassy Palo Duro Canyon, trailed in a herd of 1600 cattle, located them along the water, and with line riders to keep back the buffaloes and with the canyon bluffs to keep the cattle in, had founded what was to become one of the most historic ranches of America, the J A Ranch. When I reached the Plains in 1878 Goodnight had already entered into partnership with the moneyed Adair and was buying cattle and staking off land in wholesale quantities. The firm eventually controlled more than a million acres of ground, and J A cattle still graze over more than 300,000 acres of land, though Colonel Goodnight has not for forty years had an interest in the ranch.

About the same time that I located the Spur Ranch, Leigh Dyer located on Tule Canyon, which empties into the Palo Duro. A little later he moved east and with Coleman established the Shoe Bar, ⊃ —, Ranch, where in '79 I was to have some dealing with him. Our nearest neighbors were Baker and Wiren twenty miles away on the Quitaque. They had about 2000 head of cattle and gave the Lazy F brand, ⊏ɪ. With twenty miles between their herd of 2000 cattle and our bunch of 1300 cows it can be seen that the country was not as yet overstocked. Looking on a present day map, I judge that the Spur Ranch was only a few miles north of what is now Roaring Springs in Motley County.

When we turned the cattle loose, scattering them up and down the waterings in small bunches, and had no night-herding to do, we almost felt lost for a few days. The lost feeling, however, did not apply to our appetites, and I think we had about the most luscious eating that I have ever enjoyed. After riding out on the range all day, having eaten nothing since a breakfast of coffee, I got into camp more than once to find Sam grinning and gloating over an oven of buffalo steaks, another oven of roast bear meat, better than pork, a frying pan full of the breast of wild turkey in gravy of flour, water, and grease, and then antelope ribs barbecued on a stick over the coals.

"Boys," Sam would say, "wash yer faces and comb yer hairs and spruce up lak ye was goin' to a weddin'. I'se got a reg'lar weddin' feast pre-pared. It's a weddin' o' dinner and supper. Come 'long, come 'long while she's hot and juicy."

Sometimes Sam would roast a turkey in its feathers. To do this he would dig a pit, build a fire in it, and heat the ground thoroughly; then he would take out the coals. Having removed the entrails from the turkey and salted and peppered it, he would put it in the hole—a "fireless cooker"—in such a way that no dirt could touch the flesh. Next he would cover it with hot earth, then build a fire over the covering. When ten or twenty hours later he lifted the turkey out by its feet, the skin and feathers would scale off by their own weight, and we had a juicy, savory meat so tender that it almost melted at a touch. Turkeys often came right into camp.

The breaks about the foot of the Plains abounded in black bear. One day while I was out riding alone I noticed two old bears and two cubs playing in some tall grass near brush. When they saw me, they disappeared and I supposed they had made for the brush. I had an idea that I might rope one; so, putting spurs to my horse, I ran to the spot where I had seen them vanish. Instead of trying to get away, the bears had lain down in the tall grass and there they were still playing 'possum when my horse plunged among them. As they jumped out, my horse tried to fly straight up. He hit the ground bucking and kept on bucking until the bears were clean out of sight. I never knew which was more scared, the horse or the bears.

All old range men know that the finest plum thickets in the whole cattle country were on Pease and Red Rivers. The plums ripen in the fall of the year. Sam often stewed them or made a kind of cobbler out of them. One day while three of the boys were coming in towards camp they struck an unusually fine plum thicket. They got down, ate all they could, and were filling their hats with plums for Sam to cook when all at once they bumped into some Indian squaws that were also picking fruit. The squaws went one way and the boys went the other, and while the boys managed to keep their hats they lost every plum they had gathered.

We were just naturally shy of Indians, squaws or any other kind. No Indians were living in the country, but occasionally bands of them came over from the Indian Territory to hunt or to steal horses. More than one cowboy out alone was picked off and left to rot in the breaks while his horse was ridden back to Fort Sill. The United States officers there consistently refused to allow cowmen to seize their own horses found in possession of the reservation Indians. It was about this time that Lieutenant Colonel Davidson of the United States Army threatened to shoot Captain G. W. Arrington's rangers if they molested some Indian horse thieves. Arrington was not fazed; he was law bringer to the Panhandle, doing there what McNelly and Hall did for the Rio Grande and Nueces country.

One day while riding up a tributary of Pease River that we called Wind River, I saw the tracks of two horses. Mustangs, which were numerous, made tracks like those of any other unshod horses, but we were out two saddle horses that had been seen over in this direction, and I thought that the tracks might have been made by them. They were fresh and were following an old buffalo trail. I could not tell whether they had been made by loose horses or by horses under saddle. I should say here that we were generally rather careful about trailing horsemen, for various riders hiding out and roaming over that country were at the time strictly averse to having anyone approach them, and they had a very effective way of stopping any stranger whom they saw coming too near.

Anyway, I determined to follow the tracks leading out of our range. They were so plain that I struck a gallop. The country was rather rough with spots of brush. As I was coming around one of these clumps of brush, two Indians not fifty feet ahead of me suddenly arose and fired in my direction. I was riding a horse that "could turn on a quarter and give back fifteen cents in change," and right there he turned ends so quickly that I believe he might have given back twenty cents in change. I pulled my gun but I didn't pull on the reins. When I got about a quarter of a mile away up on an open hill I looked back and I could see those two Indians riding in the other direction just about as fast as I had been riding. I never killed an Indian in my life, but I certainly have out-ridden several of them.

The Spur cows were not hard to locate, but some of them had a tendency to trail off behind drifting bunches of buffaloes. For several weeks after making camp we kept busy shoving buffaloes out and turning cattle back. According to instructions from headquarters I was to lay claim to a range considerably larger than that necessary to graze the herd of cows, for the Cimarron Cattle Company intended to bring down several thousand cattle from Colorado the next spring. I made a thorough reconnaissance of the country and soon had line riders playing the human fence to the four sides of the Spur claim.

The business of these line riders was to patrol the ranch boundaries, to turn back any cattle that they saw approaching the imaginary line from either side—though there was little likelihood in the present case of cattle's straying into our range, not before a cold norther at least—to follow any outgoing tracks until they found the strays, and to bring them back. Back and forth, back and forth, these line riders must jog their solitary beats, each man to himself. As the constant tendency of cattle in the winter time is to drift south, especially if they have been driven north from their breeding ground, the chief work of the line riders for months to come would be on the southern side of our range. Accordingly, I established a line camp on this side and put two men at it, one to ride east and one to ride west each morning. Each rider after he had reached the end of his beat would back-trail to camp, thus inspecting his line twice daily. The beats were short enough that if necessary the riders could make two round trips daily or linger along any place where the cattle threatened especially to push out.

Meanwhile some of the hands had been detailed to build two dugouts, one at the headquarters camp and one at the line camp. The only tools we had were spades, axes, and a saw; we had neither lumber nor nails. There were in the Old West two general style of dugouts, each subject to modification and variation, the dugout of the flat plains and the dugout of the broken country. The latter style of dugout reminded one of a cabin that had somehow backed into a hillside; it was a blend of cabin and plains dugout.

Our manner of constructing the dugout at headquarters camp was as follows. We dug an open-topped rectangular hole into the south side of a slope near water. Thus the back wall and a part of each of the two side walls were formed by the ground. The remainder of the two side walls and the front wall were made of logs, chinked with mud. The flat roof butted against the hillside, but a line of mounded earth prevented water from running off the slope on to it. The roof was made first of a layer of logs, next a layer of brush and weeds, and then a layer of dirt well tamped. Such a roof when well settled would turn water—though it might leak tarantulas or even rattlesnakes. At the back end of the room we dug a fireplace and a chimney vent up through the solid wall of dirt. We had no stove pipe to run down through this vent and to stick up on the outside. A blanket did service for the door. If the roof did not leak, the only water that came into a dugout like this was through the chimney hole. A fire made such a room very snug and warm even in the coldest weather. A brush arbor could be built in front of the dugout for use in summer.

About a year after I went to the Panhandle another vaquero and myself were staying in a dugout of this kind that belonged to Leigh Dyer over on Little Red River. One morning I got up very early, having to go on a long ride. I made some coffee and then rode off up the hill, leaving my partner still asleep. When I got about a hundred yards away my horse began pitching, and, whirling on me, went plunging down towards the dugout. Before I could stop him he jumped on it, chugging about a barrel of dirt in on the sleeping occupant. In no time the cowboy came out "a-raring and a-snorting," but no worse frightened than I was. I had felt sure that the horse would fall through the roof and kill us all three; however, he lunged upon solid ground before he had damaged himself much or us at all.

The plains dugout was made by digging a pit with a stairway leading to the bottom of it. Then a roof of logs, brush, and dirt was mounded over the open hole. From a distance, such a habitation, except for perhaps a wagon and a horse or two near, looked very much like an enlarged prairie dog hole. Such a dugout required the minimum amount of timber. Fifty years ago it was the typical habitat of squatters in western Kansas. Storm cellars in north Texas, Oklahoma, and Kansas still preserve its architecture.

With the Spur cows located, boundaries of the ranch established, and winter quarters finished, there was not much left to do except routine riding. I discharged all but four hands, appointed one of them, Dick Hudson, as *caporal,* and prepared to go to Trinidad, Colorado, to meet the boss. The letter I had received at Fort Griffin directed me to come to Trinidad as soon as the ranch was established. I was to bring back a herd of cattle from the Dry Cimarron the next spring or summer. The prospects were for an idle winter, and I was well pleased with the idea of spending it in town. I was counting my chickens before they hatched.

CHAPTER XI

FROM HELL TO BREAKFAST

SOME men who came to our camp on Pease River one night had told me that Trinidad was about ten days' ride to the northwest. They said that I had better go by Tascosa, but their directions were very general. I had in my mount a horse named Gray Dragon. He had never been tired in his life, could climb rocks like a goat, and was very gentle. I decided to ride him and to leave Payaso to winter on Pease River. I knew that the boys would take good care of him. The day before I was to set out, however, a mule kicked Gray Dragon on the hock, crippling him badly. I told Payaso that, after all, we should keep each other company. With enough provisions in my saddle pockets to last two or three days and with a change of socks in my morral, I struck for Baker and Wiren's ranch on the Quitaque. As the Baker boys had come from Colorado, I counted on their giving me some specific directions.

They told me that a loaded wagon had come to their ranch from Tascosa several weeks previously and advised that I ride straight for the rim rock, top out upon the plains, and then follow the wagon track. After I had spent the night with them, they very hospitably sent a cowboy to guide me until we should pick up the wagon ruts. From that place on to Tascosa my route lay far from any human habitation.

Late in the evening I got to Tule Canyon, where I watered and camped. The canyon is still noted for being a boneyard of a thousand or so horses that General Mackenzie captured in 1874 from the Comanche and Kiowa Indians and shot to death in order to keep the Indians from regaining them. At the time I saw the slaughter ground, the bones of the horses were still well preserved and were scattered over several acres of ground.

The next water after Tule Canyon was the Palo Duro, and in riding between these two immense gashes in the Plains floor I saw the most fantastic forms of nature imaginable. It was late Indian Summer, the running season for deer and antelopes; they were chasing each other and dodging everywhere. Mustangs and buffaloes mingled in the scene. Mirages hung in the air, and when animals came between me and a mirage they had the appearance of traveling through space; antelopes appeared as large as buffaloes and buffaloes out in the distance looked as large as so many wagons heaped with hay. At noon while my horse, which I always unsaddled when I stopped, grazed and rested, I became so engrossed in watching the wild animals that I almost forgot to resume the journey.

Despite the fact that buffaloes were still to be seen, they were too scattered to make skinning them a profitable business. Nearly all I saw were moving about restless and miserable, some of them crippled, and among them many poor, motherless dogies. Buffalo bones bleached on every side. The scum of the buffalo hunting fraternity was still in the country, following the remnant around; most of them had nothing but plugs and needed good mounts. I determined if possible to keep out of range of their Sharp's .50 guns. But during the entire ride from the Quitaque to the Canadian River I did not see a soul.

As I approached the south bank of the Canadian I could see some houses across the river about a mile away—Tascosa. It was late afternoon and a fresh norther was blowing. I had anticipations of a dram and some hot coffee. One entrance into the wide, muddy waters of the river looked as good as any other and I went in where I first struck it. I had passed midstream with water only half-side deep to my horse when he stepped into a hole and plunged, wetting me to the waist. That water was cold and the wind seemed to blow the cold right into me. I felt thankful that I could get some dry clothes at the Tascosa store and struck a lope. But when I got within a few hundred yards of the houses I became aware of bullets passing over my head and on either side of me. I could see some men standing out in the street, or road, in front of one of the houses and shooting. They apparently had not seen me. Certainly they were not shooting at me. They were just practicing, I saw, aiming at some kind of target down the road in my direction— and apparently seeing how far they could miss it. I decided to go behind a small rise to one side and wait until the target practice was over before riding on in. I was an utter stranger to this country, and, as the reader must have seen already, I was on the watch-out. Most men, in those days, were on the watch-out.

While I waited I nearly froze. I felt rigors such as I had felt that rainy night when I put my trousers on hind side in front. Finally the firing ceased and I rode forward. I threw my bridle reins over the hitching rack of the first saloon in the row and stepped through the door. About a dozen men were inside, and as I entered I saw several of them flop their hands around towards their hips. Ignoring the gesture, which I took to be one of protection, I said, "Come on, boys, and take a drink with me. I am wet and freezing to death."

They all lined up, and while the barkeeper was mixing their drinks and while I was explaining that I was from a ranch over on Pease River I gulped down the fire water. The bill was three dollars, two-bits a drink, and I paid it and left before some of the other men had got to their liquor. My excuse was that I had to get some dry clothes.

Just as I started for the door, I heard some fellow laugh rather heartily and another fellow applaud him with the words, "Now, Billy." I turned. They were not laughing at me; in fact, they had apparently lost all interest in me. I noticed particularly the features and physique of the laughing youth called Billy. He was very young; he had peculiar teeth. Before many months had passed I was to see him again and learn that his full name was Billy the Kid. I was wondering if my horse would still be hitched outside. The type of most of the men inside the saloon, the type that seemed to be in possession of Tascosa, was familiar to me. They were the leavings of the buffalo hunters.

Payaso was still at the hitching rack. I led him around to Howard and Rinehart's general store—the only store in Tascosa at that time, I believe—and as I faced the man behind the counter I did what I had never done before and have never done since. I gave him the grand hailing sign of distress of my lodge. To my surprise, he jumped over the counter and grasped my hand.

"First, I want my horse fed," I said.

My newly found friend called an old Mexican and told him to put the horse in the stable, feed him grain and hay, and then to lock the door. Next he showed me his sleeping room in the back part of the store, where I immediately took off my wet clothes while he brought some dry underwear. My top clothes were hung by a fire to dry and I went to bed, still shaking with a chill. After I had warmed up a little, the old Mexican brought me a piping hot supper of coffee, beans highly seasoned with chile, and tamales. The very fumes of the food put life into me.

While I ate I laid my plans and talked. I gave the Mexican a five dollar gold piece and told him to go to the saloon— the one I had just left—and to tank up. I told him to tell the men there that I was sick in bed and would probably remain in bed for two or three days—while that mottled-faced horse ate his head off. The Mexican was to be back within an hour.

As soon as the store man—I am sorry I cannot remember his name—closed up, he came back and told me that he had guessed my troubles as soon as he saw the horse I was riding. He confirmed my estimate of the buffalo hunters by telling me that some of them had practically forced him to sell them supplies on credit and that he had already charged the account to profit and loss. In addition to the buffalo hunters in town, there were, he said, about twenty-five of them camped not very far out on the trail that led to Trinidad.

"I don't need a trail to go to Trinidad," I said. "I am used to cutting across country."

"Well," he replied, "if you do not take the road, which leads through the range of the buffalo hunters, you can follow up the Corrumpa River to the north. You will find a kind of trail for a part of the distance, at least. The big objection to that route is that all the Ute Indians are on the Corrumpa on a hunt. They are presumably at peace, but if they can surprise a white man alone, especially if he has a good horse, they will have no hesitation in killing him."

"I prefer the Utes to the buffalo hunters," I said.

"Very well, I will have a wallet of food prepared for you to take. You had better leave early."

The Mexican now returned, boozy but not too boozy to talk. He said that the men in the saloon had asked all manner of questions about me and my horse. He said that some of them were at that moment playing freeze-out poker to see which one of them should have my horse and saddle. Just for curiosity, I asked him if the young man called "Billy" was in on the game.

"*El Chivato* (The Young Billy Goat), *no.*"

The manner of my leaving was then quickly arranged. The Mexican was to pilot me until he could point out a mountain that would guide me to the Cimarron River. We were to leave at three o'clock.

At three o'clock we left. About sunup the Mexican, who was riding in the lead, halted.

"Yonder is the mountain," he said. "Leave it to your left. When you get even with it you will find some trails that lead down to the Corrumpa River."

The Corrumpa is a branch of the Canadian. I must cross it, then cross the Cimarron, then turn west. The mountain was a long, long way off.

As we were about to part, I asked my guide if he had brought the wallet of food. In our haste to get off we had both forgotten it. It was two days' ride to the first settlement on the Cimarron. On the route was an abundance of grass and a sufficiency of water. I could afford to go without eating. I did not propose to betray my presence to some Ute Indians by shooting at game.

Riding over the plains, I passed several holes of gray-tinged alkali water. About noon, however, I came to clean water. Payaso and I got a good drink and he grazed for an hour. The mustangs and antelopes coming in to water were company.

At the Corrumpa, which I reached late in the evening, there were plenty of Indian signs. The water was good and I took a "Spanish supper"—tightened my belt up a notch. I rode on out about a mile, then back-tracked half that distance and turned sharply off at a right angle. This device was to throw any watching Indian off my track. The night was cold, my blanket light, and I dared not build a fire. Once I heard the horse make a noise. I crawled out to where he was staked and watched for an hour, but no prowler appeared. I slept very little. About daybreak I rode back to the river and had plenty of water for breakfast.

Pursuing my general course now, I soon came into some buffalo trails. While I was following them through a rough, brush country, I heard some kind of strange noise to my right. I could see nothing and kept on riding. All at once I came face to face with two big Ute bucks sitting on their horses and laughing.

"How! how!" they said. *"Quire Vd. tratar caballos?"* (Do you wish to trade horses?)

They were very anxious to stop me, but I pulled my gun out and rode on, looking back to watch them. Then I rode smack into the whole Ute tribe of women and children, among them a few men. They were gathering some kind of berries. They were all afoot and two of the old women had their noses cut clean off. No mortal ever saw a more hideous sight. I learned later that among the Utes as well as among other tribes of Western Indians infidelity of women was punished by cutting the nose off. As I got among them, the Indians all began to jabber at me in Spanish. I noticed that they kept glancing in the direction from which I had come and I deduced that they were expecting more Americans to follow me.

"Cuidado! Ahi vienen los novillos," I shouted. (Look out! There come the cattle!)

The ruse worked. The squaws grabbed their papooses and ran. The bucks turned back to see the expected cattle. I rode quietly ahead until I was well out of sight and sound. Then I struck a rapid gait that I kept up for several miles.

The buffalo trails petered out and I entered some exceed-ingly rough country. More than once after getting down into a canyon and following up it a mile or so, I had to turn back and go down it in order to find a way out. When I topped out on the plains I found other canyons that had no crossings. I rode hard, for I was really beginning to think that I was hungry. As soon as I got well away from the Corrumpa I made up my mind to kill something to eat, but I went on for hours without getting a shot. When I reached the breaks of the Cimarron, it was dark. I staked Payaso and made a fire of piñon wood. By keeping it replenished and lying near it, I got some sleep.

It took me a long time next morning to find a way down to the river, which I could see far below me. After crossing and going a short distance up the valley, I came to a house. No one but a rather young woman was at home. I asked her to sell me a feed of corn for my horse. She said that she would not take any pay for corn but that I must feed as much of it as I liked. She and her husband had an irrigated field on which they had raised a big crop of feed stuff.

While the horse was eating, she asked me where I had stayed the night before. When I told her, she, country like, asked me if I had had breakfast.

"Yes," I replied, "I drank some coffee about three o'clock in the morning at Tascosa two or three days ago."

At once she arose to go to the kitchen, apologizing for not having any meat in the house but adding that she had plenty of butter and that if I would wait she would cook some bis-cuits.

I would wait! While the bread was cooking I learned that she was from South Texas. We had plenty to talk about, but I must admit that my mind was on the biscuits rather than on South Texas or this gentle lady—the first decent white woman that I had seen in many months.

Finally a big pan of hot biscuits, a pot of coffee, cream,

milk, and a crock of hard butter were set upon the table. I quit talking. I cut the butter into chunks, took a biscuit in one hand and a chunk of butter in the other. Sometimes I had butter on my bread and sometimes bread on my butter. I stopped only when the platter was "licked clean." But I was satisfied. I told my hostess that I understood now what was meant by "riding from hell to breakfast," and being as she was a Texan she understood too.

After riding up the Cimarron all the remainder of the day and then riding the most of the next day, I went through the noted Trinchero Pass. About dark I came to a scattered settlement of Mexicans. The first man I met was a negro. He said that he would sell me corn for my horse and would furnish a room for me to sleep in. He said that he had a Mexican wife who would prepare supper and breakfast, but that everybody in the settlement was going up the valley that night to a *función.* Unless I wished to go along, I should be by myself. I thought that my best plan would be to feed my horse, get supper, and then ride out somewhere and camp. But I was tired of "covering my back with my belly" and shivering all night. I decided to stay in the proffered room.

After supper the negro showed me a good place some distance out to stake Payaso. I took my saddle and other equipment into the room with me. I could not keep from wishing that there were space by my side for Payaso.

Some time after midnight I heard a commotion in the room that joined mine. It seemed to be full of Mexicans all talking at once. A woman was crying. I made out that something dreadful had happened to her husband because he was a negro. I decided that he had either been killed or run off—and that my horse was gone.

Before dawn I went out, and surely enough Payaso was not there. The rope had been untied from his neck and left on the ground. While I was picking it up I saw a bunch of horses coming in a long run from across the valley in my direction. As they drew nearer I made out my horse among them. I hurried to the negro's crib and put some corn in the

Mexican morral that I carried for a nosebag. When the horses got near, they held up and I began shaking the bag of corn and calling to Payaso. He galloped to me whinneying. He wore an old rotten headstall and a rusty bit from which the reins had been broken, perhaps by his stepping on them. My conclusion was that the negro had tried to ride him off bareback and had been thrown. I paid my bill and left.

My route now turned up the stream known to early-day Spaniards as Rio de las Animas; to the French as the Purgatoire; and to the Mountain Men and American bull-whackers as the Picketwire. Tradition has it that a large band of Spaniards long ago disappeared mysteriously while traveling down this river; hence the name Rio de las Animas—River of Lost Souls. The French trappers translated Las Animas into Purgatoire; and the American frontiersmen turned Purgatoire into Picketwire! At the time I became acquainted with the stream all three names were used.

The first train of the Atchison, Topeka, and Santa Fé Railroad, which was being constructed across the continent, had just reached El Moro, five miles from Trinidad. Trinidad was on a boom. I reported to Jim Hall, manager of the Cimarron Cattle Company, and told him of the range I had located on Pease River in the Panhandle. He seemed satisfied and advised me to rest up and have a good time. He seemed to be having a good time himself. I set about following his advice and his example.

About the first thing I did was to buy a buckskin suit, the conventional garb. Christmas was at hand. The town was full of cowmen and their families and cowboys. On Christmas Eve a group of us young people drove down in buggies to attend a Christmas tree on the Picketwire. In the group was a cowboy named Fred Davis. Fred decided that he would put a little horse of his named Big Enough on the Christmas tree for his girl. I need not add that he was pretty well "lit up." He led Big Enough inside the room and tied him to the tree and put a label on him. Then somebody lighted a firecracker. Big Enough must have thought that the firecracker was a six-

shooter; he had heard six-shooters before. He left, dragging
the tree after him. Some of the boys jumped on their horses
and followed him for a mile before they could catch him. The
folks who had presents were a week gathering them up. The
girl accepted the horse all right—but not the man. I knew the
fellow she afterwards married.

CHAPTER XII

BILLY THE KID INTERPRETED

WITH the first big snow storm of the winter, word came in that cattle on the Dry Cimarron, the range of the Cimarron Cattle Company, were drifting badly. Word came too that rustlers were stealing drift cattle on the Canadian to the south and selling them to tie-cutters and graders for the Santa Fé Railroad about Turkey Mountain in New Mexico. According to our information, the rustlers, made up mostly of ex-buffalo hunters, were under the leadership of a young man called Billy the Kid, who had just made something of a reputation in what is now styled "the Lincoln County War" and whose recent depredations on the herds of the great John Chisum along the Pecos were probably making it advisable for him to seek a fresh source of supplies.

In January various members of the Cimarron Cattle Raisers' Association met at Jake Taylor's Kiowa Springs ranch to take measures against the cattle thieves. After not very much talk they passed resolutions to the effect that every cowman represented would if necessary take his entire outfit and do his best to hang any cow thief who made sign north of the Canadian. The resolutions were to be forthwith printed in the Trinidad paper and copies of the paper were to be mailed all over the country so that the rustlers might read and take warning. The Association further decided to send a man to Fort Union, which was on the west side of Turkey Mountain, there to keep an eye on the rustlers and the cattle that the railroad construction gangs were eating. I was selected to be this man. Prominent among the cowmen at the Kiowa Springs meeting was Senator Stephen W. Dorsey, who owned a large ranch in New Mexico.

156

The senator informed me that if I would come to his ranch he would give me a letter that would be of aid to me in my work. I did not know at the time that I was making the acquaintance of a man whose name was shortly to be notorious to every newspaper reader and tobacco chewing circle in America.

This was the Senator Dorsey of Star Route fame. As the prosecution showed in subsequent court proceedings, the "Dorsey Combination," which included the Second Assistant Postmaster General, had increased the compensation for carrying mail over star route contracts controlled by them from $143,169 to $662,808—without, however, increasing the amount of mail to be carried. Most of this increase went into the pockets of the "Combination." One route conspicuous in the investigation was that from San Antonio to Corpus Christi. However corrupt he was, Senator Dorsey certainly had energy and personality. He knew the power of publicity and, not content with the publicity that the Trinidad paper gave the Cimarron cattlemen in their war against lawlessness, he established the *New Mexican Stockman* at Springer, New Mexico. To edit the paper and wage an editorial campaign against outlawry he employed a man named Charles F. Martin. Martin made things so hot for cow thieves that his life was time and again threatened and finally United States troops were sent from Santa Fé to keep order in Springer. It may be added that Martin lived long enough to get out one of the three or four most valuable books that deal with the cattle business of America. The title of it is *Prose and Poetry of the Live Stock Industry.*

The average old time range man would not have known a "folk-tale," by name, from Adam's off ox; just the same the open range was "lousy" with folk-tales, and one of them was about the way a cowman sold cattle to a greenhorn and in delivering them had the buyer count the same animals over and over. This tale has been told many times in connection with many cowmen and many greenhorns—generally some unnamed Englishman; but perhaps the best of all versions of the yarn fastens the trick on Senator Dorsey. It is to be found in a small, rollicky, and long out-of-print book called *Cowboy Life on a*

Sidetrack, by Frank Benton. It seems appropriate here to quote the story as Frank Benton, a thoroughgoing waddie, spun it.

"Then old Packsaddle Jack got to telling about Senator Dorsey, of Star Route fame, selling a little herd of cattle he had in northern New Mexico. He said the Senator had got hold of some eyeglass Englishmen, and, representing to them that he had a large herd of cattle, finally made a sale at $25 around. The Englishmen, however, insisted on counting the herd and wouldn't take the Senator's books for them. Dorsey agreed to this; he then went to his foreman, Jack Hill.

" 'Jack,' he said, 'I want you to find me a small mountain around which a herd of cattle can be circled several times in one day. This mountain must have a kind of natural stand where men can get a good count on cattle stringing by but where they can't possibly get a view of what is going on outside. Sabe?'

"Jack selected a little round mountain with a canyon on one side of it. Here on the bank of the canyon he stationed the Englishmen and their bookkeepers and Senator Dorsey. The Senator had only about 1000 cattle, and these Jack and the cowboys separated into two bunches out in the hills. Keeping the two herds about a mile apart, they now drove the first herd into the canyon. . . . It was hardly out of sight before the second bunch came stringing along. Meantime cowboys galloped the first herd around back of the mountain and had them coming down the canyon past the Englishmen again for a second count. And they were hardly out of sight before the second division was around the mountain and coming along to be tallied again. Thus the good work went on all morning, the Senator and the Englishmen having only a few minutes to snatch a bite and tap fresh bottles.

"At noon Dorsey's foreman told the English party that his men were yet holding an enormous herd back in the hills from which they were cutting off these small bunches of 500 and bringing them along to be tallied. But about three o'clock in the afternoon the cattle began to get thirsty and footsore. Every critter had already traveled thirty miles that day, and lots of them began to drop out and lie down. In one of the herds was an old yellow steer. He was bobtailed, lophorned, and had a game leg. When for the fifteenth time he limped by the crowd that was counting, milord screwed his eyeglass a little tighter on his eye and says:

" 'There is more bloody, blarsted, lophorned, bobtailed, yellow crippled brutes than anything else, it seems.'

"Milord's dogrobber speaks up and says, 'But, me lord, there's no hanimal like 'im hin the other 'erd.'

"The Senator overheard this interesting conversation, and, taking the foreman aside, told him when they got that herd on the other side of the mountain again to cut out the old yellow reprobate and not let him come by again. So Jack cut him out and ran him off a ways. But old yellow had got trained to going around that mountain, and the herd wasn't any more than tallied again till here come old Buck, as the cowboys called him, limping down the canyon, the Englishmen staring at him with open mouths and Senator Dorsey looking at old Jack Hill in a reproachful, grieved kind of way. The cowboys ran old Buck off still farther next time, but half an hour afterwards he appeared over a little rise and slowly limped by again.

"The Senator now announced that there was only one herd more to count and signalled to Jack to ride around and stop the cowboys. . . . But as the party broke up and started for the ranch, old Buck came by again, looking like he was in a trance. That night the cowboys said the Senator was groaning in his sleep in a frightful way, and when one of them woke him up and asked if he was sick, he told them, while big drops of cold sweat dropped off his face, that he'd had a terrible nightmare. He said that he thought he was yoked up with a yellow, bobtailed, lophorned, lame steer and was being dragged by the animal through a canyon and around a mountain, day after day, in a hot, broiling sun, while crowds of witless Englishmen and jibbering cowboys were looking on. He insisted on saddling up and going back through the moonlight to the mountain to see if old Buck was still there. A cowboy went with him and after they had got to the canyon and waited a while they heard something coming. Sure enough, directly in the bright moonlight they saw old Buck painfully limping along, stopping now and then to rest.

"A week later a cowboy reported finding old Buck dead on his well-worn trail. No one ever rides that way on moonlight nights now, for the cowboys have a tradition that during each full moon old Buck's ghost still limps down the canyon."

But to get back to the business of the "cowboy detective" —and I was a year ahead of Charlie Siringo in playing detective on Billy the Kid. About the first thing I saw after I got well into the Dorsey range was a bunch of old F O S cows; I found that they were scattered all over the country. The sight of them made me feel at home, for the F O S brand belonged to Frank Skidmore in South Texas. I had branded many a calf for him and brought a goodly number of his animals out of the brush west of the Nueces. Dorsey had bought a big string of cows from Skidmore and they had been driven up the Goodnight-Loving Trail. He gave me a letter addressed to the officer in charge of Fort Union, telling me that I should read it. It merely stated that the bearer was in the employ of the writer, that no questions were to be asked of me, and that any request I made was to be granted, even to the use of soldiers. The words "U. S. Senator" were at the tail end of the signature.

From Dorsey's ranch I went on to headquarters for Hall Brothers on the Dry Cimarron. There the Halls gave me two letters, one to a ranchman in New Mexico named Cameron and one to another ranchman farther on named Lewellyn. Each letter contained a statement of my mission and a request for aid and secrecy. I exchanged Payaso for a little Spanish pony that looked like something the cats had dragged in, exchanged my new Frazier saddle for an old hull patched with rawhide, hung up my prized Stetson hat and in its place put on an old floppy piece of headgear that even a Kansas nester would have been ashamed to wear. Then I announced that my name was no longer John Young but A. M. Rider—and I hit the rocks for Turkey Mountain. The A. M. in my assumed name stood for "A Mule," and I was the Rider. My plan was to look for some kind of job that would allow me to watch what was going on. Only one thing worried me—that flop hat, which always signifies slouchiness and not infrequently an unfurnished upper story. Oliver Wendell Holmes summed up the cowboy point of view when he wrote:

> Wear a good hat. The secret of good looks
> Lies with the beavers in Canadian brooks.

I'll say right here that the little Spanish pony I set out on

—with a detailed map of Mexico branded into his shoulders, his hips, and his thighs on both sides—belied his outward appear- ance. He had a bottom that no amount of riding could plumb, and he was a whirlwind after a cow. I named him Whirlwind.

At the end of the third day I unsaddled Whirlwind in the corral back of the Cameron ranch house. I found Mr. Cameron to be a fatherly old Scotchman; and after he had read the letter addressed to him and we had eaten supper and were sitting alone in front of his roaring fire, he fairly exuded canny informa- tion and beneficent caution. He warned me that I was in a country where the slightest suspicion of my business on the part of the rustlers would put a bullet through my back, for they were "positively the most cold-blooded gang of men in the West."

"You have heard, young man," Mr. Cameron went on, "that 'there is no law west of the Pecos.' You have heard the truth, and the most lawless and the most murderous outlaw of the trans-Pecos country is Billy the Kid—the man you have come to spy on. You do not know him, you cannot know him as I know him. Do not speak his name. You cannot tell when you are speaking to a friend of his or an enemy. If a man is his friend he dares not mention the fact; if a man is his enemy, he is even more silent."

Such talk naturally led me to confide to Mr. Cameron that I had another letter, similar to the one just delivered, addressed to a Mr. Lewellyn farther down the trail. When I told him about this letter, Mr. Cameron was silent for a long time while he gazed into the fire. Then he spoke.

"If you will take my advice," he said, "I will save your life."

I was ready to trust him and told him that I was relying absolutely on what he said.

"Then," he replied, "throw that other letter into the fire. The Halls thought that they were aiding you when they wrote it, but they do not know their man. Throw the letter into the fire. To deliver it would be like firing a pistol into your own brains."

Without a word I pitched the letter into the fire. I subsequently visited the Lewellyn ranch and when I saw the layout that Lewellyn had around him I was profoundly thankful that the letter was in ashes. My Guardian Angel had once again saved me.

After the letter was burned Mr. Cameron told me the full story of Billy the Kid. In general it followed the accounts that have since been made familiar to the world by Pat Garrett, Walter Noble Burns, and other biographers of the notorious outlaw. I shall repeat only such parts as relate directly to Mr. Cameron's and my own experiences. I cannot vouch for the accuracy of all the details. According to Mr. Cameron, Antrim, the step-father of William Bonney (Billy the Kid), Mrs. Antrim, and the boy, had several years before come by his ranch in an ox wagon; there a snowstorm held them for several days, and during this time Cameron became fairly familiar with the family and their past. They were looking for a place to locate, and he advised them to open a restaurant at Fort Union, a few miles on down the old Santa Fé trail.

The Antrims set up a restaurant at Fort Union, and for a while the boy, Billy, waited on the table, making friends of the cowboys, who patronized the place liberally and took to calling their waiter "Billy the Kid." Now there were a lot of negro soldiers at Fort Union and soon they were calling the boy "Billy the Goat," or simply "Billy Goat." Sometimes when Billy passed these negroes they would bleat at him in the manner of a goat. Such teasing did not sit well with his proud disposition, although he liked the name the cowboys had given him. One day when a negro soldier bleated at Billy, Billy threw a rock at his tormentor. The negro went for a gun and so did Billy. As a result there was one less negro for the government to support and Billy the Kid was fairly launched on his man-killing career. Before he became a really bad man, however, Mr. Cameron kept him on the ranch for a while, employing him as a cowboy.

Skipping the murders of Indians and Mexicans and the various killings connected with the Lincoln County War, we find Billy the Kid next refusing to trust himself to Governor

Lew Wallace, who offered amnesty if Billy would give himself up to the courts. Instead of surrendering, the Kid rode with five men through the Turkey Mountains and across the Plains to an Indian camp, where they stole a bunch of horses. They sold the horses on the Canadian, the gang split up, and the Kid, with Tom O'Phalliard and Charlie Bowdre accompanying him, went to Tascosa to make an alliance with some buffalo hunters. He had discovered a new field for operations. He had found cattle on the Canadian to steal and tie-cutters and railroad-graders to buy them.

It just happened that I had entered Tascosa at the time he was beginning operations on the Canadian, though I did not then know anything about him and had no interest in his affairs.

I rode away from the Cameron ranch with a much firmer comprehension of affairs than I had when I rode up to it. When I got to Fort Union I presented Senator Dorsey's letter to the commanding officer. He looked at me in my flop hat, looked at Whirlwind and looked at the letter again. Finally he said, "The fort is yours." As matters turned out, I had no occasion to command the fort, but the welcome was reassuring. From Fort Union I went directly to the grading camp on the Canadian River and there got a job herding the beef cattle that the contractors were buying from rustlers.

Beyond all doubt the cattle were stolen cattle, but none of them bore the brands I represented. During the course of my employment I helped the contractors purchase several small bunches of cattle, all of them from rustlers; but evidently the thieves were not bothering stock belonging to the Cimarron Cattle Raisers' Association. If they were depredating on stock north of the Canadian I never heard of it. My job was a sinecure. I kept the cattle in a pen at night and during the daytime I would frequently leave them to graze in sight of a saloon where I spent long hours among the rustlers, from whom, however, I learned little, as they were a tight-lipped crew. Twice I saw Billy the Kid and recognized him as one of the men I had treated in the saloon at Tascosa; I did not form any acquaintance with him. One evening I settled with my employers and, without saying I had quit, rode away. By daylight Whirlwind and I were forty miles north on the route to the Dry Cimarron. And so *adios* to Billy the Kid.

What was there about this killer of men, this pariah of society, this product of Bowery slum and Western lawlessness that has made him the object of such wide and undimming interest? He has been the subject of half a dozen biographies —one of them by Pat Garrett, the man who killed him, and now Pat Garrett's book has been revived and annotated by a college professor. In the Pecos country legendary tales concerning him are as numerous as legendary tales concerning Sam Houston are in East Texas and Tennessee. A monument marking his burial place at Fort Sumner has been proposed. Whereas once his purported "trigger finger" was exhibited for two bits a peep, Philip Leloir's bully ballad of "The Finger of Billy the Kid" is now read in public libraries, and in ten thousand homes and drug stores the phonograph wails out a dolorous folk song of the Kid's deeds and death.[1]

> I'll sing you a true song of Billy the Kid,
> I'll sing of the desperate deeds that he did,
> Way out in New Mexico long, long ago
> When a man's only chance was his own fo'ty-fo'.
>
> When Billy the Kid was a very young lad
> In old Silver City he went to the bad;
> Way out in the West with a gun in his hand
> At the age of twelve years there he killed his first man.
>
> Fair Mexican maidens play guitars and sing
> A song about Billy, their boy bandit king,
> How ere his young manhood had reached its bad end
> He had a notch on his pistol for twenty-one men.
>
> 'Twas on the same night that poor Billy died,
> He said to his friends: "I'm not satisfied.

[1] Words of the song here printed are taken from a record of the Brunswick-Balke-Collender Company (Brunswick record).

There are twenty-one men I have put bullets through
And Sheriff Pat Garrett must make twenty-two."

Now, this is how Billy the Kid met his fate:
The bright moon was shining, the hour was late.
Shot down by Pat Garrett, who once was his friend,
The young outlaw's life had now come to its end.

There's many a man with a face fine and fair
Who starts out in life with a chance to be square,
But just like poor Billy he wanders astray
And loses his life in the very same way.

Billy the Kid "was the Fairy Prince of New Mexico," sentimentalizes Kyle S. Crichton, the charming and exuberant biographer of another New Mexican hero, Elfego Baca. "The Robin Hood of New Mexico," shouts Walter Noble Burns, who has just made something of a reputation on his *Saga of Billy the Kid.* Even that fine English gentleman, seasoned scholar, and gallant adventurer, R. B. Townshend, whose *The Tenderfoot in New Mexico* should become a classic in the literature of the West, was, after a personal encounter with the Kid, inclined to regard him as "a mitigated ruffian" of delightful humor. Charlie Siringo, who led an expedition of cowboys in an attempt to recover cattle that the Kid had stolen, relates how when the outfit heard that Billy had killed two guards and escaped hanging, one of the men yelled, "Hurrah for Billy the Kid!" and dived into the Pecos with his boots on. Sheriff Pat Garrett, who in writing his *Authentic Life of Billy the Kid* had the advantage over all other biographers of knowing his hero personally, seems to have been strangely attracted by "his pleasant manners and openhanded generosity" and he proposed to "dissever the Kid's memory from that of meaner villains whose deeds have been attributed to him."

On the other hand, upright and clear-eyed peace officers like James B. Gillett and the law abiding, virtue preserving, though not generally imagination cultivating, citizens who give

New Mexico its stamina are apt to regard all laudations and condonements of the West's most spectacular outlaw with disgust. To such people the Kid was a stark murderer and a mean thief. As a matter of history the Kid was a professional gambler, a professional thief, and a professional gunman. He was never much of a cowboy and he cannot at all be classed as "a cowboy gone wrong." He gambled with negroes; he cheated Mexicans; he helped to ambush and murder three Apache Indians for their store of pelts and blankets. His followers were for the most part ignorant, sordid, vicious toughs. As for the polished Don Juan figure that more than one journalist has sought to mould him into, the only basis for this conception seems to be the fact that a few Mexican girls of the *pelado* class danced with him. However much may be made of his loyalty to his friends, the truth remains that he shot in the back one man who had been his friend. When his "right bower," Charlie Bowdre, dying from a bullet wound, staggered into the hut where Billy the Kid and his crew were besieged, the Kid shoved him out again with these words: "They've got you, Charlie. You're about done for. Go out and see if you can't kill one of those sons-of-bitches before you die." As to the end of the outlaw's life, he had warned Sheriff Garrett that he would shoot him on sight. There would be, there could be, no quarter on either side. According to all laws that govern such business, Pat Garrett shot Billy the Kid honorably, justly, and wisely. There have been honorable and noble and admirable outlaws *against tyranny and injustice,* like Rob Roy, like Wallace and Bruce, like Dull Knife, the great Cheyenne warrior; but when measured alongside such men as these, Billy the Kid appears tawdry.

It's not the "writer fellers" with their talk of "Robin Hood" and "the Fairy Prince" who keep the memory of Billy the Kid alive in the Kid's own country. It's the men who have themselves ridden the blood-spattered trails that Billy rode. Mostly the tales of these men are impersonal without suggestion of glorification; mostly also they are unverifiable. Sometimes the tales get into print, as the persistent one about Billy the Kid's being alive today[2] and in hiding among the Mogollon Mountains, or down in Guadalajara, Mexico, or somewhere else. In 1926 a book of reminiscences called *Frontier Dust*, by a loose-memoried old timer, John Lord, came out of Hartford, Connecticut, and in this book is an excellent example of the apocryphal tales that circulate so freely to keep Billy the Kid's memory fresh.

"Billy was working for Chisholm [Chisum]," says Mr. Lord. "He and the camp cook got into a row. The cook had a frying pan on the fire with a lot of hot grease in it. He grabbed it and either struck or threw it at Billy and some of the grease burned the Kid severely. Billy didn't do a thing but jerk out his pistol and kill the cook—got on his horse and rode away, an outlaw."

Bill Cole of Valentine, Texas, is fond of telling this anecdote—an example of scores of other anecdotes that have never been printed. One time a Texas cowboy named Dave Martin was riding from somewhere west of the Pecos to old Fort Concho, now San Angelo. He crossed the Pecos a little while before sundown, intending to stake his horse and stay all night at the deserted ruins of Fort Lancaster. When he got to the old chimneys he saw a rider coming west. The two men met, greeted each other, and both unsaddled and ate supper. The

[2] Nothing could be more absurd than these reports of Billy the Kid's being still alive; yet the amount of attention paid to the reports is astonishing—provided a human being retains the capacity of being astonished at journalistic absurdities. Not long since a young and ambitious newspaper cub talked with the writer of this book about going into New Mexico and finding the hidden Billy the Kid! He was eager for "a story"—and the Kid's name seems to have lost none of its potency in "story" making, as the following extract from an El Paso paper, dated June 24, 1926, will evidence:

"Leland V. Gardiner . . . believes Billy the Kid, notorious outlaw of pioneer days, still lives, and has thought so for the past ten years, he said. He is not the El Pasoan, however, who communicated his belief to the New Mexico Historical Society. That informant said he had seen the Kid about ten years ago [in an eastern city].

" 'I am not certain, but believe I have seen the Kid,' said Mr. Gardiner. 'I am told that he is on an isolated ranch within 500 miles of El Paso. When strangers come to the ranch he disappears until they are gone. . . . He can't take chances on being detected.' "

Hardly!

rider going west had no blanket, and Dave suggested that they make their beds together, for Dave was leading a packhorse loaded with bed roll. As the men were pulling off their boots the stranger said:

"By the way, if you have occasion to get up in the night be sure to nudge me and wake me up before you stir around any. I might wake up suddenly and shoot if I detected a man walking up to our bed."

"Well, I'll shore wake you up before I get out of bed," Dave replied laughing.

"You're going to Fort Concho, did you say?" the stranger went on.

"Yes."

"Well, when you get there you'll see my mark. I'm Billy the Kid."

At daybreak the men parted, Dave Martin going on east and his cautious bedfellow going on west. When two days later Dave got to Fort Concho, Billy the Kid's "mark" had been put under ground but there was plenty of talk about both mark and marksmanship. The mark consisted of two men who had worked for John Chisum, victims of the Lincoln County feud.

When the Kid was tried in Mesilla for the killing of Sheriff Brady and found guilty, the judge of the court, so a floating story goes,[3] pronounced the death sentence with a gathering emphasis that was highly elocutionary.

"I do hereby sentence you to be hanged by the neck," he intoned, "until you are dead! dead!! dead!!!"

"Yes," Billy the Kid calmly retorted, looking the judge straight in the eyes, "yes, and you can go to hell! hell!! hell!!!"

So much are relics of Billy the Kid prized and talked about that Charlie Siringo said "it would be a safe gamble to bet that there are a wagon load" of pistols purporting to have belonged to him "scattered over the United States." At the meeting of the trail drivers in San Antonio in October, 1928, Gus

[3] Walters, Lorenzo D., *Tombstone's Yesterday*, Tucson, Arizona, 1928, p. 118. According to the clerk of the court, George R. Bowman, Fort Worth, Texas, the Kid after having been sentenced remained silent.

Gildea of Arizona told a group of men, not without pride, that he and Billy fought in opposite ranks during New Mexico troubles for three years with a gentlemen's agreement that neither of them would shoot the other.

Thus the Kid's trigger finger goes shooting on. After all, Billy the Kid was more than a common killer and thief, more than a common leech on society. He was an uncommon killer, he was an uncommon thief. He had something in him that has called to the imagination not only of writers but of the people at large. He was indisputably brave and he was, in his own sphere, absolutely supreme. In preserving his own life and in taking the lives of his hunters he was a sheer genius. He was as single-minded in this business and as economical as Napoleon; hence his hard way with the dying Charlie Bowdre. He was probably the quickest and surest man on the trigger anywhere south or west of Wild Bill Hickok. His nerve never broke; his alertness never wavered; his determination never flagged. He had extraordinary personal magnetism, for without personal magnetism a mere boy could never have led and held in check a gang of hard, seasoned men. He controlled himself as well as he controlled others; never impetuous, he deliberated every act, every robbery, every murder. Although revengeful, he was generous hearted—particularly generous with property that belonged to other people—and, being generous hearted, he had a certain winsome care-freeness. Above all, he possessed to an unusual degree what Mirabeau finely called "the art of daring." Because he possessed this "art of daring," because his daring apotheosized youth—youth in the saddle—youth with a flaming gun—and because his daring kept him running and balancing on the edge of a frightful precipice, as it were, for an unprecedented length of time, Billy the Kid will always be interesting, will always appeal to the popular imagination. Despite facts, he seems on the way to become the Robin Hood, the Fairy Prince not only of New Mexico but of the Old West.

CHAPTER XIII

MANY TRAILS

WHEN, following my excursion to the haunts of Billy the Kid, I reached the ranch on the Dry Cimarron, I found the boys gathering up saddle horses, which always scatter in the winter, the cook scrubbing the rust off his tin plates and iron pots, and other preparations under way for spring work. The Cimarron Cattle Company had 15,000 head of cattle, but it was approaching dissolution. The truth of the matter is that one or two of the head men had literally drunk and gambled away the holdings. The partners were all in a bad humor and everything was in confusion. I looked forward to cutting loose from the outfit, but first a vast amount of work was to be done. All of the cattle had to be gathered, some of them sold off, and the remainder divided. Jim Hall was to take for his part a third of the saddle horses, about one hundred head, and 4500 heifers. These he proposed that I drive to Pease River and locate on the range where I had already located the 1300 Spur cows. We began gathering.

I felt a little lost at times, for Payaso was not in my string of mounts. During my absence he had taken to loco weed and had died.

The one event of the spring riding that I recall most vividly was roping an elk. John Duncan and I were hunting cattle on the Mesa Mayo. This Mesa is a remarkable feature in the landscape of southern Colorado. For fifteen miles it juts out from the mountains into the plains of the Picketwire valley, its western extremity three hundred feet perpendicular above the land below. In places its flat surface is miles wide. From it in one direction Pike's Peak looms visible close to a hundred fifty

miles away, while in another direction the eye can follow for
fifty miles the expanse of the Picketwire valley.

One night while John Duncan and I were camped on this
mesa a light snow fell. The next morning we saw fresh elk
tracks leading across a narrow neck of land out upon a prom-
ontory. We followed them and were still on the narrow neck
of land when the elk saw us. They were hemmed up; they
could not get down the precipitous bluffs; to escape they would
have to come by us. They were evidently bent on escaping, and
as they drew near we naturally pulled down our ropes. Their
antlers made them look like a bunch of dead tree tops running.
Both our horses stampeded. Duncan undertook to hold his
horse and missed his throw. I let my horse run along ahead of
the elk, and then as a big stag passed me with a snort I twined
him about one horn and half of his head.

He was bounding along with great leaps and at the instant
he reached the end of the rope was in midair. The jerk whirled
him around and he hit the ground flat. He bounced to his feet
like a rubber ball and ran on the rope again, but this time I
did not throw him. I could see that he was getting mad. He
quit running; his hair stood straight up; he looked at me
viciously for a few seconds; then he shook his head and came
straight for me. I realized that I must either cut the rope and
move or else shoot him. I did not want to lose my rope. I
reached for my six-shooter and already had it out of the holster
when I heard Duncan yell. He had made a run and had roped
the charging elk by the hind legs. We had no desire to kill him,
but we had to throw him down in order to take my rope off
him. We tied him in such a way that we could loosen him
from a mounted position. When he got up he had blood in his
eye, and right there we had to do some tall riding before he
got his mind again on freedom and the open spaces. It is likely
that other elk have been roped by other cowboys, but this is the
only one that I ever knew of being roped. Elk usually keep in
country too rough or brushy for horses to run in, and very few
horses could catch one on level ground anyhow. The horse I

was riding certainly could not have caught this elk had there been anything like a race between the two.

We had worked only a few weeks on the Dry Cimarron when the owners shaped up a little herd of some three hundred cows and calves, which they had sold for expense money, and turned them over to me and John Duncan to deliver at Denver. We had an easy drive, and after getting rid of the cattle we took in the town. We went to a show, I remember, and were waiting uneasily for the curtain to go up when the manager came out on the platform and apologetically announced: "The leading lady has lost her tights. There'll be no show tonight." I supposed that announcement was part of the program; but while the audience was sitting perfectly still, not knowing exactly how to take it, a fat Irish woman, who sat on one side of me, exploded with such a laugh that the whole house went laughter wild and actually we had no show. Laughter is catching, and when the audience dispersed, still uproariously laughing, the people in the streets joined in. That night Denver laughed itself to sleep. The next day as we rode down towards Las Animas one of the cowboys in our outfit made up a song that he entitled "There'll Be No Show Tonight." It was not a printable song, but it got itself adopted into the repertoire of the trail men, and within a year or two it was being sung from the Gulf of Mexico to the Canadian Rockies. We stopped at Las Animas long enough to see a badger fight, but as this institution of practical Western jokers is, like the song, too "technical" to be expounded in polite print, we'll let it pass.

The drive of the big herd of heifers from the Dry Cimarron to Pease River was uneventful. The Spur Range now had 6000 head of cattle, not counting a fine calf crop; the prospects were good, but the cattle were heavily mortgaged, and almost immediately a new set of owners took them over. The great Spur ranch, located in Dickens County, one of the best known cattle ranches in the world, can trace its lineage back to the Spur cows I placed on Pease River.

As I said in the beginning of this chapter, I was eager to cut loose from the outfit I was with. As soon as we got the 4500 heifers on their range and I got my investment out of the company, I quit and went to working for Leigh Dyer, who was running the Shoe Bar brand on Little Red River. But I did not stay there along. The nearest post office was at Clarendon. Clarendon used to be called Christian Colony, on account of some good but impractical Christians who had settled there and tried to farm. The post office, however, was established by some man—his name has escaped my memory—who drove into the "colony" with a wagon loaded principally with bandanas, a case of sardines, a box of soda crackers, and a caddy of "spit-or-drown" tobacco. He took the cracker box, made it into a post office, and called the name of it Clarendon. Every cowboy within a radius of seventy-five miles at once wrote home announcing that he now received mail regularly and that his post office was Clarendon.

I wrote and within record time, about two months, received a letter from the brown-eyed girl I had left behind me. Before I parted with her in South Texas a year and a half before I had given that girl a ring and had got her to promise that when she quit loving me she would return it. She said in her letter that she was still wearing it. She wears it yet, but it was to be several years before she put on the other ring that I see with it every day.

I told Leigh Dyer that I was going home.

"That's all right," Leigh said, "but you had just as well go by Dodge City. I've got a hundred and fifty big steers ripe for the market and have to drive them up there. Will you help me?"

Spending a month driving a herd of steers two hundred and fifty miles farther north before I headed south did not then seem anything out of the way; so I told Lee that I would go with him. Leigh Dyer was brother-in-law to Charlie Goodnight and had helped Goodnight put the first herd of cattle into the Panhandle only three years before. Only one year before, in the fall of 1878, he had with Goodnight driven the first herd of cattle out of the Panhandle to Dodge City. Goodnight had about 150 big fat steers that he wanted to send to market with Dyer's. We threw the two bunches together, and set out.

There was no trail to follow, but Leigh knew the waterings, and as for keeping our course all we had to do was to head towards the north star and bear a fraction to the right. From Palo Duro Canyon to Dodge City we did not see a soul; but deer and antelopes, prairie dogs, prairie chickens, coyotes, and wild turkeys were visible by the thousands with now and then a lonesome buffalo. I had a profound attachment for the canyons and plains and all this wild life. As we trailed along day by day with only the sounds of the tramping cattle, of the swish of grass beneath my horse's feet, and of the creak of saddle leather to disturb the silence, I felt that attachment. But something stronger than the plains and the canyons was pulling me back to the brush and prairies of the Nueces River country. Whether I stayed on the Plains, however, or drifted west into the mountains, or rode until I smelled the salt in the bayous off Matagorda Bay, my freedom would not be hampered by crowding population. From the Canadian Rockies to the Platte, from the Platte to Dodge on the Arkansas, from Dodge to the Gulf of Mexico, the land was free and open and it belonged to the cowboy. I was free too and, therefore, I was happy.

A day or two out from Dodge City Leigh Dyer rode on ahead to see about cars. When I arrived with the herd, the cars were ready, and about dark we began loading. Loading cattle at night, the sparks flying from the smokestack of an old time coal-burning engine, the lanterns of trainmen swinging and occasionally shining into the frightened eyes of the cattle, the sound of the cattle's deep breathing mixed with the yells of cowboys in one's ears, is a kind of romantic business. When we had spiked the door of the last car shut, Leigh and I climbed on board the caboose, yelled *adios* to the boys, who were going back to the Palo Duro, and pulled out for Kansas City.

We got to the Kansas City Stock Yards about daybreak and found that we had to walk some distance in order to catch a street car. Walking on hard ground with people all about—for the laborers in the stock yards were already astir—gave me a very peculiar sensation. I did not seem to be myself or to be in the world. I noticed that the people were all staring at me, but

I was too engrossed in the strange world about to consider why
they were staring. The strange world did not become less strange
when we had to get out of the mule car and help push it up a
steep hill, for the mule could not pull it even when empty.
While we were getting out, we met a bunch of dude niggers.
(There is a difference between *niggers* and *negroes,* and these
were *niggers.*)

One of the niggers pointed his finger at me and said, "What
is that?" Then the whole gang began to laugh. Here was a kind
of colored man that I had never met before. I had my six-shooter
in my pants and I immediately jerked it. Right there I would
have started a negro graveyard had not Leigh Dyer caught my
arm.

He was laughing himself. "John," he said, "you don't know
what a comical sight you are."

Then he turned me around so that I could see myself in a
window glass. I was a sight. Before I left the ranch I had given
the boys all the clothes I had except those that I was wearing,
for they needed clothes and had no place to buy them. A month
on the trail had not added to the appearance of the clothes I
started with. My beard was six inches long, and my hat was
worse than the one I had worn to Fort Union. The brim had
lost its stiffness, and to keep it from flopping in my face I had
tucked the sides of it in, making the hat sharp-pointed in front
and behind like a French loaf of bread. I had not gazed into a
looking glass for months.

I turned my gun over to the Kansas City hotel clerk,
shaved, took a hot bath, put on a new outfit of clothes, boots,
and hat, and for a week had one of the times of my life. Just as
I was about to leave for Texas I met Buffalo Bill, who was taking his show to San Antonio. We traveled on the same train
and I became well acquainted with him. At that time there
were only five people in his troupe, himself, his wife, and three
Indian bucks. The performance, which I saw in San Antonio,
consisted of some fancy shooting by Buffalo Bill, and then a
rescue of his wife from an old stage coach attacked by the Indians. Thus began one of the greatest shows on earth and by

far the most popular that ever exhibited in the western part of the United States.

Some years after this when I was living in Dog Town, Buffalo Bill came to San Antonio recruiting cowboys to go with his show to Europe. I wrote him about Tom Webb, who was then roping wild cattle on the Nueces and who was, I thought, about the best hand in the country. A letter came back inviting me and Tom both to try to qualify for the European tour. The show had no attraction for me, but Tom Webb went up. He told me afterwards that when he introduced himself at the corral, Buffalo Bill's men directed him to get on a horse and rope out a mount. They wanted to see him handle a rope. He missed three fair throws and the men told him that that would do. He started to leave, but decided to sit on the pen fence a while and watch some of the other applicants. Some of them had to show their skill at riding pitching horses as well as at roping. After the day's trials were over the boss showman walked over to Tom and nearly knocked him down by telling him that he was accepted. It was Tom Webb's individuality that won him the place. Although an uneducated product of the brush, he had a remarkable personality. He was tall and handsome; on horseback he was indeed a striking figure. The last time I saw Buffalo Bill he told me that Tom Webb always distinguished himself from other riders. Over in England, Buffalo Bill said, Tom would retire to his dressing room after the performance was over, take off his cowboy clothes, emerge in attire of the latest fashion, including a beegum hat, and then mingle with admiring nobility.

Well, I got home, which was then Beeville, in time to dance with my girl at "The Cowboy's Christmas Ball." I was still restless. I made preparations to go on the trail with horses.

CHAPTER XIV

WHEN THE BRUSH POPPED

OF treatises and chronicles concerning trail driving there is no dearth, but somehow they treat almost exclusively of the trailing of cattle. Yet in the palmy days of the trails, horses were driven over them by the hundreds of thousands and many men made horse driving their business. On the old maps of Texas the broad lands between the Nueces River and the Rio Grande were simply marked "Wild Horses." The whole of Southwest Texas was a natural horse country. The horses (mustangs) were here when the first Anglo-American settlers came, and it was not until well along towards the opening of the twentieth century that horse-raising became an occupation of the past.

As the metropolis of Southwest Texas, San Antonio was during the eighties the greatest horse market in the world; it was a clearing ground not only for horses of Southwest Texas but for tens of thousands of horses imported from Mexico. Herds of horses from New Mexico and Arizona came to San Antonio to find a market, and horse traders and speculators from Europe as well as America came to San Antonio to buy. No matter whether a man wanted a single burro, a car load of mules, or a train load of mares, he could get what he wanted in a day's time on the San Antonio market.

Many of the big buyers shipped their horses by rail to Louisiana, to Tennessee, to the New England states and elsewhere; along in the late eighties, when the country was being fenced up, immense numbers of horses went out of San Antonio in stock cars to be unloaded in North Texas and thence driven across the Indian Territory into Missouri, Arkansas, Kansas, and other states. Numerous buyers, many of them comparatively small operators, bought horses to drive through the country, peddling as they went. This class of horse traders existed until the era of the automobile. A very few still try to do business.

In short, horse traders in San Antonio were as thick as fiddlers in hell, and probably a good many of them are keeping company with the fiddlers now, for, taken on the whole, they were a slick lot. I knew them well, for along in the late eighties I was living in San Antonio as a horse trader myself. I controlled the Fest Yards on South Flores Street and did an immense business in buying and selling horses both on commission and on my "own hook."

Among the peddlers were many fly-by-night horse traders. An individual of this class generally had a wagon and camp outfit. Also he generally had a horse or two to match in scrub races. He would go to a town or a settlement and then after he had plucked all the goslings that he could, would move on. Frequently he kept a supply of "hot drops" about him. A little of this material could be carried in the palm of the hand and, without much risk of detection, applied to an opponent's horse. It would make any kind of horse go crazy, cause a race horse to fly the track or an old gentle plow horse to pitch like a bay steer.

These tricksters, however, were far from having everything their way. Every countryman in the land considered himself a horse trader and delighted in trading. In many towns Saturday, the first Monday in each month, or some other day, was designated as tradesday. On that day the town would be filled with men and horses. A man who was a good judge of horses and a close trader might begin trading in the morning with nothing but a "crow bait," before night make a dozen swaps, and then with several dollars in his pocket ride home on a good pony.

Every boy who rode a horse was willing to match a race. It was not an uncommon thing for two strangers who happened to meet each other in the road to match a race on the spot, using the public highway for a race track. Many of the big cowmen kept race horses and raised running stock, quarter horses being the favorite breed. Probably the greatest sire of the time or of any other time in Texas was Billie, owned by Foster of Lockhart. At one time Bud Malone and I bought one of Billie's colts, Jim Brown, and kept him at Dog Town, where we beat everything matched against him, running for 300 yards and allowing a handicap of 40 yards. We finally traded him away and he was raffled off in Matamoros to four old dons for $2000.

But let us get on the trail with the horse herd. Uncle Henry Clare, of Bee County, was a horse man, and I had not been home from the Plains long before Uncle Henry's three sons, Gus, Hilary, and Dave, and I persuaded him to put up a herd of horses and let us drive them. We left Beeville along in March, 1880, with something over 500 head of unbroken horses and mares, all grown stuff, excepting a few young colts that we did not count, and all as wild as bucks. We knew that if they stampeded and got away from us we should stand a mighty good chance of losing them for fair, and we had to handle them like a basket of eggs. We headed north, not caring whether we went to 36 or 54-40. We were hunting a market for horses. Uncle Henry Clare was along as boss, and no better one could be found. He could always be depended upon to run up and say, "My stars, boys, don't let 'em run!"

In many ways a herd of trail horses was managed like a herd of trail cattle. The average distance to be covered in a day was about the same as that to be covered by cattle, from ten to fifteen miles, depending on the condition of the stock, the lay of the land, and the ideas of the boss. We herded our horses at night just as we herded cattle; however, some drovers turned their horses loose at night headed in the right direction. Horses do not need to lie down as much as cattle do, and they graze at least twice between midnight and dawn. Of course we kept our saddle horses separate from the main herd. The wrangler, whose business it was to furnish us with fresh mounts on short notice, day or night, generally followed along behind the herd with his remuda.

Some of the mares already had colts when we started out, and pretty soon there were nightly additions to our stock. We could get more money for a fat mare than for a poor mare and colt, and we did not want to bother with colts anyhow; so when we got among the German settlers around Yorktown, Uncle Henry ordered all colts given away. The announcement that we had colts for free distribution brought men, women, boys, and girls alike to the herd, each with a rope. As we did not pen, they had to come to us on the prairie. A cowboy would rope out a colt, drag it to the edge of the herd, put the German's rope on it, and then we would all watch proceedings. When an old woman started out to lead a wild colt across the prairie, there was a performance to match anything seen in a high priced rodeo. Very often the colt seemed to be more master than subject. We gave away over a hundred colts.

At Gonzales on the Guadalupe we struck the blackjack country and here our troubles began. The trail through this brush was some forty or fifty yards wide with "openings," or "natural clearings," few and far between. However, at the end of the first day's drive in the brush we found a little prairie of perhaps twenty acres. Here we camped and held the herd, but there was no grass or water. That night the guard was doubled. When daylight came we found that our wagon horses were gone. We hunted them without success until noon. A couple of stranger boys had come to camp about sunup and they kept sitting around and telling the cook that they could find the horses if we would give them five dollars. Uncle Henry finally told them that he would pay the price, and in a short time they brought the horses in. They had evidently stolen them during the night and tied them out in the brush. Men have been hanged for playing that trick, but these boys got nothing but their five dollars. I later heard that they played that old trick once too often.

What with being close-herded all night and half a day without grass or water, the herd was naturally restless and nervous. By the time we started, along about two o'clock, those range horses were certainly ready to travel. Now, nearly any kind of horse can outrun a bunch of cattle, but when a horse carrying a man races with a hell-bent herd of his own kind he has to be genuinely good to outrun them. Gus Clare and I took our places in the lead to hold the herd back; we were expecting something, and each of us was on his choice mount.

Traveling along with the herd was a fellow by the name of Lewis. I can not call him a hand, for he knew absolutely nothing about handling stock. However, he was owner of fifteen or twenty mares, and Uncle Henry had permitted him to throw in with us. We kept him out of the way as much as possible, and on this particular occasion he was left behind to help the cook pack up. As soon as the wagon was loaded, so we afterward learned, Lewis got on his plug and struck a gallop to overtake the herd. Now, in any and every herd on earth, whether of men, goats, cattle, or horses, there are always some drags. The draggiest drag of our herd was an old gray mare; she was always behind and always seemed to be asleep. Lewis woke her up with a slap of his rope; she tried to jump out of her skin. Her lunge among the other horses of the herd was like the flip of a match into a dry pan of powder. The stampede was on.

Gus and I knew that the only chance to check the mad herd was to give them room. We had to let the horses run and at the same time we had to hold them down. This is a difficult thing to do; it requires skill; the ability to do it is one distinguishing difference between a cowman and a cowboy. The trail we were racing down was lined on either side with brush too thick to cuss a cat in. We simply could not check those horses, and directly the leaders of the stampede broke out into the brush on my side. The main herd followed.

It was then that I made the ride of my life. I have ridden for my life and I have ridden for money, but I never made another ride like that. I rode like a drunk Indian and a madman moulded into one. I knew that five hundred wild horses were about to get away; I knew that if they did get away and scattered through the brush of Gonzales County we should never get them together again; I realized that holding them up depended on my efforts alone. They swept forward, tearing up the brush like a cyclone. No rider by merely racing along behind them in the trail they were opening could turn or stop them.

If they ran far they would scatter. I must ride around the leaders. In another chapter the extraordinary technique of the brush hand will be dealt with. I shall have occasion to tell of how one of my friends was killed while running in the brush. Many men have been killed by the brush of Southwest Texas. The blackjack brush through which I was now running was not only thick, but the limbs of it were close to the ground. They stood like a rampart of gnarled and splintering lances to thrust back any rider who attempted to get through them.

My Guardian Angel may know how I made that run; I don't. In about half a mile we came to a small, round prairie perhaps two hundred yards across. The leaders of the stampede and I struck it at the same time. My ducking jacket was torn off; there was little skin left on my face; my arms and body had snag cuts all over them that might have satisfied any Sioux warrior about to dance the Sun Dance; the horse I was riding had a bunged knee that was to cripple him for life. But neither my horse nor I was conscious of any mutilation. I could feel his heart pounding against my legs and I could feel my heart jumping into my throat. We had found an opening and here was a chance to circle the stampede. I literally picked my pony up with the spurs, and before the leaders reached the brush on the other side of the clearing I headed them and set the herd to milling.

Directly Gus Clare and another hand came—and then Uncle Henry, shouting, "My stars, boys, don't let 'em run again!" But our troubles were not over. One old "willow tail"[1] had got the limb of a blackjack fastened into her long mane, which hung down to the point of her shoulders and was matted into a "witch knot"; and she was tearing around and around among the horses trying to outrun that tree top. As soon as the other boys came up I roped her and we threw her down and roached the mane with the brush still in it.

As horses have, normally, infinitely more sense than cat-

[1] A horse might be "willow-tailed," but "willow tail" generally meant a mare. The term is descriptive of the loose, long, coarse, heavy tails carried by some range horses—never an indication of good breeding.

tle, they have when they stampede less sense to the same degree. Their fear becomes so overpowering that they have absolutely no judgment; they will run over bluffs and into obstacles that a stampede of cattle would either dodge or halt at. They are so high-strung that, once they have made a desperate run, they are very slow to regain calmness. Getting our herd through the brush that separated our little prairie from the trail was ticklish business now, but we were successful. At the first good opening we camped on, we cut Mr. Lewis' horses out of our herd and separated from him. Our stock were so badly spoilt that they would try to run every time a stick popped, and we could not afford to have such a blunderer as Lewis around them.

When we got to the Colorado River at Webberville, below Austin, we found the water spread over the bottom lands so deep that we could not locate the main channel of the stream. We were compelled to lie over several days. Meantime several herds of cattle were also waiting to cross. One of them belonged to my friend Bing Choate, who was a few months later killed in Dodge City, Kansas, where he took his herd. After the river had run down somewhat and we had got our horses over, Bing Choate and his men helping us, Gus Clare and I went back to help Bing cross his cattle.

The water was still three or four hundred yards wide, but what made it mean to cross was a bluff just below the going-out place. The landing was narrow and boggy and we had to make sure that no cattle got under the bluff. Bing decided to cross them in small bunches, a few hundred head at a time. I took my place in the water, swimming out with each bunch on the lower side until I saw that the cattle were pointed safely and then turning back to direct the next bunch. Now, to turn a horse in swimming water is not always an easy matter. No man should ever ride into deep water with the bridle on his horse, for if the reins are pulled the horse will sink, and then if the rider quits him the horse will more than likely get his feet tangled in the slack reins and drown. The way to turn a horse in swimming water is to slap him on the side of the head. Generally, but not always, a horse will veer around from the slap.

I had already crossed three bunches of cattle and was well satisfied with my horse's behavior in the water. However, when I attempted to turn back the fourth time he refused to turn. I suppose he was getting tired of swimming. While I was slapping him hard, trying to force him, a floating tree top that I had not seen brushed me from the saddle and sent me to the bottom. As I was naked, the brush scratched me considerably and I must have been thinking of my skin rather than of the water, for I strangled badly.

Without my knowledge Gus Clare had seen the accident from the west bank and immediately started towards me. I had swum and drifted several hundred yards downstream and was leisurely angling across to "the yan side" when I heard him call almost over me. He seemed to be having some trouble getting his horse to me, and, just as he came near, the current suddenly became swifter and downstream we shot. As the horse passed me, however, I managed to catch a hold on his tail. The current carried us against a bluff on the wrong side of the river. We just had to let it take us on downstream until it cut towards the other side and then we pulled for shore. The end of the episode was all right, but once or twice I was mighty near what they call "a watery grave." No feature of nature is more pitiless or fearful than a dark, silent, swirling, swollen river.

East of the Colorado we hit open, rolling country; the sun shone and we could almost hear the grass growing. Trail driving was again nothing but pleasure. At Taylor we got our mail, the accumulation of a month. Among the letters was one for me from Grandfather Duncan on the San Saba. He said that he had some men located who wanted to explore the Devil's River country and start a ranch out there. At that time the range along the Devil's River and up its head draws was still unappropriated; I had a very good knowledge of the whole territory. Grandfather said that these men had capital, that if I would help them establish the ranch they would allow me an interest in it and engage me to run it. I sold what horses I had in the Clare herd, told the Clares goodby, and rode west.

On the San Saba I found three men with money and eagerness to invest it in 2000 cows. We formed a tentative company, packed two mules, and set out for a month's tour of exploration. We explored from the head draws of Devil's River down to Beaver Lake, across to Fort Lancaster on the Pecos, and then up and down and across the whole country. We visited the water holes that the Seminole Indian had shown me four years previously, but concluded that they were too far from good grass and too limited in their supply of water to be counted on for many cattle. After riding hundreds of miles we found what we wanted—plenty of grass and plenty of water in holes and lakes. But our plans were blasted when an old hunter on whom we happened told us that during drouthy years all this water dried up, that it was not dependable. A great part of the Devil's River country was not utilized until the advent of windmills.

We turned back, but I was in love with the range I had gone over so carefully, and ten years later I was to return as well driller and locate a ranch. Meantime I lived on the Frio River, and rode for life and livelihood through some of the brushiest brush in North America.

CHAPTER XV

BRUSH COUNTRY

ONE day along in the early eighties a long, lanky, thirsty cowboy from up on the Esperanzas rode a Mexican bronco into the only town of McMullen County. He fetched up at the main store of the place with a yell that made the old mesquite tree outside shake its leaves, dragged his spurs inside, took three deep swigs of undiluted "white mule," and then announced that he was going to wake up everybody and every dog in town. He did. After he had yelled a while, interspersing his "ya-hooing" with more drinks of straight whiskey, he got on his bronco, let out what he proposed to be a climactic whoop and dug in his spurs. The bronco began pitching and with each jump the cowboy gave a merry squall.

The dogs, which had been awakened, soon gathered around the horse and rider, all yelping. There were more than fifty of them. The natives seemed to be enjoying the show as much as the dogs, for they gathered also, joining in the noise to encourage both dogs and cowboy. Some of the dogs began to bite at the horse's heels and others at the rider's toes. The horse pitched a little higher and the cowboy yelled a little louder. He was having a bigger celebration than in his dreamiest hours out beyond in the ascetic prickly pear and black chaparral he had ever dreamed of having. Then he quieted down and his horse quieted down and the dogs fell silent, but they kept a ring around the mounted man just the same. "What next?" their ears and noses seemed to be saying.

The answer was a pretty hoarse squawk that the cowboy meant for a farewell, and he headed his bronc down the road. Perhaps the bronc did not understand. He went to pitching again, and the dogs again began snapping at his heels and at the toes of the rider. The whole performance was repeated; when the cowboy had again quieted the horse, the dogs quieted too but still kept their watchful circle. After a while the rider, who was sobering up a little, told the dogs very plainly to go home. If they understood they made no sign of understanding. Then the cowboy talked to the dogs in a language that not even some of the men could understand; apparently the dogs did not understand it either.

Finally, however, a good Samaritan broke the circle of canine beleaguers with a stick. The cowboy rode off, and had he ridden on away slowly and quietly all would have been well; but he could not resist the temptation to express the buoyancy of his unconquerable soul. At the first whoop all the dogs took in after him. They outran him and out near the Boot Hill Graveyard—nobody had heard of a "memorial park" in those days and "cemetery" was still a literary word—they rounded him up again and kept him there for an hour. At last, however, he got ahead of the pack, and the music those dogs made behind him would have set any old fox hunter wild with delight. How far they chased him nobody ever knew; some of them did not get back home until the next day.

Home was Tilden, on the Frio River, but before the presidential election of 1876 the name of Tilden was Dog Town, and Dog Town, despite the post office department, it was for many years still called. The old name was much more fitting than the new, but so far as one of the early postmasters of the town was concerned there was no difference between the two—at least in print. When the stage brought the mail in, he would dump it on the floor of the post office and then shout: "There's your mail, boys! Pick out what belongs to you."

The half dozen or so pioneer ranchmen of McMullen County who built their log houses in a bend of the Frio River, coming together for mutual protection against the Indians and Mexican bandits, had no intention of establishing a town. Eventually, however, some man put in a few groceries and a barrel of whiskey; then a stage route that was established between San Antonio and Laredo passed through the place. It had to have a name, and as every cowman had a pack of dogs with which to catch wild cattle out of the brush, it was logically and naturally christened Dog Town. Forty miles southwest of it was Fort Ewell on the Nueces in La Salle County, and, excepting Pleasanton to the north, Fort Ewell and Dog Town were the principal stage stands between San Antonio and the Rio Grande. From the big bend of the Nueces River in McMullen County to the thin line of Mexican *ranchitas* on the Rio Grande sixty or seventy-five miles southward, the country fifty years ago was practically uninhabited.

The stagecoaches, which were light, were drawn by six little Spanish mules that usually went in a long lope and often in a run. These mules had to be circled by the driver and checked by the helper at each stage stand before they would come to a halt. If anybody wanted to get on or off at a point between the stands, all the driver could do was to circle the mules, thus reducing the speed somewhat, while the passenger jumped as best he could. Stage robbers could make a hold-up only by killing the mules. The few passengers that rode the stage always got a thrill for their money.

Fort Ewell, the only stage stand between Dog Town and the Rio Grande that could possibly be called a town, was not and never had been much of a fort, troops having been stationed there only for a brief period about the time of the Mexican War. It was made up principally of Mexicans and Peg Leg Stuart, storekeeper. All that is left of Fort Ewell now is the adobe foundations of a few houses and a little graveyard fenced in with barbed wire. Hunters for buried treasure have dug into most of the graves; cattle in the Callaghan pasture of 60,000 acres, which includes the site, graze over the ruins.

In its prime, during the early eighties, Dog Town, or Tilden, had a population of perhaps 1500 people and furnished supplies to ranches over a wide territory of brush and prairie. It had a newly established "college" under the direction of Professor J. V. E. Covey, whose institution at Concrete, already described, had been run out of business by the rise of public

schools. Today Tilden has a population of two or three hundred
people. It is still the county seat of McMullen County, but the
brush, rather than the plow, has encroached upon the prairies
around it until it takes a good brush hand to find it. In late
summer a horse tied to one of the mesquites in front of the
court house can still pick a feed of mesquite beans. An ancient
Mexican with cart, barrel, and burro still supplies many of the
residents with water. But there is a public school to which
Professor Covey's college long since gave way.

The early settlers of McMullen County were, as a class,
moral, law-abiding citizens. Of course most of them carried
guns, many of them drank whiskey, and not a few gambled.
Six-shooters, whiskey, and poker, however, were within the
code: these things had no connection with morals; indulgence
in them was neither moral nor immoral, but natural to the
times. Some of the most upright, honest, and generous-hearted
men that ever lived carried—and on occasion used with deadly
effect—six-shooters, drank whiskey straight, and staked high
sums on spotted cards.

McMullen County is on the border. Because of its limited
rainfall its lands were late in being sought by westward-push-
ing home-seekers, and, indeed, the dry farmer has not yet to
any considerable extent succeeded in growing crops on its soil.
Its brush makes excellent covert for anything, man or beast, that
is hunted. Hence it was in the early eighties a refuge for outlaws
not only from the counties to the north and east, where law was
becoming established, but from Mexico, where President Diaz's
rurales were running bandits into their holes. Some of these
outlaws purported to be mustangers; all of them stole horses
and cheated at cards.

With such a class of men in the country, Dog Town, like
old Tascosa and Dodge City, soon had a Boot Hill Graveyard.
One day a harmless fellow was asleep in the shade of a mesquite that grew in front of one of the combination stores and
saloons of the town. A professional gambler and horse thief
saw him and announced that he could put a bullet through the
fellow's hat without touching his head. He shot too low and

Boot Hill had another citizen. The old timers decided that life had become just a little too cheap and that property was entirely too communistic. They did not send for the rangers or complain to the governor. They merely organized themselves into a vigilance committee and one fine morning told the undesirables around Dog Town to hunt a fresh range. Before dark most of the outlaws had crossed the Nueces and were swallowed up in the Brasada.

It was at this Dog Town, where cow dogs hemmed up cowboys, where stage mules had to be circled to a halt, and where a population of opposing ideas as to the rights of property had not yet been sifted by the promoters of law and order, that I settled in the fall of 1880, there to live for nearly a decade. My father had accumulated a fair amount of property, although he still preached on occasion, and I had saved some money. Under the name of L. D. Young and Son we went into the general mercantile business. One year our sales totalled $100,000, much of it on credit. Often we had to take cattle on debt, and, although a merchant, I was really more in the cattle business than I had yet been. My brother-in-law, James Drake, and I operated the old Marcao Ranch. Thus I was frequently away from Dog Town for months at a time, living in camp and in the saddle.

Dog Town was the capital of the brush country. I won my spurs as a vaquero while helping to snare mossy horns out of the thickets inland from St. Mary's Bay. I have been snagged by the stubble brush of northern New Mexico and southern Colorado—and that brush is bad. I have dodged through the splintering cedar brakes of the Llano hills—and that brush is bad too. I made what I consider my record ride after a stampeding herd of five hundred wild horses through a great blackjack thicket east of the San Antonio River—and that brush is worse. I am acquainted with the *tornillo* tangles on the upper Rio Grande. I worked for years in the *mogotes* of huisache and mesquite down the Nueces in San Patricio and Nueces counties, sometimes following cows and sometimes cow thieves—and that brush is so bad that it could hardly be worse. Nevertheless, by and large, taking it thicket after thicket, the worst brush in the

United States of America that I know anything about is what
the Mexicans used to call the Brasada, in McMullen, Webb,
Duval, Live Oak, and other counties between the Nueces River
and the Rio Grande.

Perhaps no widely dispersed tree growth responds more
apparently to climate, altitude, and latitude than the mesquite.
In the southern part of Live Oak County, where it seems generally to reach its maximum growth, it develops into great
trees; on the Llano River and out on the Edwards Plateau it
is gnarled and black-barked, the tops conspicuously thin; on
the Plains it is just "switch mesquite." Again, far out in the
sandy draws of the Sonoran desert against the Gulf of California
the mesquite's leaves are very small, to lessen evaporation, and
many of them, defying winter freezes, hang on the branches
until spring; here, too, the top of the tree is a bunch of dozens
of stems, or limbs, that run up from the trunk-base, sprangle
out like the stems of the *ocotillo* and, when the tree—generally
covered with an enormous amount of mistletoe—attains age and
size, bend over like the limbs of a weeping willow or a pepper
tree. The thorns on the mesquite vary in number and size as
much as the tree itself varies. In the Brasada, the heart of the
mesquite country, this extraordinary growth ranges from little
switches to big trees, and the multitudinous thorns on it are long
and sharp.

The mesquite is just one among many thorned growths that
characterize the Brasada, most of them known to the people of
the region only by their Mexican names. They give the land a
character as singular as that afforded to Corisca by the *maquis*
or to Florida by the everglades. Here are *mogotes* (thick patches)
of the evergreen, stubborn, beautiful *coma* with dirk-like thorns,
and, in season, with blue berries which the Mexican dove likes
so much that it constantly coos—if we are to believe the Mexican
folk—"*comer comas, comer comas*," saying that it wants to eat
coma berries. Here are vast *cejas*—another term of the vaqueros
for "thicket," usually coupled with the adjective *barbara* (fierce)
—of the green *brasil* and *clepino;* of the wand-like *retama,* green
also of bark and leaf, its adder-toothed thorns disguised all

summer long under yellow flowers that give it another name, *illuvia de oro* (shower of gold); of *retama chino;* and of the *junco* (the all-thorn), which, naked of leaves, was, according to Mexican belief, woven into Christ's crown of thorns, and, as a result, has ever since been shunned by all birds of the air save one—the butcher bird, who alone will alight upon it. *Granjeno,* which grows succulent yellow berries; cat's claw, which never releases its hold; balsam-breathed *huajilla,* over-spreading and making soft to the eye ten thousand hills, its diminutive and sparse thorns powerless to prevent its leaves from affording the best browse in North America for horses and cattle or its bloom from imparting to honey a flavor that only alfalfa can equal; *agrito* (wild currant), every leaf an armada of spines, first of all shrubs of the *campo* to anticipate spring by its buds; sweet-scented white brush, and sweeter *vara dulce,* cousins, prickly without thorns, and fine for bees; bitter and sharp *amargosa,* famous for its medicinal tea; black chaparral (*chaparro prieto*), the name of which is not generic to borderers as it is to East-erners but denotative of a particular growth that in many places spreads high, thick, and unbroken over thousands and thousands of acres; prickly pear, often growing higher than a man on horseback; *tasajillo* (rat-tail cactus), which, excepting the *cholla,* has more thorns per square inch than any other growth known to vaqueros, which in winter is bizarre and beautiful with a studding of red berries that are fancied by blue topknot Mexican quail and wild turkeys; the accursed devil's head; the proud Spanish dagger, which affords a poison effective in antidoting rattlesnake bite—all these growths of thorn and fiber show their thorough adaptation to the country by diverging into many varieties and to each other by locking lances, as it were, to ward off any intrusion.

Long ago when herds were sparse, when the turf of curly mesquite grass was dense, and when Indian fires periodically swept the ranges, the brush was kept in check. But since the coming of the ranchero the brush has been winning possession of the soil for a thousand miles up and down the Rio Bravo, and the more fertile the soil the more rapid has been its spread.

It knows how to make war according to the Napoleonic code; *i.e.,* to make offense. It knows too how to make a war of defense. During the past fifty years terrible drouths have decimated noble live oaks, a tree that thrives west of the Nueces but does not reach the Rio Grande except towards its mouth; no drouth has ever killed out a chaparral thicket. The drier the spring, the heavier the mesquite bean crop will be in late summer. Prickly pear requires a little moisture, it is true, but a leaf of it tossed into the crotch of a tree will find enough soil there to put roots into and to live on. In a drama that moves too slowly for volcanic spectacularity but nevertheless with a lethal finality comparable to the incessant beat of ocean surf or the ceaseless crawl of glacial rivers, the brush is stabbing a vast range to death. In addition to hiding and keeping secret many things, the Brasada has a story of its own that is here only suggested—not told.

To work effectively in this brush a vaquero had to have *tapaderos* (toe-fenders) on his stirrups, boots on his heels, heavy leather leggins (never called *chaps* in Southwest Texas) on his legs and up to his waist, ducking jacket for the protection of his arms and the trunk of his body, gauntleted gloves for his hands and wrists, and stout hat for the protection of his head. The hat frequently had a *barboquejo* (chin strap), but even when strapped on it was likely to be torn off a vaquero's head in fierce struggles against the tenacious brush. Such was the skill of the brush hands, however, that they could dispense with much of this armor and still "tear a hole" through the worst thickets. A good gun alone does not make a good shot; a good saddle does not make a good rider; nor does a pair of high-heeled shop-made boots give a man the true cowboy walk.

Perhaps in dealing with the art of the brush hand the present tense rather than the past should be used. The Brasada is still a *brasada,* the openings in it fewer and smaller. It is still a cow country, and brush hands, mostly Mexicans now, still "kill up" their horses running wild cattle. However, the wild cattle are few indeed compared with their former numbers; the country is all cut up into pastures, and the waterings are controlled by fences. Perfection in any art requires constant practice, and present conditions do not demand so much hard running in the brush as formerly. Nevertheless, although this account is of times and conditions that have passed away forever, the thorned land and the class of men who ride through the thorns have not, like so many other things, utterly vanished. As nearly as the present day cowboy on the wide broken ranges of Arizona approaches the old time cowboy, the present day brush hand of Southwest Texas approaches the brush hand of the time when the Brasada was as wild as the cattle that hid in it.

In running in the brush a man rides not so much on the back of his horse as under and alongside. He just hangs on, dodging limbs as if he were dodging bullets, back, forward, over, under, half of the time trusting his horse to course right on this or that side of a bush or a tree. If he shuts his eyes to dodge, he is lost. Whether he shuts them or no, he will, if he runs true to form, get his head rammed or raked. Patches of the brush hand's bandana hanging on thorns and stobs sometimes mark his trail. The bandana of red is his emblem.

If the brush is low and thick, the brush hand, while he may not have to dodge it with his head and body, still has to ride with every muscle active in order to stay on his leaping, crashing, swerving mount. Now the horse, in a bound that curves in midair so that he may secure footing on the other side, shows skylight under his belly. Here is a race with thorns for handicaps and every step a hurdle. It is a race that the Derby or Newport would hardly recognize.

Unseen and unapplauded, the brush hand almost daily exerts as much skill and grit as any rodeo star ever displayed in conquering the most savage outlaw horse. The bronco buster is constantly on exhibition. Millions of people have seen him and thrilled at his daring. Bold painters, skilled photographers, and able writers have glorified him. He has become the darling of the cowboy tradition. But nobody ever sees the brush popper in action. When he does his most daring and dangerous work he is out of sight down in a thicket. An "observer" might hear him breaking limbs, but that is all. He has never been pictured on canvas or in print. If in the romance of range tradition he ever

comes into his own, he will come through the record of someone who has himself "split the brush" and not through per-
formances before rodeo fans.

A brush hand can work on the prairie as well as any prairie-
trained cowboy, but a prairie-trained cowboy is as helpless in
bad brush as any tenderfoot. After struggling in the brush, any
kind of horseback work on the prairie seems as "soft" to a brush
hand as a cushioned rocking chair seems to a leg weary ditch
digger. No ditch digger ever exerted himself more or sweated
more profusely than a brush hand in a thicket on a hot day.

Like the brush hand, the brush horse is a distinct type. A
horse raised and trained on the open prairie is no more to be
depended upon in the brush than in steep gorges and rocky
mountains, though a brush horse is all right on the prairie, provided it is clear of prairie dog holes. These require a special
skill. The chances are that the untrained hand who gets on a
good brush horse and starts after a wild cow through a thicket
will soon be knocked or dragged from the saddle. A good brush
horse is not going to stop when he gets after something in the
thorns any more than a game hound will stop when he gets hot
on the trail of a panther. A little horse is better for dodging
under low limbs; a big horse is better for clearing the way for
his rider. A few horses, powerful and fearless, have a way of hitting the brush sidewise. Plenty of brush hands are afraid to ride
these powerful horses. In the heat of the chase they are apt to
become "cold-jawed" (hard-mouthed) and uncontrollable. A
rider who trusts to one will get there—if he does not get killed.

Let us draw a picture. Down in a *ramadero* of spined
bushes and trees that seem to cover all space except that occupied by prickly pear, a man with scratched face, frazzled
ducking jacket, and snagged leggins is sitting on a horse, one leg
thrown over the horn of his saddle. He is humped forward and
seems almost asleep. The horse has gray hairs in his flanks; his
knees are lumped from licks and thorns of past years. He is an
old timer and knows the game. He is resting one hip and he
seems to be asleep. The man is waiting, for some other vaqueros
have entered the *ramadero* above him to start up the wild cattle.

Presently he thinks that he catches the high note of a yell far up the brush; he feels a quiver in the muscles of his horse. The horse thinks that he hears too; he no longer appears to be asleep; his ears are cocked. A minute later the sound of the yell is unmistakable. The brush hand takes down his leg; the horse plants down the leg he has been resting and holds his head high, ears working. Again the yell, closer.

Pretty soon the popping of brush made by the running cattle will be heard. There will not be many cattle in the bunch, however—just three or four or a half dozen. Outlaws like company but they are not gregarious. The vaquero's feet are planted deep in the stirrups now. *Pop—scratch*—silence. In what direction was that sound? The old horse's heart is beating like a drum against the legs of his rider. *Pop—scr-r-r-atch*—rattle and rake of hoofs. Man and horse hit the brush as one. They understand each other. They may get snagged, knocked by limbs that will not break, cut, speared, pierced with black thorns, the poison from which sends cold chills down the back of the man and makes him sick at the stomach. No matter. The horse and rider go like a pair of mated dogs charging a boar. The brush tears and pops as if a team of Missouri mules were running through it with a mowing machine. The brush hand is in his element.

Walter Billingsley used to say that "if Sam Dickens was running a cow across a prairie a section wide and there was a chaparral bush in the middle of it, Sam would head his horse right through the bush." Sam was a brush popper. Like many another brush whacker, he was wont to emerge from a thicket with enough wood hanging in the fork of his saddle to cook a side of yearling ribs.

Winter has always been the best time in which to run wild cattle. Then some of the brush sheds its leaves, allowing greater visibility, although much of the brush, like the coma and black chaparral, is evergreen. Wild cattle that have been run hard and have become "over-het" often die. In hot weather they will literally run themselves to death; running them in cool weather is much less disastrous. In winter time, too, a horse can run farther and work harder without becoming *solado,* or "solyowed" (*solaoed*), as the border people have anglicized the Spanish word meaning "wind-broken." Half of the cow ponies of the brush country used to be *solado.* The heat and exertion suffered by a horse that is ridden recklessly and relentlessly through the brush of southern Texas in summer time are killing.

A brush popper does not ask for room in which to swing his rope. He is lucky if he strikes a little opening big enough to allow him to toss a clear loop over the horns or head of the animal he is running. If he misses his throw at this little opening, he will probably not get such an opportunity again. Often he is right at the animal's heels without space in which to cast any kind of loop. If he can keep up with the animal long enough, however, he is almost sure to come to a place where he can rope it by one or both hind legs. Sometimes he leans over and pitches the loop up instead of down, as is done on the prairie, thus avoiding low hanging limbs. This kind of side-and-up throw generally catches a cow *media cabeza*—by the half head. To rope in the brush a vaquero wants a much shorter rope—one twenty-five feet long is about right—than is used on the Plains, where ropes forty, and even forty-five, feet long can be managed. Carrying a rope in the brush without getting it entangled is an art in itself. In the old days the rawhide reata was used a great deal, for it could, on account of its weight, be thrown through the small brush much more effectively than lighter ropes of fiber.

Sometimes we of the Brasada put cases of rawhide on the front legs of our horses to protect them from thorns, but these horse leggins were never very successful. If put on tightly they chafed a horse; if put on loosely they were apt to work around so that a snag could get between the rawhide and the horse's leg, causing him to stumble. They seemed to make horses reckless.

The number of horses required to mount a man who was running regularly in the Brasada was very large—probably three times the number required in an open country, for they were always getting crippled. As long as a horse keeps warm he can run, no matter how many thorns are in him; he becomes crippled after he has cooled off. The morning after a *corrida* of men had run all day in the brush, a third of their horses would sometimes be unable to walk to the corral with the remuda.

Prickly pear poultices and kerosene oil were with us the principal remedies against thorns in the flesh of either man or horse, though "Volcanic Oil" and "Sloan's Liniment" were widely used. When a horse got a thorn from the *viznaga* (devil's head) in his foot, no poultice or caustic could draw it out. The devil made the *viznaga* thorn so that it will work in, in, and it is plated with a hard substance that will hardly decay. A big mesquite or *coma* thorn in the joint of a horses's leg is as bad as a *viznaga* thorn in his foot.

Thorns were just one item that we had to contend with in the problem of keeping enough horses to work on. Horse thieves were another item. Mustangs, constant enticers of gentle horses, were still another. Then, sometimes our saddle stock would wander from their accustomed range looking for better grass. A few months later they might return fat; again they might never return. Sometimes a rancher even in the midst of cow work might find himself afoot and compelled to buy a new remuda. The plausible question, "Why did not the rancher catch some mustangs and break them to ride?" will be answered later. There were plenty of mustangs to be caught.

There was a plenty of many kinds of wild life. The Brasada is still a harborage for great numbers of white-tailed deer. The turkeys, though, that used to fatten on elm mast and acorns along the streams have disappeared. Mexican (or blue) quail, rattlesnakes, and javelinas (peccaries, or musk hogs) were the most numerous forms of wild life in the brush.

When I came to Dog Town there were, compared with what there had been and also with what there were three or four years later, few cattle in the country. The "Breakup," coupled with the "Big Steal," had cleaned it. The amazing story of these range phenomena will be told in the next chapter. Most of the cattle left in the country were literally wilder than the deer. When Pat Garrett, in his *The Authentic Life of Billy the Kid,* wished to give an idea of how fast some outlaws ran on a certain occasion, he said, "They ran like a bunch of wild Nueces steers." *To run like a Nueces steer* used to be a common—and expressive—saying to keep company with *kicking like a bay steer.* These native wild cattle of the Nueces did not know that the brush grew thorns. Among them were old maverick cows and bulls that belonged to anybody who could catch them. Some of the cows and steers that bore brands were not worth catching. If roped they would only "sull" and fight; they weighed nothing and "looked as if they had but one gut in them." The best thing to do with them was to shoot them in order to prevent their spoiling other cattle. Out in the Brasada ten and fifteen miles from permanent water were old Mexican longhorns that could subsist for months on prickly pear and dagger blooms without coming to water at all. Such cattle were exceedingly wary. Only dogs could rouse them. A popular nickname for the wild brush cattle was "cactus boomers."

It used to be a common saying that Texas was all right for men and dogs but was hell on women and horses. In the Brasada country the dogs had as hard a time as the women and horses. Every cowman had his pack for trailing and rallying the wild cattle, and when we were working regularly we had to change dogs just as we changed horses, for thorns, rocks, and the prevailing warm weather would soon wear down the hardiest of dogs. Three dogs were regarded as the right number for two or three vaqueros working together to run with. In the brush we could have no round-ups; we just "worked," "hunted," and "ran" cattle. Running them with dogs did not make them any gentler.

On moonlight nights we often took stands near the river and roped *ladinos.* Low-hanging elms and other growth line the banks of the Frio and Nueces in this part of the country; then there used to be—and to an extent yet are—openings between the river brush and back-lying thickets. Outlaw cattle that stayed in the thickets all day grazed out on these openings at night and crossed them on their way to water. It was best to let them drink their fill, so that they would be less active, before "tying into them." Often we had to run through scattering brush in order to get onto the cattle; night-roping then became dangerous business. Old Dan McCloskey was right. He used to say that it took just two things to make a good brush roper, especially at night—"a damned fool and a race horse."

A few of the waterings in the country could be controlled by pens. The gates would be left open and the pens undisturbed for weeks at a time; then some night a brush popper or two would hide near the gate and shut it on a bunch of wild cattle while they were drinking. One night another vaquero and I were squatted in a clump of bushes at one of these pens, watching. We saw a little bunch of mighty thirsty and mighty skittish cattle go inside and then we ran to the wide gate to close it. It was just a wire gap. While we were getting a strand of wire that had caught untangled, a two-year-old maverick heifer came dashing back. I could see her plainly. I had my rope in hand and, uncurling a big loop, I roped her. She got one foot through the loop and the rope drew up on her shoulders. The ground was sandy, and I hitched the loose end of rope around my waist and let her drag me. After I had plowed a furrow with my heels about two hundred yards long, the heifer suddenly turned and came at me full tilt. She had horns too. I managed to jump to one side of a little mesquite and, as she came by, took a twist around it and drew up the slack. The other cattle, following the lead of the heifer, all got away, but we tied her.

When an outlaw animal was roped out in the brush it was tied to a tree and then later necked to a lead ox and thus brought in. The lead oxen were, of course, gentle. They were kept around ranch headquarters, and one of them with a rope around his horns would lead, following a vaquero, as well as a horse. After an outlaw "critter" had been necked to a well trained ox, the ox would be turned loose and left alone to make his way back to the ranch, frequently through many miles of brush. In the course of a day or two he would come in, his mate considerably subdued. However, many of the lead oxen with their yoke mates had to be driven.

At the ranch the outlaw cattle, some with forked sticks on their necks, some with heads tied down to a front foot, some necked together, might be held in a small pasture until enough cattle were gathered to make a bunch; or they might be held under herd with gentler cattle during the day and then penned at night. Getting them out of the country even after they were caught was a job. We generally drove them out in a herd of manageable cattle.

Excessively wild cattle in a brush country are not money makers. In order to gentle our cattle we of the Brasada kept our cows and calves in a pen, turning out the cows to pasture by day and the calves by night. Several months of this sort of handling would gentle the cows, and the calves would start life in a civilized manner. Sometimes a ranchman would have two or three hundred head of cows and calves up at one time. A few of the cows were so wild that they would not come to the pens even for their calves. In that event the calves might be released to their mothers, or they might be suckled to other cows and thus raised as *sanchos* (dogies).

Little has been said concerning the experiences that trail men had in taking their herds through the brush; one reason is that most trail drivers went around it. However, A. Collatt Sanders, now of Littlefield, Texas, took a big herd right through the Brasada in 1884, and the account of his troubles as he has written it seems an appropriate conclusion to this chapter.[1]

The herd was made up of 3200 longhorned steers varying from three to fifteen years in age. They were off the M K Ranch in Cameron County, owned by Mifflin Kenedy, from whom J. H. ("Uncle Henry") Stephens had bought them.

"Now, Collatt," said Stephens, as he told his trail boss goodby, "if you have only fifty head when you reach your destination, do not take any cattle but those belonging to me."

Collatt Sanders shall tell his story without interruption.

"Three days after leaving the ranch," he says, "I crossed

[1] Taken from *Frontier Times*, Bandera, Texas, July, 1926.

the narrow-gauged railroad [the Texas-Mexican Railroad running from Corpus Christi to Laredo] at Peña Station, now Hebbronville, on the edge of the brush, and then there was no trail. We watered the cattle there Friday at noon, and they did not drink again until Monday morning, when we reached Black Water Creek; the drags did not trail in to water until noon. All that saved the cattle on this dry drive was prickly pear, which has considerable moisture in its leaves. At that time there was no grass in all that country. Nothing but rattlesnakes and chaparral.

"When we reached old Fort Ewell on the Nueces River, April 20, we met a cold rain from the north, and that night between nine and twelve o'clock thirty-six of my saddle horses froze to death. The horses had all been ridden hard, and without grass to eat they had become too poor to stand the cold rain. Those that did not freeze to death were hardly able to strike a trot. I went to the storekeeper at Fort Ewell and told him what a predicament I was in with 3200 steers and my men all afoot. He told me there was a widow living three miles down the river who had saddle horses to sell. [This was Mrs. Amanda Burks, one of the few women who went up the trail, a remarkable representative of frontier womanhood.]

"I went to see her, introduced myself, and then made her a little speech, not the kind that men usually make to widows, however. I told her that I had to have horses but that I had no money.

" 'You can get all the horses you want despite the fact that you have no money,' she said.

"So I bought a remuda from her and gave her in payment a check on Uncle Henry Stephens. Then we mounted and hit the trail—the brush, rather, for there was no trail. If we found a place to bed the cattle where the prickly pears were no higher than the stirrups of our saddles, we thought we were doing fine. After driving two days we found where a few herds had preceded us and had made a trail. We followed the trail; then we came to where it entered a man's pasture a little below Uvalde. Before we reached this fence, however, the owner of the pasture had barred the gap with logs and put up this sign: 'All herds keep the main road to Uvalde.' When I saw the sign I went back, camped the wagon, and stopped the herd. I then rode up the main road towards town and saw that it would be impossible to take a herd that way, as the brush along it was from ten to fifteen feet high and as thick as it could stand.

"About midnight I got back to camp, wakened the cook and all the boys that were not on guard, and started the herd. Then I sent two men ahead to tear down the logs that barred entrance into the pasture. No one made a noise; all you could hear was the cattle walking. After getting them through the gap and giving the boys orders to keep them moving, I turned back, for I thought that the owner of the pasture might discover the trespassing and try to have me arrested. The boys later told me that he came up on them just as they were going out on the opposite side of the pasture. He asked who and where the boss was. The boys told him my name; then he burned the breeze for Uvalde and had a warrant issued for my arrest. The sheriff set out to find me.

"After hiding a while, I rejoined the herd, now safely out of the man's pasture, about noon. The first thing I did was to disguise myself. I put on a pair of the cook's old shoes, his old slouch hat, a pair of pants frazzled out around the bottom, and a pair of suspenders, made from a piece of rotten tarp, to hold them up. About the time I got my rigging on, the cook announced dinner; the relief in camps[2] ate, then went to the herd. When the guard that had been relieved came in, the sheriff was with them.

"One of the boys said to the cook, loud enough for the sheriff to hear, 'Who is that man here in camps?'

" 'Oh,' the cook replied, 'it's just a farmer who owns an apiary up in the canyon.'

"I ate dinner by the side of the sheriff, and he never did find the boss. I had the boys posted to bring the cattle on; so I told the cook goodby, thanked him for the dinner, and urged

[2] The phrase *in camps* instead of the singular, *in camp,* is very common with old time Texans.

him to stop so that I could give him some honey when he got to my place up the canyon. As I rode away, I saw the sheriff chinning with the boys in as friendly a way as one could imagine. I could see all along that he did not think very hard of a man for taking a herd of cattle through a pasture in order to keep out of the brush. I felt that he would not hang with the outfit long or give me a very hard chase.

"Our route was up the Nueces Canyon. . . . The day we topped out of it into the divide we struck the first really open grazing ground that we had seen since leaving Peña Station."

The remainder of Collatt Sanders' narrative is without applicable interest. His hands killed a stray yearling worth ten dollars, and some hombres wearing big six-shooters prevailed on him to pay twenty dollars for it; his cook bogged the chuck wagon down and got all the flour wet. He went on to Dodge City, but despite stampedes, high water, and Kansas grangers, he met no further troubles comparable to those of the Brasada.

CHAPTER XVI

THE BIG STEAL AND THE BREAK-UP

It has already been said that at the close of the seventies cattle had become scarce in the Brasada country. They had become scarce all over Southwest Texas. For instance, on the prairies from Barlow's Ferry to Lagarto in Live Oak County, reports the Galveston *Daily News* of July 28, 1877, "hardly 100 cattle could be gathered now where two or three years ago 2000 or 3000 might have been rounded up."

What had become of the cattle? Some had died from drouth, for the country was too poorly watered by nature to furnish stock beyond a certain limit, and artificial waterings —to come with fences and individual control of their own lands by ranchmen—were yet scarce. But more cattle than had died had been driven off—great numbers of them by men who "neglected to pay for them." [1] When cattle were cheap they were easy to steal; as they advanced in price they were worth stealing, and west and north an unappropriated empire of grass was being wrested from the Indians and buffaloes to be stocked with cattle. With fencing only well begun in the settled counties, the range along and beyond the frontier fringe was still out of control. One of the periodical booms of sheep was on. Thus the assessment rolls of Webb County—an extreme case—for 1878 showed only 8000 cattle against 239,000 sheep and 19,000 Mexican goats. [2] Other counties, like Bee and Karnes, to the north and east of Webb, still had large numbers of cattle but not nearly so many as formerly.

This extraordinary depletion, which was temporary, of the

[1] Report from Atascosa County in Galveston *Daily News*, Aug. 8, 1877.
[2] Galveston *Daily News*, Dec. 18, 1878.

range cattle of Southwest Texas, resulting as it did in the financial ruin of many stockmen, was locally called "the Break-up." It was concomitant with what is still alluded to as "the Big Steal." The individual who contributed most towards bringing it about and who was most tragically affected by it was James Lowe.

Like many other notable men, he is often remembered for a trifle—his experience with a slicker, long a familiar item in range lore. "I had a new slicker," Lowe used to tell. "I had always heard how warm a slicker was and so when I had to lay out one cold night in the Frio bottom, I had no fears about keeping warm. Well, all I can say is that if I had had two new slickers I positively know that I would have froze to death."

James Lowe settled with his family on the Frio River in 1858 and helped make Dog Town. According to a high authority on the cattle industry of Texas,[3] the McMullen County ranges at that time "were covered with old cows and bulls, fifteen to seventeen years old, without an owner or a brand of any sort upon them." Wild horses ran in herds numbering as high as a thousand head each. The Lowe stock increased and multiplied until he became one of the half dozen most extensive operators in the cattle world. In one year alone, along in the seventies, James Lowe branded 20,000 calves. According to the old way of counting five head of cattle for every calf in the brand, 20,000 calves meant a herd of 100,000 cattle. For fifty miles around him in all directions Lowe's cattle grazed at home. His activities were gigantic. In 1873 he advertised [4] that "in view of the great inconvenience to stockmen of transporting specie to different and distant parts of the country to pay off stock claims," he would pay and accept currency. Bank checks were yet to be introduced and the advertisement, even with James Lowe's name to it, failed to change immediately the demand of range men for gold and silver. It reflects the dissatisfaction of a man who was constantly being burdened with coin. Before the decade

[3] James Cox, *The Cattle Industry of Texas and Adjacent Territory*, St. Louis, 1905, page 605. Fortunate, indeed, the person who possesses a copy of this very rare and very valuable book!
[4] *Western Stock Journal*, Pleasanton, Texas, June 10, 1873.

was out this man who found it a great inconvenience to transport his funds and who was branding 20,000 calves in one year possessed absolutely nothing on earth but a mongrel bunch of 300 cattle, which he was keeping under herd by day and penning at night. He had never owned much land; he had depended on free grass in the unfenced world.

Like the majority of cowmen, James Lowe, as he saw his herds increase and multiply, knew but one ambition—to get more and yet more cattle. He resembled somewhat the old Texas settler who, upon being accused of trying to "gobble up" all the land in the country, stoutly asserted that he did not want *all* the land. "Oh, no," he said, "all the land I want is just what belongs to me and my boys and everything jinin' it." But it took money to buy more and more cattle. However willing he was to accept currency in lieu of weighty coin, James Lowe kept neither very long; he kept cattle. He did not want to sell off his cattle in order to get money; and the time came when he considered that he could swap cattle more advantageously than he could sell and buy. Small owners, who were finding it increasingly difficult to keep up with their scattered stock, would come to him and express a desire to sell out, *range delivery*—"sight unseen." They would show their books, in which were recorded their brandings for the past several years and also any sales they had made. The brand tallies, multiplied by five, minus the number of cattle sold and delivered, ought to show fairly well the number of cattle bearing the brand of the man who wished to sell.

Now, Lowe figured that while he was working his own brand scattered over far flung ranges, he could work just as well any number of additional brands in the same territory. The prospective seller did not usually want to go out of the cattle business. He usually wanted to move on to a better range or a more open range or a range where he thought he could keep his cattle together better. If he could have gathered up his own cattle and have taken them to the new range, he would have done so; but he did not know where his cattle were; in fact, very often he did not know whether he had any cattle or not.

He had the tally books. In the end James Lowe would take over the little man's brand, receiving a bill of sale; in payment he would authorize the little man to gather up a stipulated number of his (Lowe's) cattle, which were accessible, and drive them out of the country. On the books at least, Lowe always got more cattle than he gave.

The trouble with this kind of dealing lay in the fact that James Lowe was an honest man, and, being an honest man of simple, undesigning mind, he considered other people honest. First, he trusted the tally books of the men from whom he bought. Secondly, he gave these men permission to gather his cattle themselves and to count out for themselves the number he had agreed to deliver. Thirdly, he did not realize until too late that times were changing, that in order to maintain his own a cowman must henceforth hold land as well as cows,— and that the Big Steal was on.

How generally the many men with whom he traded counted the Lowe cattle into their herds may be imagined. To the new ranges on the Concho and the Pecos, to the great plains of the Texas Panhandle, to New Mexico, Arizona, California, Colorado, Kansas, Wyoming, Montana, to the hide and tallow factories on the coast—wherever cattle could be disposed of the Big Stealers drove them—and James Lowe, along with plenty of other honest cowmen of Southwest Texas, was left cowless. He owned lots of brands but he did not own anything that was branded. He had lots of tally books but he had nothing to tally.

The whole business was absurd, fantastic, incredible. Many of the men with whom Lowe traded were too slow in the mad scramble to gather all the cattle they wanted and in consequence they made haste to gather other men's. A considerable group of men from whom the rustlers were stealing under guise of gathering Lowe brands became very much incensed with the McMullen County cattle king. One day a mob of about fifty of them met him in the road and told him that they were going to hang him. He was riding horseback alone and unarmed. He asked why they were going to hang him. They could not answer. Then he got down off his horse and, walking up and down on his tiptoes, with flaming wrath told the men of the mob, severally and collectively, what he thought of them. They faded away. They knew that they were unjustly accusing a man of character and honor, however unfortunate he might have been in his business judgment. Even in the desperation of losing all, James Lowe remained honest and upright. In 1904 he died at Tilden—old Dog Town—among his own people, respected and loved, though he had never "come back." It may be added that men of the Lowe name, for James Lowe had a fertile brother as well as sons, are prominent today in the cattle business of Southwest Texas.

James Lowe probably bought out more brands than any other cowman that ever lived in Texas. It is said that some of his representatives carried with them to distant round-ups books in which were recorded as many as two thousand brands owned by Lowe. He was unique in the extensiveness of his operations, but in buying out hundreds of "little fellows" over the country, range delivery, he was following a highly speculative custom of the times. A complete account of cattle stealing in the country that Jim Lowe's cattle ranged over would make a big book. One episode of the Big Steal will have to represent much. This episode sounds incredible, but it is based on the written testimony of two living participants, A. M. Nichols and S. O. Porter.[5]

The year 1874 was marked by a terrible drouth over most of what was then called West Texas. From Wilson County south, however, through the counties of Karnes, Bee, and Goliad, the rainfall was sufficient to make grass and put out water. As a result, during the fall and winter of the year cattle from the drouth stricken territory to the west drifted and were driven by the thousands into this region. The spring of 1875 opened with rain, and as early as possible the cowmen from the west began rounding up the ranges on which their stock had win-

[5] This testimony is contained in two articles that appeared in the Kenedy, Texas, *Advance* in 1926, one under date of April 15 and the other, which was sent to me clipped and undated, of a few weeks later. The accounts were written by a native son, S. C. Butler, who took down the words of A. M. Nichols and S. O. Porter, two of the cowmen who helped to put a quietus on the rampant cattle thieves.

tered. It was a big country, far from an open country, and every man worked how, when, and where he pleased. There were no well organized and accurately dated round-ups such as were soon to be a feature of cow work on the Plains. The strangers working down the San Antonio River seemed most pleased when working unobserved. It is presumed that they did not find so many cattle as they expected to find, probably not so many as they should have found. The demand for hides was fairly good. At any rate, in taking herds back home they showed an utter disregard for brands, driving off more cattle that did not belong to them than did. Meantime the ranchers over the territory that was being combed were becoming mightily stirred up, though as yet they had not acted in any concerted manner.

Then one bright moonlight night in March thirty-one riders from the west made a clean sweep through a fine country south and east of what is now Kenedy, in Karnes County. They were led by a man named Henry Fountain. Fountain detailed fifteen of his men to spread out fanlike and work up Escondido Creek which runs into the San Antonio River at Falls City; he made a fan of the other fifteen for winnowing cattle out of the country along the San Antonio River. Thirty men well disposed can cover a wide strip of ground. While the dew was yet on the grass the forces drew to a focus. They had "a herd of 9000 cattle," three times as large as a herd should be for proper management. How any number of men could have collected that many cattle at night in a country cut by brushy creeks and draws is amazing. The number seems incredible, but good men have testified to it. The night riders at once started west on a forced drive; by dark they were at the Peacock Ranch on the Atascosa Creek in Atascosa County.

Now, Bill Irvin, a rancher in the country, happened a day or two after the night round-up to be riding out on his best horse. He never made any bones about inspecting any herd that passed through this range. There was no danger of his overlooking this one driven by Fountain's crowd. By the time he had read all the brands, the sun was getting low. He had "better be riding," he said. He headed east, and as soon as he was well out of sight of the herd he loosened the reins and pressed his heels against his horse's sides. He happened to know that Bill Butler was going to camp that night at Conquisto Crossing on the San Antonio River, five miles below Falls City. As everybody knows who has ever heard of the once notorious Butler-Elder feud, Bill Butler was a warrior; the Butlers owned more cattle than anybody else in Karnes County. As soon as Bill Butler learned about the brands in the Fountain herd, he sent a man south to notify J. M. Nichols, another cowman much concerned. Nichols, in turn, was to send runners to notify cattlemen in Bee and Goliad counties. The clans were gathering.

It was just good dawn when Irvin rode into Butler's camp at the Conquisto Crossing; it was an hour after dark before Jim Nichols arrived with his men, all on good horses, all well armed. He waived leadership in favor of Butler and immediately the combined forces set out. They were ten in number; they were riding against thirty-one; and they were ready to fight. They might have waited a day for reenforcements from Bee and Goliad counties, but they did not want to wait. They did not figure that Fountain and his men were going to wait long over on the Atascosa.

An hour after leaving camp Butler struck the trail of the stolen herd. It was easy to follow in moonlight, and the trailers made good time. About four o'clock Butler ordered a halt so that the horses might rest and graze a little while the men caught a bit of sleep. At daybreak they were in the saddle again. The sun was still aslant in the east when they topped a high hill that gave them an outlook over a valley a mile or so away. The valley was dark and spotted with cattle. Apparently the cow thieves had been unable to get very far with their enormous herd on the day after the forced drive. Also, as it turned out, they were shaping up a trail herd.

Butler's men paused only long enough to shift saddles and examine pistols. "Go on, Bill, and beard the lion," one of them called. "We'll back you up." They rode down to the herd and without any trouble located Fountain. As A. M. Nichols, who was along, remembers the talk, this is what Bill Butler said:

"My name is Butler and I understand that you have some of our cattle in your herd. Also, I have been told that you would not allow your herd to be cut. We have come to cut out our cattle."

"Why, Mr. Butler," Fountain replied, "you or anyone else who has cattle in my herd can cut them out. I am no fighter and no cattle thief, as Jim Calvert, who is there with you, very well knows."

Fountain had recognized Calvert as a boyhood friend, and here Calvert laughed in a way to break the tension.

"I told them all along," he said, "that if you were the same Fountain I knew in school you would not fight and that you were an honest man."

It developed that Fountain was not gathering cattle for himself but for another man who was preparing to go up the trail. He proved to be a most accommodating fellow. He ordered his men to bunch the cattle up, and in no time the Butler men were cutting. Of course they cut not only their own brands but the brands of all men south and east of them. By sundown they had 2700 head in the cut and were not nearly through. A man can not inspect brands in the darkness, however, and so the cut was moved off about a mile for night herding. Butler and his nine men took turns in standing guard. At sunrise they were cutting again, Fountain having promised to have the cattle ready. By noon they said that they were through; they had 1800 additional cattle to add to the original 2700, making a herd of 4500.

Now, ten men are a small crew to handle a herd of 4500 cattle, especially when the cattle are hungry, thirsty, and feverish from having been ginned about, especially also when the men have been in the saddle almost constantly for sixty hours. Fortunately, they had brought plenty of horses. They managed to get the cattle to the Lipan Creek by dark, camping near Dan Brister's ranch.

That night word came in that another herd of cattle fresh

from ranges to the east was over on Atascosa Creek to the south. In the morning Bill Butler took four men with him, leaving five to ride around the 4500 cattle. Towards the close of day he returned with 1200 head that he had cut out of this second herd.

The men had now been in the saddle for three days and most of three nights. They had not had time to cook anything to eat, but had merely "snacked" off cold biscuits and meat that they had brought along in morrals. That morning before leaving the camp at Brister's ranch, however, Butler had detailed A. M. Nichols, sixteen years old at the time, to butcher a cow and cook her. Nichols had borrowed an axe and a spade from Brister, had dug a trench, made a fire in it, and then built over it a scaffold of green poles. The meat of the cow had barbecued all day over the coals, and Mrs. Brister had cooked up a washtub full of biscuits. Also in borrowed utensils young Nichols had made five gallons of coffee. The cowmen from Goliad and Bee counties were hourly expected. At dusk they dashed in.

They came a hundred strong. At their head rode Sam Porter. He had neither slept nor eaten for seventy-two hours. He made a picture. His horse was covered with foam. Two long six-shooters hung from his belt and a .44 Winchester slung in a scabbard from his saddle. Great Mexican spurs clanked on his heels. A bandana of flaming red waved about his neck. He looked as vicious as any lion, and he roared. Frank Fountain had been let off entirely too lightly, he said; nothing short of hanging should have been given him. Porter did not calm down until he had eaten several pounds of barbecued meat, but he was not ahead of his companions in consuming food. In a little while not an ounce of the cow was left. Another was cooking.

There were enough hands now to do anything they wanted to do. The leaders divided them into four groups. One group was to take the cattle home. A second group was to ride on west and go up the Nueces River; a third group was to work up the Frio River, and the fourth group went up the Atascosa River. These several squads were not only to cut any and all herds found and to look through what range cattle they could, but they were to warn in emphatic manner all parties who had been driving cattle out of the counties to the east. Every man was armed to the teeth. Yet many of them were very quiet men, spare of words, noted for avoiding trouble and for honesty.

The expedition that went up the Atascosa was typical, and only it will be followed. Sam Porter was the leader, but he had with him a dozen cowmen who knew how to lead better than to follow—J. M. and Bing Choate, John and Henry Clare, Ples Butler, Tobe Wood, Darius (always pronounced Die-reece) and Albert Rachal, Will Lott, Bud Jordan, A. Martin, and Fate Elder. They found few cattle up the Atascosa, and after they got above Pleasanton they decided to go to San Antonio, where they were sure to find some of the cow thieves they wanted to lecture. As they rode on to Main Plaza they made rather a sensation, blasé as Main Plaza was to men, horses, and arms.

At the old Hord Hotel they ran smack into a half dozen of the men they wanted to see. J. M. Choate did most of the talking, and he concluded by saying that if any of his auditors ever drove off another cow belonging to a man in Bee, Goliad, or Karnes County their bones would be found bleaching on the hillsides—even if the thieves and cattle had to be followed clean to Montana. To emphasize these remarks, Tobe Wood and Darius Rachal, who had taken a few drinks, walked out on Main Plaza and emptied their six-shooters into the free air. Sam Porter calmed them down; the police had "scattered like wild turkeys."

The next morning the crowd left for Karnes County. In Wilson County they struck a man that the majority were for hanging, but wiser counsel prevailed and he was only "lectured." Then they turned off to inspect a cow pen on West Weedy Creek that a man named Crunk was reputed to be using for branding other people's cattle in. They surrounded Crunk's camp before daylight, and when Crunk's fifteen men awoke they were looking down the muzzles of twenty-eight Winchesters. No blood was shed, but the Crunk gang disbanded right there and stopped gathering "Lowe's brands."

Thus the Big Steal met obstacles. The conditions that made

possible both the stealing and the retaking of great herds of cattle made possible also the Break-up. It is true that the Break-up did not mark sharply the end of the old order, for more than a decade was to pass before the trails were fenced across and the free-grass men were entirely fenced out; and in that decade the range industry boomed as it had never boomed before—the decade of the eighties. In Southwest Texas, however, great changes were at hand. These changes did not mean that all grazing land was to be plowed into fields. The changes consisted of barbed wire and windmills and the results.

CHAPTER XVII

THE BRASADEROS

As HAS been made clear, the Brasada—the brush country—marked the meeting of the East and the West. Desperadoes from eastern states as well as from Texas counties to the east sought the border brush and its security. Raiding Mexicans from below the Rio Grande slipped over the unguarded river, rendezvoused with the American bad men, stole, murdered if necessary, and rode back into Mexico before they could be discovered, though plenty of them were trailed far beyond the borders of Texas and there ceased making tracks forever. In short, the Brasada was a strategic point for stealing and smuggling.

The white men who operated with the Mexicans were worse thieves and more hardened criminals than the *bandidos;* in some ways they were worse than the Comanches had been. They could steal a bunch of horses as far east as the San Antonio River, ride hard all night and a part of one day, and then, having crossed the Nueces River, lie up in some wild thicket of the Brasada. There Mexican confederates with a bunch of "wet" horses—horses stolen in Mexico and smuggled across the river—would meet them; the two outfits would exchange stolen stock; then each would turn back with horses to trade. Such operators could afford to offer horses at attractive prices. Many a Texas cowman bought Mexican horses for which his own remuda stolen a week or ten days before had been swapped.

The Brasada had its "Four Horsemen." These four men "just happened along" and took up headquarters at Dog Town. They were all middle-aged, all gamblers, horse racers, and gunmen. One of them gave his name as Russell, from Kentucky; we called him the Kentucky Colonel, and he looked the part.

Another was known to us only as Gotch. He had a bullet hole
through his ear. A third went by the name of Slim. The last was
just Dan. They got no mail that anyone knew of. Slim sometimes referred to happenings in Arkansas. When he got about
three sheets in the wind, the Colonel would babble vaguely of
moonshine and a fight with revenue officers back in Kentucky.
If the others had a past, they never referred to it.

The Four Horsemen seemed inseparably united. They had
a pack horse on which they loaded all their possessions. They
kept a few race ponies about their camp; they generally had a
horse to trade. Sometimes after camping around Dog Town for
weeks they would suddenly disappear. Then in a few days they
would be back with a string of Mexican ponies that they claimed
to have bought down in Mexico. They usually found a ready
sale for them; if not, they drove them on to San Antonio.

A circumstance that I began noticing was that though they
were always very visible when they drove their *caballada* north,
nobody ever saw them when they went south after the *caballada*.
Of course the ranch people of the border country were continually losing horses. Sometimes we knew when they were stolen;
sometimes it was weeks after they disappeared from the range
before we found that they were gone. It took me a good while
to put two and two together.

Now, McMullen County had Six Horsemen who were
almost as close together as were the Four Horsemen. They were
Tom McCoy, Jim Morris, Ben Corder, Ike Hill, Lee Pope, and
myself. We mustanged together, cow-hunted together, played
monte together, danced together, drank together, and sometimes
fought together. To this gang I confided my suspicions as to
who was stealing our horses. We at once decided to investigate
on our own responsibility.

One day five of us met at the S E Ranch on the Nueces
River. Taking two horses each and a single pack mule, we swam
the river and then proceeded up to the mouth of the Arroyo
Meta Sol (Sunflower Creek), where we found Lee Pope awaiting us. He had come down the river from Fort Ewell. We rode
up the Meta Sol until we reached the divide between the Nueces

and the Rio Grande. This country was usually without water, but it had rained a few days before, and on a brushy hollow we found a water hole. Good grass for our horses was at hand, and we struck camp. For several days we rode around over the country, returning each night to the same camp. Wild cattle and mustangs that, following the rain, had beat back on the fresh grass were plentiful.

Then we found what we were looking for. It was a brush corral deep hidden in a thicket. It showed to have been much used for holding horses, but the sign was at least a month old. Immediately in front of the corral was a little opening. Leading away from it into the thicket was a distinct trail. We followed it. At the end of it we found an old camp. Judging from the amount of ashes on the ground and the number of empty cans and greasy, sharp-pointed sticks used to broil meat on, the camp had evidently been used to a considerable extent. More interesting to us, it was evidently going to be used again, for secured in a mesquite tree was a store of provisions. They were carefully put away so that neither weather nor prowling animals could get to them; plainly, they had been there for a good while. The owner might appear at any time! I spied an old gunny sack sewed up with a rawhide string. I recognized that sack the moment I laid my eyes on it. It had come from the store of L. D. Young and Son, Dog Town, Texas. In our expectation we talked in whispers and stepped about so that our spurs would not jingle.

We had located, we were sure, the place where the Four Horsemen met and swapped stolen ponies with the Mexican smugglers. But, after all, the trail was cold. It was too cold even for Ike Hill, the best trailer as well as the best brush hand in Southwest Texas; on the trail he was what the Mexican vaqueros call *muy perrito* (like a very dog). Maybe all we had found was a "mare's nest." The horse thieves might not show up here for a month or two. They might get wind of us and not show up at all. We ceased to whisper and our spurs clanked. We "borrowed" some peaberry out of the mesquite, took water from our canteens, and boiled coffee. Then we rode back to our camp.

Each morning for three days we eased up to the brush corral, hoping to find something. Still there was no sign of any other human beings than ourselves in the country. One morning we decided to make a final round and then, if we discovered nothing further, to return home.

Before we got to the brush pen we saw fresh sign. We approached very cautiously. We need not have been so cautious, for all we found was twenty-seven horses staked and hobbled outside the corral. All but two remuda mares, which were securely picketed, were saddle horses. Every animal bore a Mc-Mullen County brand—and among them were half a dozen horses that actually belonged to us—horses that we had seen in our remudas the day we left home! The sign told us that the *caballada* had come in the evening before.

It took us only a few minutes to put the horses in the pen and to cut the hobbles. The thieves would surely show up soon. With the recovered stock strung out in front of us, we hit the trail for home. We felt confident of being followed.

We had gone only a few miles and, after crossing a wide prairie, were entering a heavy thicket when we saw four horsemen following us at a run. Before they were well within range they began shooting. Perhaps they saw only one or two of us and thought to bluff us into abandoning the horses. At the distance we were apart, brush between us and all of us moving at a sharp pace, it was probably impossible for anybody on either side to recognize any one of the opposing party, though I recognized the Kentucky Colonel's favorite mount.

We returned the fire, as ineffectually as it was given, and the men veered into the brush, where they seemed to halt for a parley. We held a short parley also. As Ben Corder and Jim Morris carried only six-shooters, we decided that they should keep the horses moving, while the other four of us, who had Winchesters, should cover the retreat.

We took our stand in a kind of swag down which we felt sure the horse thieves would come if they were coming any farther at all. The brush here was rather spotted, very thick in some places with open intervals between the *mogotes*. We had hardly got our horses tied and ourselves well placed when we heard a limb break and caught sight of the Four Horsemen. About the same time they located us. We were four to four. My partners were in a kind of line, I on the right end. Our understanding was that we would, if possible, take the enemy in order, I to give the signal. I was flat on the ground, and when I aimed at the first man the barrel of my gun was resting against a mesquite limb. I could not miss. We fired almost at once. Two men fell. We had not missed.

The third man was the Colonel. He turned his horse broadside and began shooting. I shot at his horse while the other boys centered on him. He and the horse both went down.

The fourth man's horse was either gunshy or he had been hit by one of our bullets, for he kept pitching and whirling around and around so fast that his rider could not shoot and we could not draw a bead. Slim, for that was who the rider was, finally got his horse on the run and disappeared in the brush. In the few seconds of time that the performance covered we got in several shots, and from the way in which we saw Slim drop his gun we felt confident that he had also been hit.

We waited a few moments; then, no move being made by any of the enemy, we mounted our horses and rode on. These men had been following us and if they chose to discontinue the chase we were more than willing.

The fight was away out in the brush in a no man's land without roads or settlers. We could not know whether the Four Horsemen had recognized us or not. We did not know for a certainty whether we had killed any of them or not, though our belief was that we had killed three of them and perhaps mortally wounded the fourth. If one or more of them were alive, we did not want to advertise ourselves as the men who had caught them stealing horses and then fought them. So we agreed to go home and say nothing. Not one of us was an officer of the law. We had investigated on our own hook. No one would question where we had been or what we had been doing. It was a time when Texans tended strictly to their own business and let other people alone to tend to theirs.

About midnight we crossed the Nueces River near the mouth of Cañada Verde and struck camp, almost a day's ride from Dog Town. The next morning each of us caught out his own horses, turning the others loose, free to drift back to their accustomed ranges. Lee Pope went to Altita, where he ranched, forty miles from Dog Town. Ike Hill and Tom McCoy went to their camp on the San Miguel, twenty-five miles from Dog Town. Ben Corder and Jim Morris struck for their ranch on the Guadalupe, twenty miles from Dog Town, and I just drifted back to Dog Town itself.

We were neighbors. We came together a few more times and then our trails forked, dimmed, faded. Lee Pope was killed in a pistol duel in Laredo. Tom McCoy, I heard, was killed in Cuba; I never learned the particulars. Ike Hill was killed in the brush by his horse running under a limb. A quarter of a century ago Jim Morris died in Sonora, Texas; I was by his side. Ben Corder died in London. I *must* be next. It is something to have ridden together; it is something to have been one of six *brasaderos* in the great Brasada.

After that encounter in the brush no news of the Four Horsemen ever came to our ears. However, several days after we got back home a horse that had been stolen from somebody in the country showed up with a saddle on; the saddle was never claimed. Later on a Mexican over in the San Casimero country found another horse carrying an ownerless saddle. We six frequently spoke of going back to view the scene of our experience, but we never went. That particular section of the country is still in brush; the pastures that contain the brush are large. Probably to this day no vaquero has chanced upon a bit of evidence of the skirmish now made public for the first time, for though we eventually told a few friends what we knew, no inkling of the episode ever got into a newspaper.

In those days there was generally more exciting news outside of the newspapers than in them. A majority of the ranch people seldom saw newspapers. The San Antonio *Weekly Express* came my own way more regularly than I had opportunity to read it. Then there was *Texas Siftings,* just being started in

Austin by Alex E. Sweet and J. Armoy Knox. Sweet and Knox seemed to have consecrated themselves to caricaturing in all possible variations the typical Texan as a long, lank, walking arsenal. They certainly did their part towards extending the old tradition that people in Texas grow horns. *Texas Siftings* proved so popular that the owners of it moved it to New York. It was one of the American literary bubbles that in the wake of Bill Nye's success as a humorist expanded and then burst.

In time Dog Town—or Tilden, as it should now be called— came to have a weekly newspaper, though it has none today and the county of which it is the capital has none. It was the newspapers that came near leading the *brasaderos* into an adventure of international concern.

In the summer of 1886 a Texan by the name of A. K. Cutting was apprehended in Mexico and charged with having committed in Texas a crime against a Mexican citizen who was living on this side of the Rio Grande. The Mexican government was about to try Cutting when the United States raised a protest. The affair lasted over a considerable period of time with much hullabaloo in the papers. It came to be known as the "Cutting Incident." I did not know Cutting from Adam's off ox, but as a border Texan I was highly indignant that an American should be apprehended in Mexico for something that he was supposed to have done in his own country. All over the Southwest feeling ran high.

I said that I felt highly indignant; I probably felt as venturesome as indignant. The *brasaderos* began talking about entering Mexico and releasing Cutting. As I remember the affair, he was at this time in jail in Piedras Negras across the Rio Grande from Eagle Pass. I made a trip down to Monterrey and looked the country over. When I returned, a bunch of us brush hands got together and agreed that if Cutting were not released by a certain date we would go get him. We had no doubt that we could whip whatever Mexicans got in our way. We organized: I was elected captain; Jim Morris was elected first lieutenant, and Tom McCoy, sergeant. When the question of a flag came up, we decided that it should be black—no quarter asked or given. Lee

Pope declared that he would carry it. On the date stipulated we were to meet at a ranch between Carrizo Springs and the Rio Grande, each man furnishing his own horse, guns, and ammunition. We would depend on Mexico for food and forage. The lonely crossing on the river that we would make, the line of march, the attack were all planned. Then Cutting was released, and we were spared the venture. Had we made it, I suppose that most of us would have got killed. Well, we loved living more than we loved life.

CHAPTER XVIII

MUSTANGS

THE long, open divide between the Frio and Nueces rivers in McMullen and La Salle counties was one of the last ranges of Southwest Texas for large herds of mustangs. The mustangs would, of course, when closely pressed, take to the brush, and in the brush they made their final stand; but their favorite habitat was the mesquite sprinkled prairies. Here on this divide of prairie and mesquite I saw the year after I went to Dog Town fully a thousand mustangs in one bunch; they had run together from many directions ahead of a big round-up of cattle. When they left the plain where they had gathered, they all left at once in one direction, passing not far from where I was riding. The rumble from their running was deafening and they fairly shook the earth; a stampede of five times as many cattle could not have caused such disturbance.

Many people have wondered why at a time when horses were highly prized and sorely needed the ranch people did not domesticate more mustangs. Yet history shows that in the very years when mustangs were most numerous gentle horses were at peak prices and horse thieves and Comanche raiders were most active. The Comanches would ride, or walk, for days through vast numbers of mustangs in order to steal, at the risk of their lives, a few horses from the settlers. The wealth of the Plains Indians lay largely in horses, but they never went on the warpath over the extermination of the mustangs as they did over the extermination of the buffaloes. The lives and livelihood of the settlers were dependent upon horses, but most of them would have been glad if all the mustangs in the country had been run off.

Ranchmen in general regarded them as a great nuisance, good for nothing but to entice off gentle horses, to tramp up the range, to ruin water holes by their pawing, and—after barbed wire came—to tear down fences. The mustangs were continually running and when they came to the newly strung fences they never veered. In tearing the fences down they cut themselves all to pieces. A wire cut at any time of the year except in the middle of winter meant screw worms, and screw worms in horses are generally fatal. The toll of mustangs taken by the first fences was enormous. The remnants were cleared out of the pastures either by bullets or by men who drove them off as a joyful gift from the pasture owners.

While the country was still unfenced, captured mustangs had generally to be driven away from their native range before they could be released to graze in freedom. Otherwise, even after they were "broke," they were extremely likely to hear the call of the wild and rejoin what Will James calls "the Wild Bunch." Among the native steeds of the prairies were fleet, hardy, and beautiful animals, some of which, like the Pacing White Stallion, Star Face, Black Devil, and the Blue Mare of the Washita, achieved legendary fame. As the frontiers advanced, the best mustangs were sought for with increasing eagerness and the proportion of inbred and poorly shaped mustangs increased. There were many of this class. At a distance, one of them with arched neck, distended nostrils, and flowing mane and tail looked graceful, even magnificent, but near at hand he was likely to appear gimlet hammed and narrow chested. The best horses among them were generally domesticated horses that had gone wild, and these were warier than the mustangs themselves. Occasionally a well bred stallion escaped to them; then he and his offspring became marked prizes. By 1880 the wild bands of horses had been picked over by mustangers until good animals among them were not so common as they had formerly been.

As long as there were free mustangs to be caught, however, some men made a business of catching them. Many a cowboy killed a fifty-dollar horse trying to rope a twenty-dollar mustang. Sometimes in slack seasons the cowboys spent a good deal of time setting rope snares across trails in order to catch the wild horses, but they seldom caught anything that way. The mustang that was snared was usually a stallion leading his *manada,* and he was likely to break either the rope or his own neck. On some of the horse ranches the men caught colts and raised them on cow's milk, but they were barely worth the trouble. The professional mustangers were the only men who caught mustangs in considerable numbers.

The biggest mustang drive that I ever heard of was on the Cibolo Creek in La Salle County. This was before I came to the Brasada. In preparation for their drive the mustang hunters built a very stout corral capable of holding a hundred and fifty or two hundred horses. Out from the corral they ran brush wings a half mile or so long. Near the corral the wing fences were stout. The hunters intended for the corral to serve them a long time. When they had it ready, they got an outfit of cow hunters who were in the country to help them with the first drive. More of the mustangs headed in than was expected and they headed better. Something like a thousand head pointed in between the wings on a dead run, and the narrower the lane became the harder the horses ran. The pen at the end of the lane filled, but the stampeding animals from behind never checked. They poured on into the seething corral, climbing over the horses that had got there first. The corral and the well fenced entrance to it became a veritable shambles. Hundreds of the mustangs were smothered and trampled to death. In some places around the fences the dead and maimed were piled up so high that the plunging horses on top of them climbed over and got away. The only mustangs that the drivers got were the dead ones. I often passed by the ruins of the old pen and saw the whitened bones of its victims.

The most noted mustanger in the country during his time was my good friend and fellow *brasadero,* Ike Hill, who ranched on the San Miguel Creek. He was the best brush hand that I have ever known and he was a born horseman. He owned many gentle horses, but he was always after mustangs. His way of catching them was to place a large bunch of gentle horses in a thicket through which a *manada* of mustangs could be run. He would leave a couple of good men to hold this gentle bunch and see that they got headed out right at the proper time. Then he would take his other men and make a run on the mustangs, directing them into the thicket. The two bunches would mix when they came together, the whole herd would rush on, and the men would have them in a corral before the mustangs realized what was up.

Ike would now rope out the mustangs and tie a long rawhide strap to a front foot of each one. After he had worked with them a while and got them properly strapped, he would turn them out under herd. If one tried to run off, he stepped on the rawhide strap with his hind feet, thus throwing himself. After a few falls he no longer tried to run. When a sufficient number of horses had been caught and "herd-broke," Ike drove the bunch to San Antonio, where he found a ready market. He had the reputation of having caught and handled more mustangs than any other man in Texas. He was absolutely fearless in running through any kind of brush, and it was while he was after mustangs that he was finally killed by his horse running into a tree, near Loma Alta in McMullen County.

Watching the habits of the mustangs was with me a frequent source of interest. Their breeding season was the early spring months, and then the stallions were in continual combat. Every old stallion would be busy fighting the young stallions, including the yearlings, out of his *manada*, and the young stallions would be manoeuvering to steal a mare or so each; in addition to fighting off these young upstarts the old stallions had to guard against each other. The strongest and best stallions kept the most mares. Thus, under conditions undisturbed by man, the breed would have a tendency to improve, selective breeding rather than inbreeding being the natural tendency.

I have watched two old stallions meet midway between their *manadas*, usually near some watering, and fight for hours. Rearing on their hind legs, they would paw each other, each sparring for a chance to whirl and plant his feet in the belly or on the hock of his opponent. One well directed kick might turn the tide of battle. Or if a stallion could seize with his powerful jaws the jugular of his opponent he might kill him. A fight to the death was not unusual; a fight that resulted in one or both horses' being badly crippled was common. Sometimes, while the old stallions were in mortal combat, an eager young stallion would slip into one of the herds and begin driving off mares, but as soon as the lord of the *manada* discovered that his harem was being disturbed he would break away from the fight and take after the stolen property.

The social unit among mustangs, the *manada*—a bunch of mares under the command of a stallion—was as well defined as the tribal unit among Indians. Day and night the stallion was on guard to keep his bunch together and to protect them. If he wanted them to run, he gave a signal snort and fell in behind them, biting chunks of hide and flesh out of any laggard or recalcitrant mare. If the mares were well trained, all the stallion had to do was to snort and take the lead; after he got his *manada* well going, he took the lead anyhow and kept it. Sometimes he had to fight from the front in order to turn the running mares back or to swerve them.

The bunches of young stallions that took up with each other were not so compact. They were constantly scattering. In nearly every bunch of mustangs were a few saddle horses with an occasional mule. The saddle horses were not afraid of man, but they were harder to catch than the mustangs, for they would run and dodge with more intelligence. Sometimes we might get a cross-run on a bunch of mustangs and cut or rope the saddle horses out, but we never caught a mule. A mule that had taken up with mustangs was always alert, ready to "whistle" when he saw a man. One could never slip up on a bunch of mustangs that contained a mule, and the mule never tired on a run.

One summer I located, out on the divide between the Nueces and the Frio, a *manada* of mustangs that I decided to capture. The stallion was a beautiful sorrel and the mares and pony stock were above the average. The bunch numbered about thirty-five head, and with them was a mule. My plan was to "walk" them down and then drive them to a corral,

In order to walk mustangs down two or more men relayed each other in riding after them until the bunch became too tired to run and grew so used to a man's following them that they would turn and drive as he directed. One man alone on one horse could walk a bunch of mustangs down if he hung on to them long enough. The time required for several men to walk a bunch down depended on how hard they rode, on whether or not they kept up the pursuit during the night, on the amount of water out, and on other conditions. There is a tradition that a party of forty-niners lost their teams while crossing the plains and, in order to replace them, followed afoot after mustangs until they were able to catch some of them; hence, tradition adds, the technical use of the word *walking* among mustangers. Long before this, no doubt, Indians captured mustangs by going after them afoot; but it is doubtful if any cowboy or American mustanger ever footed it after wild horses.

To relay me in the walking game I took along a faithful negro hand named Bill Nunn. We made camp near a water hole that was, I judged, about the center of the range over which the mustangs would run when we got them to going. Camp consisted of a few provisions, a blanket apiece, and plenty of extra horses. The horses could be hobbled; or if one of us was around camp and not too sleepy, they might be loose-herded. All mustangs had a given range beyond the limits of which they seldom went; when they reached the boundary of this range, no matter how closely pursued, they would soon circle back. Thus a mustang hunter could count on keeping within the vicinity of a certain spot. The range was seldom more than twenty-five or thirty miles across and was often much less.

Although I did not propose to do much night work, I timed our hunt to begin in the full of the moon. The morning was still fresh when I struck the *manada,* having left Bill in camp with instructions to be on the watch to furnish me with a change of mounts. The mustangs ran a mile or two and then stopped. Their next run was for four or five miles—and they really ran. I loped and trotted along behind them all day and they never went near camp. Over on Quintanilla Creek they got all the water they wanted while I was trailing far behind. At dark they appeared as fresh as they had been when I first flushed them. My horse was fresh also. I had not struck a gait faster than a gallop all day. I decided to keep on worrying the mustangs for two or three hours.

Despite the bright moonlight, I could see only a short distance ahead, and the solid turf of low mesquite grass made their tracks hard to see. As they frequently veered their course, I could not always guess in which direction I should follow in order to come up with them again. Now, some horses will trail other horses by smell almost as well as dogs can trail, provided the sign is fresh; however, a horse shows his trailing abilities, generally, only when he is eager to get with his own bunch. That night the horse I was riding seemed to know that I needed some help in following the mustangs—no friends of his. In many places he put his nose to the ground, and when he did this I let him take his course—invariably the right one. Several times the mule among the mustangs discovered their exact whereabouts by whistling. Between ten and eleven o'clock I staked my horse and bedded down on leggins, slicker, and saddle. In a morral attached to the horn of my saddle I had some bread, dried beef, and coffee, with an empty tomato can for a coffee pot; so I did not go without breakfast. As soon as it was light enough to see I was after mustangs again. About ten o'clock old Bill, who had been watching from the top of a hill, saw us and took my place.

Our bunch of mustangs would, while running, frequently dash into other bunches, but the sorrel stallion never let one of his herd get away and the bunches always quickly separated. We knew the markings on our bunch so well that we could not confuse them with other mustangs even in the distance. After they had been followed for two or three days they were noticeably slower than other mustangs in getting away. In another day or two they were so toned down that we could almost set our own pace in keeping up with them—a walk or a gallop. The mule, true to form, was the most alert and the most skittish animal among them.

We soon learned the habits and runs of the bunch so well

that Bill or I could have relieved the other at almost any hour. Some days by means of short reliefs we pressed the mustangs pretty hard, but they generally got time at night to rest a little and to graze and sleep.

Finally the bunch was so tired that we could ride along close to them and turn them—all but the mule. He would snort, stiffen his tail, and trot on ahead; apparently, he never dozed. However, I got close enough to read the brand on him and to note a collar mark on his shoulder. At the end of the tenth day I told Bill that the mustangs were walked down and that we would pen them on the morrow. I told him to take the saddle horses and camp outfit in, and with a couple of Mexican hands and a bunch of gentle stock horses to meet me somewhere about the old stage stand on the Guadalupe Creek next day. Before he left I caught an extra good horse that I had ridden but once on the entire hunt. He was unusually fat, but I did not contemplate any very hard running.

I had no trouble in pointing the *manada,* and for a while they went along fine, the mule playing in front as usual. Then he decided to turn back; so he just high-tailed himself around me, the mustangs following. I headed them right again, but again the mule led them back. He had his mind made up, and pretty soon I discovered that he, rather than the stallion, was going to manage the mustangs that day. When I undertook to force the mustangs to turn, they scattered and did not get together again until I allowed them to enter some brush. I followed them out of the brush, headed them right again, and again they turned and scattered. By now I was riding hard and fighting hard. I actually got close enough to some of the mustangs to whip them over the noses with my quirt. I pulled my six-shooter and killed two of them that were particularly wooden-headed. The mule was causing all the trouble, however. He was the most valuable animal in the lot, but after a while I realized that I could do nothing with the bunch so long as he was around. I shot him dead. Immediately the mustangs were under control again.

We went trailing along slowly and quietly now. Then I

noticed my horse quivering. At once I jumped down and took my saddle off. I knew what that quivering meant. I stuck my knife in the horse to bleed him—an old time remedy that had virtue in it—but the blood that came out was thin and actually appeared to be mingled with melted tallow. In five minutes the horse was dead. I had ridden him to death, though I had not ridden him nearly so hard or so far as I have ridden many other horses. The day was fearfully hot.

There I was afoot twenty-five miles from the pens on the Guadalupe, and not a cow ranch or a cow camp anywhere in the country. One chance and one chance only I had for a mount. About two miles from where I was, a kind of range enemy by the name of Sullivan had a sheep ranch. I did not know him personally, though I had seen him, and I knew him to be both a rough Irishman and a hard hater of all cowmen—but any port in a storm. When I walked with heels just about blistered up to his sheep-smelling shanty, the sun was two hours below the meridian. Mr. Sullivan was on the front gallery. He did not say anything about a cup of coffee, and I immediately told him my troubles.

"Do you know," he said, "what I think of a man that will ride his horse to death? I think he is a damned brute."

I agreed with him all right and said that I had no excuse except that I did not realize how fat and soft my horse was. I told him that I had ridden many horses twice as hard even in hot weather without hurting them.

"Well," said Sullivan, "what assurance have I that you won't kill my horse if I let you have one?"

"Nothing but my word," I replied.

It was plain that Mr. Sullivan did not care about lending me a horse. Then after he had finished his lecture he said that he did not have any horses up and that it would be night before any of his men came in with a horse. I merely replied that I would stay until I got something to ride.

"Now, young man," he bantered me, "can you *ride*?"

"Yes, sir," I answered, "I can ride, I have ridden, and I will ride anything that wears wool, hair or feathers, I don't care what."

I saw old man Sullivan half grin. "There's a mule staked down there in the valley," he said, "that's been rode one or two saddles. If you think you can ride him, take him. Sorry I can't let you have a saddle, but I guess you can lead him out to where your saddle is."

I thanked Mr. Sullivan and went after his muleship. It still appeared to be mule day. The mule proved to be a long-legged four-year-old, as scary as it is possible for a mule to be. When I untied the rope from the tree he was staked to, he at once wheeled and dragged me for a hundred yards. I stopped him, but could not lead him. He did not know how to lead. I would drag him a while and then he would drag me; sometimes we were going in the right direction and sometimes in the opposite direction.

I hurried all I could, for I still had hopes of getting in behind the mustangs and taking them on to the corral. The leather leggins and six-shooter I had on did not make the weather seem any cooler. The mule and I were getting a little better acquainted and we were making fairly good time when I stepped almost on a rattlesnake that had been asleep in the shade of a little bush. At his rattle I jumped forward as far as I could; the mule snorted and jumped back, at the same time wheeling for a run. He pulled me square over the rattlesnake, which was a monster, and the rattlesnake struck. He must have got a square strike, for he hung his fangs in the edge of my leggins so that he held on. I jumped, kicked, ran, and wanted to fly. The mule was not moving a bit too fast to suit me—and he was moving.

Directly the snake's fangs broke off and I stopped the mule. I pulled out my six-shooter with murder in my heart, and the only reason I did not shoot was because I could not decide which to kill first, the mule or the rattlesnake. I delayed to examine the place where the snake had struck. One of his fangs was still in the leggins, and at once I cut a generous slice of leather off with it and threw it away. Then I reflected that the mule must have been actually scared—as much scared perhaps as I was—

and that therefore he was not to blame for jumping and running. I decided further that the snake must have been considerably scared also. If I fired at the snake I knew that the mule would get worse scared than ever. I seemed to have a sympathy for scared things; so I put the gun back in its holster, pulled the rope across my shoulder, and trudged on.

When we got well in sight of the dead horse I realized that the worst was yet to come. My saddle was right at the dead horse and there was not a tree or a bush anywhere about to which I could tie the mule. No amount of work could get him up close enough for me, while holding the end of the rope, to grab my blanket and saddle. I worked until I was exhausted. Then while I was wiping the sweat out of my eyes with a bandana handkerchief that was wringing wet, I thought of a ruse that I should have thought of an hour before, a ruse that all cowboys know.

The idea seemed to freshen me, and I climbed down the rope until I got near enough to the mule to rub his nose and head. Finally I got hold of his ear, pulled it down until I got the tip of it between my teeth, and held it tight. That is the only way to hold a mule. It must be understood that I weighed at that time only a hundred thirty-five pounds. After I got the mule well eared it was comparatively easy to work the bandana over his head, tie the ends of it to the hackamore (rope halter), and then slip the adjusted bandana down over his eyes. He was blindfolded. I was now able to back him up to within reach of my rig, though backing him was no small job. At last, however, he was saddled and bridled and I was aboard.

When I leaned over and raised the bandana blind so that the mule could see, his first glance was at the dead horse almost under his nose. He whirled, kicked at the fearful object, and began pitching. That mule seemed to take two jumps to one jump made by any pitching horse that I had ever ridden. At the same time he was kicking, and he actually kicked my feet out of the stirrups. He was absolutely crazy with fear. When he finally quit pitching, he stood stiff in his tracks and snorted, just snorted. I spurred him to make him go and he began pitching again. The only reason I was able to stay on him was that I had to stay on him. I have no idea how long we had it around and around. When he finally decided to travel, the sun was nearly down, the mustangs were nowhere in sight, and I felt mighty weak and lonesome.

With that mule there was no use trying to camp out in the hope of finding the mustangs next morning. I felt it in my bones that if I ever dismounted I should never be able to ride him again. I did not want to go back to Sullivan's ranch. I pulled out for the camp where good old Bill Nunn was no doubt anxiously awaiting me twenty-five miles away. Nobody nowadays knows how far twenty-five miles is; the only way to know is to ride a wild, stubborn, idiotic mule for twenty-five miles on a dark night without a trail to follow.

The night was cloudy, and, without a start or any other object to guide by, keeping the mule in a direct course proved to be no simple matter. He had his head set on going back to Sullivan's or somewhere else. Two strata of clouds were flying overhead, one going east and one going west. Once in a while a patch of stars shone. It was only by keeping watch on the clouds and the occasional stars that I kept any sense of direction. As long as I sat still in the saddle the mule jogged along fairly well, but every time I shifted my weight, he shied and resumed his bucking. I don't think I have ever been quite so near exhaustion as I was that night. The east was lighting when I entered the stage road that ran from Dog Town to Fort Ewell. Then for the first time I struck a gallop, and by sunrise I was in camp. Bill and his Mexicans were all ready to start out on a hunt for me.

After I had drunk about a half gallon of black coffee and consumed bread pones and fried "sow belly" in proportion, I felt really generous. I called Bill Nunn over to where I was squatted, still "playing the coffee pot," and told him that I would make him a present of my interest in all the mustangs left in Texas; in addition I offered to lend him saddle horses to ride while he caught them. I had never set myself up as a mustanger; I was through with mustangs forever. Bill took me up on part of the offer, for he got one of the Mexicans to help him and not long afterwards brought in the *manada* we had learned to know so well. He sold them for a very fair price.

The spring following my round with the mustangs Amos Miles and I were ranching and keeping batch at the S E Ranch on the Nueces River. Each had a string of about fifteen broncs that he was breaking both to ride and to stay with a bell mare. Our method was to pen them at night—for we had no adequate horse pasture fenced in—and then during the day while not riding them to herd them with the bell mare—the *caponera,* as the Mexicans call her. As young horses are very fond of colts, we had picked for our *caponeras* two mares with foal. Before long we had the *potros* (young geldings either unbroken or in the process of being broken) so well trained that hardly a one of them would graze out of sound of the mare's bell. A remuda that stayed together was much less trouble and much more valued by ranchmen than a remuda that was constantly splitting up and straying apart. Amos and I considered that we were training two prize remudas.

One evening when I put my broncs in the corral, I saw among them a stray horse. He was a gentle horse that showed the marks of many saddles and of several hot irons, but he was so vicious that he would not allow one of the *potros* to come near the mare and colt. He had already peeled strips of hide off the backs of two or three of them. I cut him out and then ran him away from the pen. He came back immediately. After I had chased him away three times with the same result, I opened the gate and let him back with the remuda. Then I roped him, led him outside, tied him, and blindfolded him. I was determined to be rid of him. Hanging on the fence was the dried hide of a beef we had killed a short time before. I took it down, carried it noiselessly around behind Old Stray, and then tied the tail of it fast to his tail. He had been asleep, I think, while I was "fixing" him, but when I took the blind and the rope off him he certainly woke up. Literally and figuratively he "dragged it." As he raced out of sight down the road through the brush I could occasionally see that hide bouncing up into the air.

It was time for Amos to be in with his remuda, but I had not thought about him. As it turned out, he was not above a half mile from the ranch, driving his horses quietly along the road when he saw the run-away coming. He made a desperate attempt to turn him off and keep him from entering the remuda, but to no avail. His horses broke and stampeded with the hide-bound stray. Amos was riding his pet horse, a beautiful paint, which he thought more of than of his sweetheart. He would never run this horse in the brush for fear of getting thorns in his legs; but now he certainly had to run to keep up. With the scarecrow among them, the *potros* cut out of the bunch one at a time and left until only the mare and stray remained; even the colt had been left behind. Amos ran until after dark. Of course I knew nothing of what had happened until he finally came in long after I had gone to bed, his paint pony on three legs.

He came into my room and struck a light. I knew from sounds I had heard that something was the matter. When the lantern was lit I saw a six-shooter in his hand. He had not spoken a word. Now he deliberately told me that he was going to kill me—and I knew that he meant what he said. He was simply furious; yet I knew that he was too brave a man to murder me in bed for unintentionally stampeding his horses and giving him such a hell of a time. While he held the six-shooter and told me what he thought of me, he also told me how his horses were scattered over ten miles of country and how some of them would no doubt get among the mustangs and be lost for good. I just had to be sorry and to laugh loud at the idea of his shooting me. He agreed to put off the shooting until he had eaten some supper. Then we both laughed. It took him several hours to tell me how and where each horse had quit the bunch, how the old bell mare acted, where he last saw the stray with the hide still dragging at his tail, what his paint horse had done at a certain hollow, and a hundred other details. That run was certainly on his mind.

Of course I went with him the next day. We located the mare by the sound of her bell; the stray was at her heels and he still had his burden. We roped her, and while one of us led her towards the ranch the other ran the stray in the opposite direction. We later learned that there had been a terrible commotion among mustangs out beyond the place where Old Stray was last seen. It took us a week to get Amos' horses back together, though we got them all. For some time they "boogered" at every chance sight or sound.

In November, 1883, I married the girl that had been wearing my ring and we set up housekeeping in Dog Town; I might as well say now that we have reared seven children of our own and about a dozen orphans. I was interested with my wife's brother, Jim Drake, in a ranch thirty miles from Dog Town, and frequently I made trips to it. One night about ten o'clock I arrived to find Jim in despair and his wife in a very low condition indeed. She had been so ill for three days that Jim had been unable to leave her, and not another soul was on or near the ranch to send for a doctor.

I returned immediately for Doctor G. B. Dilworth. I told him that the Nueces River was on a big rise and that he would have to swim it. He was then past sixty years old, but he had a heart in him "as big as an ox." He said that we would not cross the river until we reached it. We delayed only long enough for me to change horses and for him to saddle his. When we got within a few hundred yards of the river, Doctor Dilworth said: "Regardless of how it looks, you ride in and I will follow. Maybe it will be down." It was up higher than it had been when I crossed it in the night. Dilworth shifted his pill bags to his shoulder and rode in. We did not stop to pour the water out of our boots. The doctor saved Mrs. Drake's life; he said that if he had been a few hours later she would have died.

Another time one of my wife's aunts was visiting on this same ranch when her four-year-old baby became very ill. They put him in a buggy and drove hard for Dog Town, but before they reached it the baby was dead in its mother's arms. These instances are told to show some of the hardships and some of the chances on life taken by the women and children of pioneer ranches.

Yes, Texas was hell on women and horses—including some of the mustangs.

CHAPTER XIX

THE BANDANA AND OTHER BELONGINGS

WITHOUT a rope the old time vaquero felt as lost as a hunter without a gun. The rope was so much a part of him that the Mexican ranch people when wishing to describe an all-around good hand said simply, though figuratively, that he was *un buen reata* (literally, "a good rope"). A big game hunter likes to recall the various kinds of animals he has killed; the old time cowboy frequently took pride in the variety of creatures he had lassoed, and there were many varieties, ranging from elks to polecats, for him to "count coup" on. At a time when his lariat was in constant use it was almost second nature for him to "hang" it on anything he saw. In his excellent book, *Tales from the X-Bar Horse Camp,* Will C. Barnes tells how a waddie out in Arizona lost a fifty-dollar saddle by roping one of the camels that had been imported by Jefferson Davis, while Secretary of War, for government transportation across the American desert and that were later turned loose to shift for themselves. The tried and true prescription for sobering up a drunken cowboy was to rope him and jerk him off his horse.

The wildest thing, however, that a cowboy ever roped—wilder than camel or another cowboy—was probably the smokestack of an engine. Nearly every old time cow town has its memory and its yarn of the cowboy who "roped a train." One time at Cotulla, on the Nueces River, a vaquero who was a little the braver for liquor roped the smokestack of an engine that was moving towards Laredo at the rate of twenty miles per hour. The rope was strong and so was the engine. After the engineer stopped the train and the cowboy got himself and his

horse separated from the property belonging to the I. & G. N.
Railroad Company, he was thoroughly sober.

Then there was Peckerwood Pete. Peckerwood Pete had
never been within sight of a railroad; so when he learned that
the Texas and Pacific was actually running trains through Colorado City, Texas, he saddled Straightedge and set out. Straightedge was a wonderful roping horse; he would squat and brace
himself for a hard jerk every time Pete cast a loop from his
back. The jerk was inevitable when Pete "throwed," for Pete
never missed. He was the prize roper on Sulphur Draw.

After he had ridden east for two days he met, coming from
Colorado City, three of the boys who lived a little farther up
the draw than he lived. They told him that the train was some
sight. What interested them particularly was that it had a cow-
catcher; they did not know exactly what the business of the
cow-catcher was, but they knew that one was employed by the
train. Peckerwood Pete tarried not. Like a true Westerner, he
was for progress, and he made up his mind at once to leave
ranch jobs behind him forever and become an up-to-date cow-
catcher for the T. and P. Certainly Straightedge could fill the
bill as a horse, and as for himself he had caught more cows
than any other hand between the Colorado and the Pecos.

Some such recommendation as this, in modest manner, he
conveyed to the conductor of the train when it pulled into
Colorado City. The conductor told him that a try-out would
be necessary before he was engaged as official cow-catcher.

"Ride up the track about a quarter of a mile," said the
conductor, "and wait for us. Then when the engine comes by,
show us how well you can rope. Rope it around the smokestack."

Peckerwood Pete rode up the track. By the time the engine
got to him it was hitting a pretty good lick. Straightedge was as
shy as a rabbit, but Peckerwood finally got him to lay in after
the clanging, smoking object. Then, when at the right distance
and the right angle, the cowboy who would be cow-catcher
whirled his rope. The loop shot true, Straightedge squatted, the
cinches broke—and really that's about the end of the story. If

anybody wishes fictitious details, he can get them out of an odd
little pamphlet entitled *Forty-Nine States Story Book* that was
written and published by Hill and Smith in Dallas shortly
before the advent of the automobile.

I never roped a smokestack, but, as has already been related,
I roped a stag elk on the Mesa Mayo, and I have roped nearly
everything else of western America that wears hair—including
antelopes. While it is next to impossible for a horse to run onto
an antelope, we used to get antelopes and deer in round-ups of
cattle and rope them before they got away. If a man ropes a
buck deer or a black bear, he had better keep his rope tight
and drag the animal down or else prepare either to shoot or to
cut loose. If given a chance, a bear will "climb down a rope,"
and a buck deer will try to gore both man and horse.

The easiest wild thing to lead that I ever had my rope on
was a buffalo calf. I roped him while I was at the Spur Ranch;
he came into the corral at the end of my rope like a broken
colt and the first cow that was turned into the pen with him
had to let him suck. If the Plains ranches had had more milk
cows, lots of dogie buffaloes would probably have been raised,
for a buffalo calf easily takes to a cow and the cow can not
prevent it from sucking her. Roping grown buffaloes was a different matter. The way to catch them was on an up-hill run.
Probably the biggest buffalo roping stunt that was ever pulled
off was in 1868 when Joe McCoy, founder of the market for
Texas cattle at Abilene, Kansas, decided to advertise it to eastern
buyers by exhibiting a carload of buffaloes among them. He
hired Mark Withers, of Lockhart, Texas, and some other men
to rope the exhibit. At the end of a strenuous week, Mark
Withers says, they had got just twelve live bulls into the car.

The outfightingest animal that I ever roped was a wild cat.
While riding one day not far from a huisache tree—this was in
San Patricio County—I saw a bobcat spring out of the branches
and land on the back of a colt. The colt bucked him off, and I
got my rope around him before he could get to the brush. For
a minute he clawed at the rope, spat, and fought like a tiger,
but I soon jerked the life out of him. Perhaps the most difficult

THE BANDANA AND OTHER BELONGINGS 243

animal to rope is a wild razorback hog; this creature holds its
nose so close to the earth that, except on open ground where the
vegetation is low, it is almost impossible to get a noose over its
head; then its head is so narrow that in order to make the loop
hold one must ensnare a leg. Still, roping wild hogs on the
prairie is a sport fully equal to that of spearing the wild boar
in Europe. Roping the big lobo, or timber, wolves on the prairie
was just as exciting.

On January 30, 1927, Howard Hampton had in the Dallas
News a remarkable article entitled "The Palmy Days of the
Texas Cowpuncher." Mostly it is a relation of the experiences
of Horace Wilson in Wilson's own words. The paragraphs on
this old time hand's career with the rope may here be fittingly
quoted. They follow.

One of the boys by the name of Green Hardison and I once
jumped a big, dry maverick cow, and Green sailed in after her and
spilled a loop, but missed. I was riding that same little Howard Col-
lier horse, and by this time he just couldn't be beat on the end of a
rope. Tie him to a freight train, and if he didn't hold it he would get
his navel into the sand trying. So when Green missed I took in where
he left off and plaited my catgut square around her neck and pretty
deep back on her shoulders.

Howard squatted, and the next thing I knew I was on my
haunkers on the sod, and the cow was gallivanting across the landscape with my saddle bobbing along behind on the end of my lariat.
The girt had busted square in two.

I had been carrying a Winchester in a saddle scabbard and when
I left the saddle the gun did too. Cows were cheap and saddles were
high in those days, so I grabbed up the rifle from right where I sat,
took quick aim and shot the cow in the back of the neck. It didn't
kill her, but stunned her long enough for Green to get his rope on her
and save my saddle. I got more satisfaction out of branding her than
any other animal I ever stuck a hot iron to.

It wasn't always wild stock that we were roping, though. Every
good cowpuncher loves to rope and will hang his lariat on almost
anything that jumps up. A good many of the old-timers roped buffalo, but that was a little before my day. Colonel Charlie Goodnight,
whose range joined the Mill Irons on the west, still has a herd de-

scended from buffalo he roped and partly domesticated during the early days. Although I didn't get in on the buffalo, I did hang my loop on an antelope, several wolves and even a wild turkey gobbler. I also killed one wolf with a rock and another with a frog-sticker knife tied on the end of a stick.

In the Mill Iron outfit was a new hand we called San Antonio because he hailed from the Alamo City.

He and I were out one day and struck a bunch of the thousands of antelope that roamed the Panhandle in those days. San Antonio took a notion to shoot one, and I rode up a draw behind the bunch and ran them by him. He opened up with his Winchester as they strung out past him and a big buck wheeled to one side and dropped out. We both thought it was mortally wounded, and San Antonio suggested that I run onto it and rope it. I was on a fast iron-gray Hashknife horse and readily agreed.

But the antelope wasn't hurt as much as we thought. For about a half mile my horse fairly flew, and I finally caught the buck after turning it into the roughs. When I made the catch and my horse sat down, the antelope jumped as high as the rope would let it go and fell flat on its side. San Antonio rode up in time to heel it and hold it down while I cut its throat. The bullet had only nicked one of its hams. Likely the wound helped instead of hindered its running.

That was about the only antelope I ever heard of being roped in the open. I know of several men who roped antelope after they had been caught in the round-up and tried to break away.

The gobbler I caught with a calf-sized loop, around the neck, over one wing, and under the other. I jumped him out of the brush on Turkey Creek in the southwest part of Hall County, where there used to be oodles of them.

Another time I ran across two panthers out on the flat at a head of a canyon, but lost them in the roughs after a hard chase.

Bob Green, general manager of the Mill Irons, had better luck. Early one morning when he was leading the drive we jumped a big boar panther out in the shinnery and the whole outfit, eighteen or twenty of us, spurred in after it. Green was the first man to get a loop on it and it took him but a few minutes to drag it to death in the brush. The old cat clawed the air and growled and spit as he bounced around on the end of the line behind Green's running horse, but it didn't take the rope long to choke him to death. He was a whopper and had had one eye shot out, evidently a long time before.

Bob Green was one of the best and most fearless ropers I ever knew. He would tie onto a 1,200 pound bull while riding a green bronc—and get away with it.

The "loafer" wolves and panthers took an awful toll from among the calves and colts in that country. Our own outfit had a $10 bounty on wolves and panthers, and Colonel Goodnight, our neighbor on the west, paid $20. For a $10 wolf scalp any of us would ride a $100 horse to death—and in my estimation most of the Continentals' horses were worth about that, even then.

A fellow by the name of Ike Inman and I were riding south from Bridle Bit headquarters one hot summer day, hunting horses. Ike was a whale of a man—big enough to hunt bears with a switch.

As we rode into the shinnery a big buck deer jumped up and Ike wanted to rope it, as they are said to be easy to catch in low brush. It was so awfully hot that I knew we might kill our horses before we caught it; so I persuaded him not to chase it. Just about that time a big lobo came loping along and swung off to the right of us a little and kept on going in the way we had come.

The deer's hide was worth a dollar or two at the most, and the loafer's scalp would bring $10—enough to keep us in chewing tobacco for a month or two. We forgot all about the heat hurting our horses, and in less time than it takes to tell it both of us had shook down a loop and were in after him, Ike in the lead.

He was right on it in no time, swinging his loop for a throw, but his rope knocked his hat off and you could have heard him cuss for a mile. Any cowboy can tell you what luck you will have if you lose your hat, rope or quirt on the run and think you can go back later and find it. So Ike pulled up and I shot by him like a streak.

In the two miles between where we jumped him and Turkey Creek I put not less than a dozen loops over that lobo's head, but we were traveling so fast that he went through every time before I could jerk up my slack. However, by the time we reached the creek he was so winded that he came to bay on a gravel bar under the far bank. The wolf, my horse, and I were all in a lather.

Times usually were not so rollicky on the Mill Irons as they had been out on the Pecos, and we went unarmed a good deal. I was carrying no gun that day, but I just had to have that tobacco money showing its fangs across the creek bed. As I quit my horse and picked up a big rock, the rest of the outfit, who had seen the race from the ranch, came riding down to meet me, hollering at me to stay in the saddle or the wolf might jump on me. But I was too hot under the collar to pay any attention to them, and whizzed the rock at the loafer and killed him dead as a doorknob with a lick over the eye. It was just fool luck, of course.

The cowboys used—over a vast area of the West yet uses —his rope not only to lasso animals, both domestic and wild, but for many other purposes. After catching his horse with a rope, he used it to hold the horse while he was saddling him, and then to stake out his horse to graze. He used it to rescue drowning men from swollen rivers. Sometimes he used one end of it for a quirt; he used a double of it many times to kill rattlesnakes. Away from underbrush it is really much easier to kill a snake with a rope than with a stick. The rope was used to pull poor cows out of the bog and to "snake" wood up for the cook. Often it was hitched on to the chuck wagon and, from the horn of a saddle, employed as a means to help the work horses pull out of bad places. The automobile of nearly any modern ranchman would if searched reveal a stout rope carried for emergencies. With two or three ropes joined together, cowboys on the range customarily make a corral for penning the remuda in. When cattle are put in a corral some cowboy takes his rope down to tie the gate fast. Most outfits furnish their men ropes—the only article excepting grub and horses that they do furnish.

The kinds of loops and throws employed by vaqueros are almost as numerous as the uses to which the rope can be put. There is a way of roping a "cow critter" going at full speed so that it will turn a somersault and break its neck. Many a cowboy tired of a frijole diet and hungry for fresh beef has roped a fat yearling in this way and charged the result to "an accident."

One of the neatest throws in common use is the *mangana*, which means catching an animal by the forefeet, "forefooting." An animal roped by the forefeet will most certainly tumble if the man at the end of the rope does not give. The *mangana* is seldom used outside the pen, but can be cast from the saddle as well as from the ground. Often the roper, when afoot, twists his end of the rope about his body and thus braces his weight as well as his strength against the pull. In roping wild horses in the pen the *mangana* used to be employed constantly. Sometimes a horse, when forefooted, will fall in such a way as to break his neck.

A fancy throw, never much used and now hardly known, was the *mangana de pie*. In order to make this cast the roper laid the loop, well opened, on the ground, put his toe under the *hondo* (the noose slip), and then when the animal to be roped —generally a horse—came by, pitched the loop straight out with the foot (the *pie*). This manner of roping was useful to Tol McNeill, of Live Oak County, who, though one-armed, was one of the best ropers and cigarette rollers in the country.

Another form of the *mangana* is called the *mangana de cabra* (the *mangana* for goats). This is a throw that *pastores* use. It is all right for little calves also, but is no good for a big animal or for an animal with spreading horns. The use of it requires a sleight that few vaqueros have mastered. The loop is thrown in such a way that it makes a figure 8, catching the neck of the running animal in the upper half of the figure and its forefeet in the lower half. When the rope is tightened the forefeet are thus drawn up off the ground, and the animal falls.

The *pial* is much more useful. To *pial* an animal is to catch it by the hind feet. This throw is commonly used for "stretching out" a "cow critter"—never a horse—that has been roped around the head or neck. When adroitly cast, the loop turns so as to form a figure 8, and one hind foot is caught in one half of the figure and the other hind foot in the other half. Thus "twined," an animal cannot possibly kick itself loose if the rope is held at all tightly.

One of the best ropers, best cowmen, and best men that Texas ever produced was John Blocker, and his name has been given to his favorite size of loop, a big loop. No doubt many people who speak of the "Blocker loop" nowadays never heard of John Blocker, although all the real cattle people in Texas know who John Blocker was. A trick that comes in handy in all kinds of roping is that of throwing a half-hitch around the top of a post after an animal has been roped but before the rope is drawn taut. With the rope thus wrapped around a post, a very small man can hold the largest animal.

Modern cowboys seem to be giving up the bandana handkerchief. Perhaps the moving pictures have made it tawdry. Yet there was a time when this article was almost as necessary to a cowboy's equipment as a rope, and it served for purposes almost as varied. The prevailing color of the bandana was red, but blues and blacks were common, and of course silk bandanas were prized above those made of cotton.

When the cowboy got up in the morning and went down to the water hole to wash his face he used his bandana for a towel. Then he tied it around his neck, letting the fold hang down in front, thus appearing rather nattily dressed for breakfast. After he had roped out his bronc and tried to bridle him he probably found that the horse had to be blindfolded before he could do anything with him. The bandana was what he used to blindfold the horse with. Mounted, the cowboy removed the blind from the horse and put it again around his own neck. Perhaps he rode only a short distance before he spied a big calf that should be branded. He roped the calf; then if he did not have a "piggin string"—a short rope used for tying down animals—he tied the calf's legs together with the bandana and thus kept the calf fast while he branded it. In the summer time the cowboy adjusted the bandana to protect his neck from the sun. He often wore gloves too, for he liked to present neat hands and neck. If the hot sun was in his face, he adjusted the bandana in front of him, tying it so that the fold would hang over his cheeks, nose, and mouth like a mask. If his business was with a dust-raising herd of cattle, the bandana adjusted in the same way made a respirator; in blizzardly weather it likewise protected his face and ears. In the swift, unhalting work required in a pen the cowboy could, without losing time, grab a fold of the bandana loosely hung about his neck and wipe away the blinding sweat. In the pen, too, the bandana served as a rag for holding the hot handles of branding irons.

Many a cowboy has spread his bandana, perhaps none too clean itself, over dirty, muddy water and used it as a strainer to drink through; sometimes he used it as a cup towel, which he called a "drying rag." If the bandana was dirty, it was probably not so dirty as the other apparel of the cowboy, for when he came to a hole of water, he was wont to dismount and wash out his handkerchief, letting it dry while he rode along, holding it in his hand or spread over his hat. Often he wore it under his hat in order to help keep his head cool. At other times, in the face of a fierce gale, he used it to tie down his hat. The bandana made a good sling for a broken arm; it made a good bandage for a blood wound. Early Irish settlers on the Nueces River used to believe that a bandana handkerchief that had been worn by a drowned man would, if cast into a stream above the sunken body, float until it came over the body and then sink, thus locating it. Many a cowboy out on the lonely plains has been buried with a clean bandana spread over his face to keep the dirt, or the coarse blanket on which the dirt was poured, from touching it. The bandana has been used to hang men with. Rustlers used to "wave" strangers around with it, as a warning against nearer approach, though the hat was more commonly used for signaling. Like the Mexican sombrero or the four gallon Stetson, the bandana could not be made too large. When the cowboys of the West make their final parade on the grassy shores of Paradise, the guidon that leads them should be a bandana handkerchief. It deserves to be called the flag of the range country.

More men have been killed on account of bluffing with their guns than were ever killed because they had no guns. Branch Isbell was probably right when he said that he had saved his life several times by not going armed. Nevertheless, most of us went armed. A man who carried a gun merely for show or because gunpacking was customary, yet who could not use it, was absurdly foolish; still many men who could not hit the side of a barn with all day to aim in were walking arsenals. The only reason on earth for carrying a gun is to use it when needed. The only reason on earth for pulling it when needed is to shoot it with lightning speed and deadly precision. I was never notorious as a gun man, but for fifteen years I wore a six-shooter buckled around my waist, and I always considered that I owed it to myself to be ready to use it effectively on demand. Also, I took a natural human satisfaction in shooting fairly well. When the time came to unbuckle the cartridge belt and put the gun aside, I was ready and glad to go unarmed.

I accidentally broke the trigger off the first Colt's 45 that I owned and was not at the time where I could have it replaced. I simply took the pistol apart and with a file removed the trigger mechanism. The gun could then be fired by merely drawing the hammer back and releasing it—one motion. After I got used to shooting this way I, like many other men, would not have a trigger in a gun. A man with a trigger had to pull the hammer back, then pull the trigger, making two motions in firing. One motion is always quicker than two. Of two men equally swift on the draw, the man without a trigger had the shade of advantage over the man with a trigger. Frequently the fraction of a second meant the difference between life and death.

Now there is a considerable difference between a triggerless revolver and a "double-action" revolver. To fire a double-action revolver one pulls the trigger, which action raises the hammer and lets it fall—one motion. But the trigger must be released so that it can be pulled back for a second shot. The danger of the double-action gun lies in the "trigger squeeze." More than one man fighting for his life with a double-action revolver has pulled the trigger once and then kept on pulling it, not allowing it to spring forward to catch before pulling it again. There he stood squeezing it when he should have been releasing it. In pulling back and releasing the hammer, an act performable with almost incredible speed, such an involuntary mistake was not likely. The novice pulled the hammer back with the ball of his thumb, but the man of experience pulled it with the second joint of his thumb as his hand closed around the gun he was drawing. The mainspring was often loosened so that the hammer could be worked more easily.

I never carried but five cartridges in my six-shooter and the hammer was always down on the empty chamber. This is the only safe way to carry a gun. The Western stories that describe "six shots ringing out in quick succession" are usually bunk. The man who carried all six chambers loaded frequently shot himself before he had a chance to shoot anybody else. I never knew a man to lose his life by having only five cartridges in his gun, although I knew one to almost lose it by having only one cartridge. It was in a fight that Captain McNelly's rangers had with some Mexican outlaws down near the Rio Grande. Captain McNelly had fired all his cartridges but one, which he was holding in reserve. He called to one of his men to bring him some shells. One of the Mexicans, who understood English, rushed at the captain with a *machete* (a heavy knife), saying, "Damn you, I got you now!" The captain fired at him with his last cartridge, hitting him squarely in the mouth and killing him instantly.

In quick action the gun was often fired from the hip as it came out of the holster, but the second shot was aimed straight at the heart, sometimes the head. The exaggerated ideas now current about shooting from the hip have been well disposed of by Captain James B. Gillett, of Marfa, one of the best known and best experienced rangers and marshals of Texas. "In all my experience with both officers and desperadoes," says Captain Gillett, "I never saw a man shoot from the hip. All of them pulled the pistol, pointed it from the shoulder level, and fired. There's a lot of stunt shooting that I never heard of until I read about it in story books. Most of those old gun fighters like Wild Bill Hickok, Ben Thompson, Wes Hardin and Bat Masterson generally fought their battles in a bar room or a gambling house at a distance of not more than five or ten feet from the man they were shooting at, and, of course, in such close quarters they just pulled their pistol, shoved it up against their victim, and touched it off. No need to aim it under such conditions. If one of them, however, was shooting at a man across the street or at a turkey in the top of a tree, I have an idea that he aimed his pistol rather carefully."

A few men carried two guns, but that was generally for

show. I have never known of an instance where two guns had the advantage over one. Men who could really use one were scarce. Lots of cowboys who carried guns let them rust and get out of order. If, with guns in such condition, they got into fast company, they were just out of luck.

"Fanning," like carrying two guns, was pretty much a piece of show business, though there were men who could "fan." To "fan" a gun the person gripped it in his left hand and with rapid passes of his right hand knocked back and released the hammer. The gun used in "fanning" had, of course, no trigger. A man might "fan" for pastime, but seldom for his life.

I have spoken of piking monte and I have mentioned Monterrey. Perhaps I had as well admit that I at times played cards pretty hard and drifted down to Monterrey—the monte capital of the two republics—every once in a while. During the seventies and eighties monte and poker were as popular on the range as bridge now is among women. The men who carried decks of cards with them were few, and consequently monte rather than poker or some other game was often played in camp so as to allow all hands to enter. Any number of people can with one deck of cards pike monte. The monte banker, whether in camp or in a big gambling house, always set a limit to the "pikers." Among us cow hands the limit was generally a dime.

Unless the banker did set a limit he would, provided he played an honest game, "go broke." Now I had a system that could beat any monte game *fairly played*. At least I thought I had such a system. It required an iron will, also capital. Like most men who gamble, I had a superstition. My superstition was against counting the money I bet. I simply shoved the money out, and thus I came to be known as the vaquero who always said, *"Todo sobre el limete va en el Viejo."* (All over the limit goes on the Viejo.) The Viejo (literally the Old Man) is the color of the card opposite to that on which one bets, but the Viejo has so many phases that only a well trained Mexican gambler could interpret all of them.

One time we six *brasaderos* went to Monterrey for the *diez y seis de Septiembre*—the Sixteenth of September—celebration, a celebration that corresponds to our Fourth of July. The plaza was full of gambling games, monte having first place. One long table had perhaps $25,000 in gold and silver piled up on it. At this table was the most famous dealer in Mexico.

I was feeling my oats anyhow, and the sight of all that gold and silver made me feel like bucking the moon. I could hardly wait to ask the dealer what the limit was. With a curious smile that was hardly a smile he replied that my first bet would be the limit. At this he passed the cards to me to cut. The lay was a deuce and a jack. Now, the dealer was smoking a cigarette that had burned pretty short, and it apparently burnt his lips. He had the deck that I had cut in his left hand and with a rapid sweep of the cards he knocked the cigarette out of his mouth. But he was not too swift for me to see the jack on the bottom of his deck. Dozens of other gamblers saw the same thing. Pikers at monte are always watching for anything of that kind. If one sees something one is said to "catch port."

I felt sure that I should win. I plugged down $500 *puro oro* on the jack for an ace. The others pikers who had also "caught port" bet on the jack until the card was buried with money to the amount of six or seven thousand dollars. When the dealer turned the deck over the deuce, not the jack, was "in port." While all of us were watching him he had, without detection, changed the cards with his little finger. The burning cigarette, the flash of the cards with his hand, and the changing of the bottom card were all an old trick. I lost, but I learned something; before riding back into the Brasada I was well ahead.

I have no idea of trying to defend gambling or gamblers. I can only plead that among moral, law-abiding frontiersmen of the border country—and most of the bona fide settlers were honest and law-abiding—gambling was, if not participated in, at least tolerated. Of course professional gamblers did not have the respect of the best citizens, but "just gambling" was not very bad.

As I think of it now, I was rather particular about my bandanas, my ropes, my boots, my six-shooter, and other equipments, but I had no feeling towards them. They were just things. My horse was something alive, something intelligent and friendly and true. He was sensitive, and for him I had a profound feeling. I sometimes think back on Payaso and two or three other remarkable horses that I owned in much the same way that I think back on certain friends that have left me. I do not believe that any Arab ever loved his horse more than I loved mine. I went hungry sometimes, but if there was any possible way of getting food for my horse or if there was a place to stake him, even though I had to walk back a mile after putting him to graze, I never let him go hungry. Many a time I have divided the water in a canteen with a horse.

I want to enter a protest against the treatment that picture-show actors evidently give their horses. In many pictures the horses of these play cowboys can be seen "wringing," or writh-ing, their tails, as if they were trying to twist them off. The effect is supposed to convey "action." When a horse "wrings" his tail it is evidence of nerve-wracking pain. The "wringing" is occasioned by the picture-show cowboy's spurring or lashing the horse and at the same time holding him in. If I were a censor I should eliminate every picture that shows a "wring tail" horse.

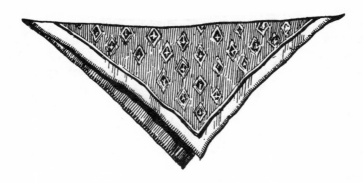

CHAPTER XX

THE MAN WITH THE IRON HAND

THE year 1890 found me trading horses in San Antonio, but I have already told something about the horse business. Town life, despite the fact that I was constantly out and going, did not seem to agree with me. One day my doctor announced that I had tuberculosis. Within a few weeks I and my family were in a covered wagon headed west. We were bound for a high and dry country that I knew well and that for many years I had yearned towards. I had first learned it while under the guidance of a Seminole Indian; I had then dodged Comanches on it and piloted a herd of cattle across it; later I had explored it thoroughly with the intention of locating a ranch in it, but had been turned back on account of the scarcity of water. We were bound for the Devil's River country.

Going up the North Prong of the Llano River we gathered a winter's supply of pecans; there was nothing to eat them but squirrels and wild hogs. We had squirrel, turkey, venison, or fish at almost every meal. I cut a bee tree and got a big bucket of honey, and could have got a wagon load from it and other bee trees. The Llanos were a land of plenty, but by 1890 the range along them had all been appropriated for grazing. I was heading for free land.

After we crossed the high divide between the Llanos and the head draws of Devil's River we came to Sonora, a little town just about a year old that was soon to become the seat of Sutton County. We did not tarry here long, but long enough for me to reecive some distinct impressions.

Its chief organization was a kangaroo court, and this court was about the liveliest thing of its kind that ever functioned in the West. It claimed its authority from "the famous Seventeenth Legislature of Texas"—though I never found out what made this particular legislature famous. The "Just Judge" that presided over it was my uncle, Sam Duncan, who claimed to be the only honest gambler in the country. The prosecuting attorney was Charlie Adams, author of a book, printed privately some years later, entitled *Forty Years a Fool*. In this court there were no juries and the decision of the Just Judge was without appeal. He frequently assessed fines, and the money was always turned over to the cause of charity.

Sam G. Tayloe, now district judge in San Antonio, was tried for theft and his wife was brought in as a witness—evidence of the fact that women sometimes took part in these mock courts on a frontier barren of social amusements. It was proved that Tayloe had stolen his wife. In another case a long, lank young man was accused of "stuttering in the streets against the peace and dignity of the State of Devil's River." He gave his name as Bob Martin. The Just Judge sentenced him to herd a flock of 1500 sheep for one day. He was to herd them on foot. At the end of the day he came in—so a story that has been told on many tenderfeet goes—and reported to the owner, who asked if the sheep had given him any trouble. Bob stutteringly replied that three lambs had given him just an awful lot of trouble but that he had finally corralled them with the other sheep. It was a time of year when there were no lambs, and the owner's curiosity was aroused. He went down to the pen to investigate. The "lambs" turned out to be three jack rabbits. On the strength of his energy and enterprise Bob got a permanent job. Today he is handling sheep of his own by the tens of thousands.

Sonora had more horse play and more varieties of horse play than any other community I have ever been acquainted with. It possessed a weekly newspaper called *The Devil's River News* and also a struggling Sunday School that was held in the one-roomed school house. The chief news gatherer for the paper was a Mrs. Hooper; she "knew everything." One Sunday morning several of us young and younger men came together in one of the dozen saloons of the town. One of the gang was Lee L.

Russell, now of Fort Worth and one of the largest cattle dealers in America. He announced to us that he had promised his sister he would attend Sunday School at ten o'clock that Sabbath morning and he suggested that we all go along. We went. The few women who conducted the Sunday School welcomed us most cordially and apportioned to our use a long bench. The teacher was an elderly woman and she began her instruction with orthodox catechism.

"Who knoweth all things?" she asked, directing her attention to Lee Russell, who was on the end of the bench.

"Mrs. Hooper," Lee replied.

The teacher at this, without a smile, rebuked Lee for levity in a house of worship and informed him that God knoweth all things. Lee told her that he did not doubt what she said, but that she evidently did not know Mrs. Hooper. Our teacher preferred not to argue, and she directed the next question to me.

"Who," she asked, "was the father of Zebedee's children?"

I plainly told her that I did not know, and as the question went around all the other "boys" said that they did not know. When the time came to sing, our teacher was visibly relieved.

For eighty-five miles above the head springs of Devil's River there was no permanent water, and this dry land averaged a width of about the same distance. It is cut through by many canyons, or prongs. The country I wanted was along one of the middle prongs; all I had to do was to lease a section of land from the state of Texas and then use the free grass all around me. That is, I could use the free grass if I could get water.

Well-drilling in many parts of the range country was at this time on a boom that may be said to have prefigured subsequent booms in drilling for oil. Cowmen were finding out that the great Plains country was underlaid with a lake of water that could be tapped at a comparatively shallow depth; hence vast areas of land that had been useless on account of the absence of natural waterings of permanence were being utilized. But there is no broad lake of water under the surface of what is known as the Edwards Plateau—the land lying between the Pecos River on the west and the Colorado River with its tributaries on the east and extending north to the Plains. The underground water of the Edwards Plateau is in veins; in that part of the Plateau known as the Devil's River country, the veins are deep down and far apart.

I had provided myself with a well-drilling machine, the "horse power" of which was a horse—or a mule. While my family wintered comfortably in a tent, protected from high winds by a brush fence, I dug for water and slept in the open. I got rid—permanently—of tuberculosis before I found water. Two, four, five dry holes I dug—two of them on Central Prong, two on East Prong, and then one over on Turkey Roost Prong. Various other men in the country were drilling as unsuccessfully as I was. Some men found what they were digging for.

Water to furnish a drilling outfit had very often to be hauled for ten miles or more. The well casing and other supplies had to be hauled from San Angelo. Drilling under such conditions was expensive, and by the time a man had gone down a few hundred feet he had spent a thousand dollars. The dry holes left by men who had to move on were marks of exploration to guide the water-seekers who followed. In the course of time, after the expenditure of a great deal of money—all the savings that many men had—the Edwards Plateau has become pretty well watered, though on many ranches of West and Southwest Texas men are still boring for water. The numerous "water witches" with their "gift" of locating water by holding a forked stick a certain way in their hands and walking over the country until the stick "pulls" down have not done a great deal towards watering the land; yet it would be surprising to know how many hard-headed cowmen have drilled at locations made by these "switchers." "Dusters"—dry oil wells—have revealed more water than the "switchers," and many a cowman has been made happy when the prospective oil well developed into a well of water.

The story of the well (of water) driller has never been told. The enormous importance of drilling machines and windmills to the range industry has never been realized by historians. A numerous class of men who owned well-drilling machines and drilled on contract became a distinct type in the cattle country. They never made much money and they never became a part of the range tradition as it has been popularized. Wells of water there were, of course, on the first Spanish ranches of Texas but they were dug by hand, and the water was pulled out of them either by hand or by a horse. In the more primitive manner— and by far the more common manner—a man rode the horse, drawing the water bucket up by means of a rope that ran over a pulley and was attached to the horn of his saddle; another man, who stood on the well curb, emptied the bucket as it came up. The jack-pump was less primitive; a horse hitched to a kind of windlass trod around and around, translating horizontal power—the power of the saddle horn—into rotary power. The "dug wells" were necessarily shallow. Along in the seventies with the advent of barbed wire came also windmills—at first very expensive—to set up over these dug wells. Storage tanks, or cisterns, of sufficient capacity to tide thirsty cattle over a calm spell were slow in coming; cement reservoirs are a modern development. When the dog days sizzled and the wind did not blow, the cattle bawled piteously; from sheer thirst, they died by tens of thousands. Fences had cut them off from natural waterings; jack-pumps and saddle horns were too slow to bring up sufficient water from the sparse wells. Sometimes the number of cattle that a ranchman put in a pasture was determined, mistakenly, by the amount of grass he saw in the spring rather than by the supply of water he could safely count on during a drouthy, calm August.

There have been three eras to the cattle industry. First was the era of the open range, where grass was free and nature supplied the only water. Second came the era of barbed wire, of land control—also, of pastures fenced in and stocked before they were even half supplied with wells, windmills, and dirt tanks. Add to these facts the fact that as the range settled up it became more heavily stocked, the sod became cut up, and flowing creeks and springs were choked with washed soil so that they no longer flowed. The western half of Texas does not today possess one-third of the living water that it possessed fifty years ago.

The first era of the range industry was the era of free grass; the second era was the era of thirst. The third era, our own, is that of a range adequately watered as well as securely fenced. Well-drilling machines, with horses for power, and windmills made this era possible. The machines could dig deep and bring water from depths that hand digging could not plumb. Now that horses have given way to gasoline, the machines can bore still deeper. At the same time, gasoline engines are so cheap and effective that they not only supplement windmills during calms but are often depended upon the year around to pump water.

It is related that one of the first windmills erected in the Big Spring country was put up by the great cattle king, C. C. Slaughter. Shortly after its erection a round-up was held near the well. Colonel Slaughter appeared in his buckboard, drawn by two fine horses. After the herd was "worked" and "shaped up," everybody went down to the well to drink. The wind was blowing hard, the windmill was racing around, and a thin stream of water was pouring out into a trough. There was no reservoir to catch the water and store it up against a dry and windless day. Colonel Slaughter took a drink from the end of the lead pipe, looked up at the revolving mill, and said:

"Boys, that there machine is going to revolutionize the cattle business of Texas. The windmill assures water on millions of acres of grass that has heretofore gone to waste."

For a minute nobody said anything; but while the Colonel was prophesying, a gangling cowboy whose mouth was considerably wider than his forehead had been guzzling water. He stopped, got a breath of air, then retorted:

"That windmill reverlutionize anything! Hell, I can drink water faster than one of them things can ever pump it."

"How long could you keep drinking before the mill got ahead of you?" Colonel Slaughter asked.

"Until I starved to death for water," and the cowboy soused his head in the trough.

Many of the cowmen who were getting windmills knew precious little about keeping them up. One such cowman had listened attentively, however, to the "windmill men" who put up his mill. They had impressed on him the idea that if the rod quit drawing water he must pack the "barrel" (pump cylinder) with leather. One day he came into the ranch to find the mill turning all right and the rod going up and down all right, but no water coming out of the pipe. He at once instructed two of his cowboys to get some leather, climb up on top of the tower, and "pack the barrel with leather." He had no idea where the leather should be put; the cowboys had no idea either. However, the day was at hand when every sizable ranch in the windmill country should have one or two windmill men as highly specialized in their work as the cook or the bronco buster, and when also the small rancher should be handier with windmill tools than with a rope. On any modern ranch nowadays one will hear twenty times as much talk about windmills as about ropes, mavericks, broncos and other things that made the old time cowboy strictly a horseman with little use for foot work and little knowledge of machinery.

In the early eighteen-nineties, however, there was still plenty of unwatered land in the Devil's River country and on west across the Pecos, across the New Mexico-Texas line, and clean to California. In an unwatered land fences are always scarce. Many people do not know that as late as 1895 herds of cattle were still being driven from the Pecos to Montana. I made one last drive before I was fenced in and roped off. It was not a very long drive and it was with a comparatively small herd; but it was about the most adventuresome and at the same time the most worrisome of all drives that I made.

As soon as I got into the run of things after moving out on Devil's River I accumulated a few cattle, which I held on watered land while I dug wells. In the fall of '92, I think it was, some of my neighbors and myself contracted with a man from Colorado City to deliver 700 long yearlings—yearlings that would be two's in early spring—to a point in Dawson County, about a hundred and fifty miles northwest of us. The cattle were poor and we had to do something with them. I was placed in charge of the outfit, which consisted of a cook and six hands besides myself, and about the middle of December we started out. We had already experienced several northers and the nights were cold.

The cattle were very little trouble. They drove at a snail's pace, but at night, except for an occasional scare, which amounted to nothing, at a polecat, a snake, or something like that, they bedded as quietly as so many infants. Then about twelve o'clock one night a "blue whistler" snorted down upon us. We were on the plains country, and no one who has not experienced a blue whistler on the open prairies of West Texas really knows what a cold north wind is like. The nearest protection was the north star, but we had to stay with the cattle and let all possibility of shelter go.

For a while the dogies slept on; then all at once they were running in every direction, not stampeding together, but scattering like partridges. It took me some time to find the source of trouble. It was a dry lake, a mile or two north of the bed ground, overgrown with a bumper crop of tumbleweeds, or Russian thistles. The tumbleweed grows to a height of two or three feet and is very bushy, the bush part being about as big around as a washtub. With the frost of winter the weed dies and when dry it is very, very light. The wind against the bush breaks the stem off at the ground and then the tumbleweed tumbles— tumbles for miles unless it rolls into some break or against some obstruction.

The blue whistler was bringing tumbleweeds from the dry lake, and our dogies were in their path. With the onrush of weeds among them, over them, under them, all around them, the yearlings naturally began dodging in every which way. The tumbleweeds came singly, in pairs, and in droves. The night was so dark, the weeds were so big, and the yearlings were so little that we could not very well tell tumbleweeds from dogies. One of the boys swore next day that he had run a bunch of weeds at least half a mile trying to turn them back before he discovered that they were not yearlings. It was both pitiful and

comical to see a dogie trying to outrun a tumbleweed and then
when the weed overtook him and rolled upon the top of his back
to hear him bleat as if a wolf had him.

At daylight we counted the herd and found that we were
out fifteen head. I took one man with me. We cut for sign,
picked up the trail, then followed it south, in front of the wind,
for about ten miles. There we came to some rocky, hard ground;
the cattle appeared to have scattered, and we lost the trail. The
man with me and I then separated, he to circle back on the left-
hand side and I on the right. I made a larger circle than I had
intended to make and did a great deal of zig-zagging. Late in
the evening I turned towards camp. I judged that it was fifteen
or eighteen miles away. I had ridden only a short distance and
night had fallen—as black as the ace of spades—when suddenly
my horse stopped. I recognized the signal. He was "give out."
I had overtaxed his strength; neither he nor I had had a swallow
of water or a bite to eat since daylight. I dismounted and began
to lead him. It was slow traveling.

I knew that camp was due north against the bitter wind;
so I could not miss my way, although I might miss the camp
in the darkness. In a little while a light snow began falling.
Fifteen miles is a long way for a tired man leading a tireder
horse to walk in snow-sprinkled darkness. Camping was out
of the question, for the only fuel in this country was cow chips
and I could not see any of them to gather up. I determined to
avoid numbness and the fatal drowsiness in which a man may
comfortably freeze to death.

A pack of lobos began howling off to the east. Their voices
are deeper and hoarser than the voices of coyotes. These lobos—
"loafers," most of the old timers call them—are now approaching extinction. They were by far the most predatory animals
that the cowmen ever knew. Many years ago while I was riding
on the Sauce Creek between Beeville and Mission, in Refugio
County, I saw four lobos attack a cow five or six hundred yards
ahead of me. I struck a run towards them, but before I got near
enough to do any good with my six-shooter the lobos had
brought the cow to the ground and were eating her. Lobo

wolves were so numerous that cowboys used to make round-ups of them in North Texas and Oklahoma, and one man has testified that he saw five hundred of them in one bunch, on the plains of the Pecos, migrating west. I was not afraid of the lobos I heard barking off to my right so long as I remained awake and could use my six-shooter; but I knew that the animals were watching me and would not hesitate to attack me if I lay down. The cold norther was making them hungry.

Then directly I heard what I took to be a coyote barking off to my left. The bark was a little like that of a dog, but as dogs sometimes go wild with the wolves, I thought that if it was a dog I heard barking it must be a wild dog. The wind seemed to veer in the direction of the lonely bark, which was occasional, and I veered slightly also. I did not know at the moment that I had shifted my position, but very soon I heard the bark again and noted that it was straight ahead of me. Then I saw a low, smouldering camp-fire. My direct route would have taken me past that dim camp-fire without my seeing it. What made me shift so as to walk right into it? I have said something before about a Guardian Angel.

A solitary man was preparing supper. Speaking in Spanish, he told me where to find the water barrel and bucket to water my horse and also where to find corn in the wagon. After watering my horse and giving him a good feed of corn, I walked around towards the fire. It was of cow chips, which when dry make a very hot fire but give out little light. As I faced the fire I noted that the man was putting dough in a large Dutch oven, the lid of which was on the fire; I particularly noticed that the lid was almost red hot—too hot for the even baking of bread. While I was still several steps away the man reached over, hooked the finger of his right hand in the iron eye of the glowing skillet lid and deliberately removed it from the coals and placed it on top of the oven. Then he shoved his hand down into the bed of live coals and placed several handfuls of them on top of the lid.

Honestly the sight of that man handling fire almost paralyzed me. I had halted to watch the actions of his hand and had not yet got a look at his face. Then as he leaned over the coals, somewhat turning his head to one side in my direction, I discovered that it was ebony black; the blackness fairly shone. I might have looked for a tail on this person, but he was wrapped in a blanket, Indian fashion, and before I could examine his right hand further he put it under the blanket. There in the night over the fire he realized to my imagination certain pictures of the devil, black and fire-fearless, that I had seen in books during my boyhood and that I had heard my father describe to his Baptist congregations. I have never believed much in the devil, but here was a Devil Man.

About this time the owner of the camp rode up, calling to the Devil Man to get on a horse and go around the sheep. The Devil Man quickly mounted and was gone. The boss proved to be a decent sheepman and a friend of mine named Donald McRae. He gave me a hearty Scotch welcome. He said that he was moving his sheep down into the breaks for winter and that the tumbleweeds had nearly run him and the sheep both to death. The night before, he said, he had been forced to turn his herd loose. Before we could talk further we fell to eating. Then he said that he must go back to his herd and stay with them until they got quieter. He invited me to take his bed, saying there was room for two if he should be able to come in. I went to sleep almost instantly.

McRae came in some time during the night, and the next morning when we got up the Devil Man, who was really the sheep herder, had eaten his breakfast and was with the sheep. After a hearty meal I told McRea *adios,* remarking at the same time that I would ride by his herd and take a look at his fine sheep. I was determined to find out in the daylight what manner of *pastor* he had that could handle fire. I might have asked McRae, but I did not.

On accosting the *pastor* I found that though he was black he could not speak English at all. Despite his color, his features were those of an Indian. He told me, upon my questioning him, that his father, a negro slave, had run away from Texas during the Civil War and joined the Seminole Indians in

Mexico and that he himself was half Seminole and half negro. While he talked he kept his hands under his blanket. As an excuse to bring them into view I offered him the makings of a cigarette. He rolled the cigarette with his left hand, not exposing at all the hand I had seen in the fire. I hesitated to ask point-blank about his right hand, but my curiosity was becoming more and more aroused. I determined to satisfy it even if I had to rope the man and tie him down in order to get the hand out.

Finally I told him that I had to be riding and offered my hand for a farewell shake. He was about to take it in his left hand, but I withdrew it as if insulted. "Friends always give the right hand," I said.

He looked me squarely in the eye and then asked, "Are you an officer of the law?"

I at once surmised that he was a fugitive from justice and that he was holding in his right hand a pistol, ready to use it. I quickly assured him that I was not an officer of the law but just a plain vaquero who had lost some cattle. This seemed to relieve him, and then I told him very frankly how I had seen him handling fire with his right hand the night preceding and simply had to get an explanation of such extraordinary conduct.

The poor fellow actually shed tears as he told me how he had lost his arm in a battle, how he had managed to get a kind of metal arm with a hook on the end of it, and how the metal when it got cold caused the stump of his arm to ache, which explained why he kept the metal wrapped up. I accepted the shake of his left hand and turned for camp, my anxiety about the cattle renewed.

When I arrived I found the cattle loose, scattered, and grazing off, though the herd seemed intact. Not a man, not even the cook, was around. While I was wondering what would turn up next, one of the cowboys came in. He informed me that the man who had gone out with me the day before had found the fifteen lost yearlings and had brought them in. When I did not return during the night, he said, the outfit had decided that something serious had happened to me and before daylight they had all set out to hunt me, leaving him to ride around in the country nearest camp so that he could more or less keep an eye on the cattle to prevent their getting away.

During the afternoon the other hands straggled in and we made plans to drive on next day. The wind had died down and the temperature had moderated, but that night a real snow began to fall, the snow of the night before not having amounted to much. By morning the snow was a foot deep and snow clouds were still heavy overhead. I thought it best not to break camp, which was near water, before the spell had broken. Of course all the grass was under snow, and in order to expose a little of it for our horses I had the boys make a drag out of the sideboards of the wagon and rake the covering off a few patches of ground. Dragging the improvised snow plow at the horns of their saddles was not very difficult work.

Our worst problem was getting fuel. The cow chips on the prairie were all covered up and even when found were too wet to burn readily. The camp cook who complained that he used up all his wages in buying hats to wear out in fanning fires of cow chips was entitled to sympathy. Among outfits dependent on this "prairie coal" it was customary for several men to scour out in different directions with gunny sacks, each bringing in what he could find. Now with no chips visible and with those that could be kicked up damp, fuel became mighty scarce; yet somehow we managed to get by. We always did manage somehow.

We had now been in camp two days, but the morning of the third day dawned clear and bright. We could see the snow melting; and the dogies strung out in fine style, their condition not so bad as might have been expected. I was figuring on a good day's drive—but troubles never come singly. After the cook had loaded up, he drove into the edge of the lake to fill his kegs with water, and there he bogged both horses and wagon so deep in the slushy mire that it took us hours to get him out. While the horse wrangler was helping the cook, a part of his horses got away. We made just about five miles before I stopped the herd for night.

The next two days were smooth going. Then a fresh norther blew up, not very cold but strong. We had passed out of the snowfall and into a country that was as dry as tinder. Along about ten o'clock in the morning of the third day I saw smoke ahead of us. I knew what it meant; it meant that nightmare of the plainsmen—a prairie fire. The wind was bringing the fire towards us at a fearful rate. A fight was inevitable. I stopped the herd, for there was no creek or break to put them across, and at once set all men to back-firing. First we burned a clearing in front of us, then on both sides, and then behind us so as to leave an island for us to stay on. We so controlled these fires that we had perhaps a hundred acres of grass left. The sky became dark with smoke as though the sun were in eclipse. Antelopes, deer, coyotes, and wolves were passing us like the wind, fleeing the fire. Many of the animals stopped on our plot.

The question now was: How far ahead of us was the country burnt off? Such a fire as we had escaped, in such a wind as was blowing, would jump any ordinary fire guard or break in the plain of grass. When daylight came next morning, we were on our way across the blackened ground of unknown extent. The smoke and soot on our faces made us look like so many negroes.

Instructing the hands to keep the cattle coming, I rode ahead to find out what we might expect. After riding a good distance I came to an island of grass around a hole of water. Beyond that as far as my eyes could reach there was nothing but black ground. On my ride I saw the charred remains of many deer and antelopes. After finding such a good place to camp I rode back, met the herd, and piloted it in. The next morning I set out ahead again. I was hardly out of sight of the cattle when I rode up on the ruins of two wagons near a water hole. There was nothing to tell who the owners had been or what had become of them. Probably they were hunters who had set the prairie afire accidentally and had then ridden the wagon teams to safety. Three or four miles on beyond the burn came to an end and we were once more on good grass.

From here on nothing eventful interrupted the drive. We delivered the cattle and came back home to our squats on Devil's River.

CHAPTER XXI

TRANS-PECOS

WHILE drilling for water on the dry canyons of Devil's River I drifted westward until I found myself on the West Prong, in Crockett County. The only settlement in this country at the time—and it is still the only settlement of any consequence—was a place called Tail Holt on Johnson's Run, a prong of Devil's River. In 1891 the country was organized, and, with a new name, Tail Holt became the county seat. The new name was Ozona—derived from *ozone,* one of the principal assets of the country. I was made cattle inspector of the county; then after serving as inspector for two years I was elected county assessor, which office I held for eight years. During this period of office-holding my family and I lived in Ozona, but I was away from home a great deal, for I was still in the ranching business. Just below old Horsehead Crossing on the Pecos River —the boundary of Crockett County for a hundred miles along its western side—Claude Hudspeth, Clay McGonigal, and I had a ranch; my chief outside business, however, was selling ranch lands and closing out big cattle companies.

As both of my partners were interesting men, a word about them may not be out of place. Claude B. Hudspeth came to Ozona when he was sixteen years old, bringing with him a little hand press that he had learned to use in Bandera County. He started the Ozona *Kicker,* a weekly news sheet that he ran for several years. He was editor, typesetter, devil, reporter, and everything else connected with the paper. Meantime he was getting interested in cattle, and within a few years he turned the *Kicker* loose in order to devote all his time to ranching. It was then that we went in partners. Our section of Texas was badly

270

in need of a state representative who had the interests of ranch people at heart, and we elected Hudspeth to the legislature. He had broken his ankle while roping a steer and was willing to quit riding for a while. The next thing we knew he had read enough law to pass the bar examination, and then we elected him to the state senate. His next jump was into Congress from the El Paso District, which he still represents. All of these years, however, he has hung with the cattle business and is a genuine cowman. He owns ranches in Val Verde, Crockett, Terrell and Brewster counties and his ranching interests are rated at around a million dollars. A Democrat, he has boldly stood for protective tariff on wool, mutton, beef, and other ranch products, and, strange to say, his Democratic constituents, who raise wool, mutton, and beef, have stood behind him.

One little experience with Claude I shall have to tell. While he and I were one day riding along a bend in the Pecos River we jumped a yearling maverick, a bull. After we had roped him, thrown him, and branded him, he was all "on the prod," and to keep him from butting me I caught him by the tail as he got up. He was pointed towards Claude, and Claude expected me to "tail him down" while he mounted his horse. But I decided not to tail the yearling down. I just let him run, and Claude ran too—towards the Pecos River. On the bank he tangled his spurs in the weeds and rolled into the water. I still had hold of the yearling's tail. I could not resist the temptation; so I tumbled him into the river after Claude. Now occurred what seemed to be a transmigration of souls. The water cooled the yearling down and he swam out on the other side perfectly docile; but Claude spluttered up the bank as "ringy" as the yearling had been. He said several uncomplimentary things to me; then for a week he would hardly open his mouth. For more than twenty-five years now, however, he has been in a good humor; so I do not mind refreshing his memory on the matter.

Clay McGonigal, my other partner, became during the time of our association the champion roper not only of Texas but of the world. His record time for running on to, roping, and tying a steer down was 17 2/5 seconds. I organized the first rodeo held in our part of the state. However, we did not call it a "rodeo"; we called it a "celebration" or a "roping contest." Clay, along with Joe Gardner and Ellison Carroll (who eventually lowered Clay's record by just one-fifth of a second), did so well that he entered other contests over the country and was soon a familiar figure whenever cowboys competed for prizes in roping. In those days the entrants to such contests had to "bust" and tie down their steers, always grown cattle. Naturally a good many steers were killed, and to some people the sport appeared almost as brutal as that of the bull ring. About 1898 the whole of Southwest and West Texas went "hog wild" over roping contests. All the boys in the country were practicing at "fair grounding" (roping and tying) steers. They often roped cattle that did not belong to them and trespassed into pastures where cowmen did not want their cattle disturbed. In fact, no cowman wants his cattle run and abused. The cattlemen were suffering so much that they prevailed on the legislature to pass a law, which was sponsored by Claude Hudspeth, against throwing cattle in contests; an animal might still be roped but not thrown. The law had its effect, and "contesting," or "practicing," on cattle has become pretty much a thing of the past.

The Pecos country will always be a cow country. Nature has so decreed. Oil wells may flow in patches here and there among its breaks studded with *lechuguilla* daggers; irrigation ditches may turn stretches of its valley into populated fields; but the on- and on-stretching plains of greasewood and grass, the rolling sand dunes of gray sage and goldenrod and dusty mesquite, the wild breaks of thorned bush and rock—an immense territory hundreds of miles wide cut into by a solitary river that winds for a thousand miles through drouthy New Mexico and drouthy West Texas—will never change its general character at the behest of man, machine, or mineral. Here Nature has written on an incorruptible tablet: "So far shalt thou go but no farther."

And of all names that the cattle country of America has given to touch the imagination of men that of the Pecos seems destined to be most enduring. Despite modern annihilation of time and space, *the trans-Pecos country* still connotes a country vasty, sweeping, and lonely, where the coyote's howl is the only sound by night, and the solitary buzzard circling above and scattered cattle grazing on the sparse grass are the only visible forms of life by day. Yet this vastness is altogether out of proportion to the size of the Pecos River. A man may ride for hours with straining eyes and burning thirst without experiencing the hope of being near the stream until he suddenly finds himself on the brink of its salt-cedar lined banks. The salt-cedars are low, and for hundreds of miles not a tree marks the course of the river.

Up towards its head springs the color of the water is silver, and it runs shining and gay. Then about Roswell and on down to Carlsbad it becomes deep and blue. Lower down it takes on the color of red, and for hundreds of miles courses turgid and sullen. As it nears its union with the Rio Grande the waters borrow the grayish cast of the rocks that for a great stretch wall them in.

At times the water is so strong with alkali that it is almost undrinkable. "It would give a killdee that flew over it the diarrhoea," so an old timer described its alkaline effect. During drouths the stream runs shallow, and thirty and forty years ago when it was the only water for stock on either side of it for many miles back, cattle used to splash up and down its bed bawling for water—water that was not an alkaline solution. When on a rise, the Pecos is and always has been, on account of its many curves, narrow channel, and swift, shifting current, the most dangerous stream to swim in the West. Thousands of cattle, swept down between its moat-like walls, have been drowned in it, and dozens of cowboys.

The lower reaches of the Pecos canyon have been cut through solid rock and are deep and impassable. Farther up, the stream cuts a ditch of perpendicular walls through hard red soil. Crossings on the Pecos have always been rare, and the remembrance of the most noted of these crossings is not likely to dim, though it has long been abandoned. That is Horsehead Crossing, the name of which connotes more than three centuries of desperate and perilous riding. The first Spaniards to find it, so legend goes, marked the approach to it with skulls of mustangs that they found bleaching on the banks. One of the early routes to California passed over it. Before the Chisholm Trail had yet been beat out by the hoofs of a Texas herd, Goodnight and Loving drove ninety-six miles westward across the desert from the Concho and brought their thirst-maddened cattle to Horsehead Crossing. It became the most noted, the most desired, and the most dreaded mark on the Goodnight-Loving Trail. Here for long decades bands of Comanches lay in wait to rob and kill travelers and herdsmen; here grew up a little graveyard, untended and uncherished, for no habitation of the living has ever been erected at Horsehead Crossing. No camper ever tarried there longer than necessary, such a dreary, forsaken place it was.

The buffalo hunters used to have a saying: "When a bad man dies he goes either to hell or the Pecos." The buffalo hunters are nearly all dead—and they are not out on the Pecos. The buffaloes had no liking for that stream; they never ranged west of it and but few of them watered from its eastern bank. As hot and dry as Yuma, birdless, shunned even by coyotes, infested with rattlesnakes, its aboriginal inhabitants matched in toughness only by a few contesting frontiersmen of alkali-parched skin who had rather shoot than shave, the Pecos country *was* tough.

"There is no law west of the Pecos," another saying went. There is law now, but to thousands upon thousands of minds the words "law" and "Pecos" in conjunction mean but one thing —the sign hung up by a singular character of old time West Texas. The sign was: "Roy Bean, Justice of Peace—Law West of the Pecos." Giving her name to legend at the same time that old Roy Bean was giving his, was the Pecos Queen:

Across the Comstock railroad bridge, the highest in the West,
Patty rode her horse one day a lover's heart to test;
For he had told her he'd gladly risk all dangers for her sake,
But the puncher dared not follow, so she's still without a mate.

Far up the Pecos, in New Mexico, was John Chisum, most baronial, most feudalistic, in many ways most individual of all Texas cowmen that gave to the West its character. He claimed the lands from old Fort Sumner down the Pecos to the Texas line. His Jinglebob mark and his Fence Rail brand were on a hundred thousand cattle. The Lincoln County War was fought over his ranges. The men in his camps and ranks have been denominated "the warriors of the Pecos." And John Chisum, with Billy the Kid in his wake, will always belong to the Pecos tradition. The Pecos requires no monument, but should it ever require one, the monument will be found in the massive shutters, interlaid with steel, of the old Tunstall-McSween store at Lincoln—where the warriors of the Pecos fought some of their most desperate battles.

If in the old days a man said of another, "He is a cowboy of the Pecos," that might mean many things. It might mean that this cowboy was unusually efficient in handling cattle or in riding horses. It might mean that he was a rustler. It might mean that he ran the risk of being "pecosed" either for his integrity or the lack of it; on the other hand, it might mean that he had helped to "pecos" some other rider of the range. To "pecos" a man one shot him and rolled his body into the river—the one river that drained an empire. Perhaps the end of the cowboy of the Pecos might be more heroic. An old song of the Pecos Trail—the Goodnight-Loving Trail—describes a fitting end:

> On the rocky banks of the Pecos
> They will lay him down to rest
> With his saddle for a pillow
> And his gun across his breast.

It is an ironic paradox that a class of men whose name is synonymous with simple honesty—the cowmen—should be destined to share in popular fame a place side by side with cow thieves. Yet, such being destiny, perhaps it is not unfitting that the last wholesale stealing of cattle in Texas over a wide territory should have been along the Pecos—the Pecos that belongs to stockmen forever. The time was about the opening of the present century. History seemed to be repeating itself. The Pecos range was still largely open, the few fences being mostly drift fences that had not been kept up. From its junction with the Rio Grande to its head draws in New Mexico the breaks of the Pecos for several years harbored cow thieves by the score and its waters slaked the thirst of burnt cattle by the thousands.

The story of the cow thieves was the old story of young men beginning their career as mavericks and ending as outright takers of other people's property. For some reason a number of big ranches along the Pecos in Texas became careless in branding their calves; they simply did not work the range close enough; perhaps some of the bosses of the cow outfits had mavericks in mind. Certainly the inevitable result of such loose management was mavericks.

The boy who got the credit for being leader of the rustlers in our part of the country was Henry Green. He had for several years been "outside man"—a man who attends roundups on ranges away from those of the home ranch—for M. Halff and Brother, and was one of the best cowmen that ever forked a horse. He was often away from the Halff ranch for months at a time, but his employers always felt satisfied that their interests were being cared for over the wide circle that Henry Green rode. He numbered his friends by his acquaintances, and he was acquainted far and wide. He knew every canyon and thicket within a hundred miles of the Halff ranch—and as the loose branding went on under his eyes he came to know that many of the thickets and canyons contained unbranded cattle from one to three years old.

Henry Green decided to start business on his own hook. He resigned his job, drew his wages, bought a few ponies, and rode off into the breaks with his branding iron. He did not need help in roping and branding whatever scattering mavericks he should find, but he wanted company. He was a sociable kind of fellow, not without magnetism. He soon had several men about him. When mavericks became scarce the gang started to burning out brands.

Their practice was to round up a bunch of a hundred or so cattle in the late evening, keeping lookouts on the watch against any riders in the vicinity, drive the cattle perhaps twenty-five miles that night, throw them in a rough canyon where they could be held securely, rest them a day or two, and then under cover of darkness drive them another twenty-five miles. After the cattle were on a distant range the Green rustlers burned the old brands into new brands and turned the cattle loose. They frequently gathered a bunch of cattle in the vicinity where they had turned the burned cattle loose and handled them in the same way. They usually employed some brand that no one in the country had ever seen. They would not openly claim this brand and they could not be indicted when no one had seen them put it on cattle. They counted on gathering and selling the stolen stock at future times after the brands were healed and the cattle had come to be considered as strays.

This kind of stealing and branding kept up until the cowmen of the Pecos were beginning to have very little faith in the power of brands to "hold" their cattle. Almost everybody knew who was doing the burning, but nobody had proof that would hold in court. Then the rangers came in; there were some grand round-ups that resulted in skilful reading of mutilated brands and in the rebranding of thousands of cattle. Meantime the suspects "made for the tules." Henry Green escaped to New Mexico, where he was before long killed in a pistol duel.

A contributing factor to this last big steal was the uncertain financial situation of some of the ranches along the Pecos and Devil's rivers. A group of California capitalists had bought a ranch on Live Oak Creek—above old Fort Lancaster—in the western part of Crockett County and stocked it with cattle. They ran the 7 7 brand and all told had around 1500 head of cattle. They owned and controlled 20,000 acres. Then they got into a fight among themselves and finally appealed to the courts to settle their business. The district judge appointed me receiver and general manager of the ranch, and I was several years getting the cattle and land all sold.

In the meantime Dull Brothers of Pittsburgh, Pennsylvania, engaged me to sell and deliver their Big Canyon Ranch in Pecos and Terrell counties. It comprised 246,000 acres of land and grazed 11,000 head of cattle and 200 horses. I sold the entire outfit—land, cattle, horses, chuckwagon, everything—to a company composed of N. H. Corder, Irv Ellis, Will Bevins, Lee L. Russell, and R. R. (Dick) Russell. The cattle were good cattle, but I got only $13 a head for grown steers and cows, all calves being thrown in uncounted. After the sale was made cattle began to go up, and Lee Russell told me later that he and his partners sold 2800 steers out of the brand for enough to pay for the string of 11,000 cattle.

About the time I got the Big Canyon Ranch disposed of some Boston capitalists who were—along with many other absentee stockmen—going out of the cattle business, employed me to manage and dispose of their Blocks Y and H Ranch in Val Verde and Terrell counties. It comprised 172,000 acres. I sold it to Leonard Hillis of Peoria, Illinois. In the sales of the Big Canyon and the Blocks Y and H ranches my commissions and fees amounted to over $27,000.

In various wanderings I had become acquainted with the fine ranges in the Davis Mountains and in the Big Bend of the Rio Grande. This country is now famous as the Highland Hereford region and is conceded to grow the best white-faced cattle in America. Much as I liked the land of the Devil's River and the Pecos, I liked this land better; it was developing. I judged that land business here would thrive for a long time. So in 1906 I moved to Alpine to deal in cattle and ranches, though I no longer rated myself as a ranchman.

The Kennedy Ranch in Pecos County of 60,000 acres and 1500 cattle I sold to Andy Nichols and Son. The N Ranch of the same county, containing 44,000 acres, I sold to Ross Peters. In Brewster County, of which Alpine is the county seat, I sold the Rosillo Ranch, embracing over 100,000 acres of land owned and leased, together with 2200 head of cattle, to J. M. Graham. Not long ago I sold my old friend and partner, Claude Hudspeth, the Altuda Ranch, which is in Brewster County not far from Alpine and which contains about 15,000 acres. All in all,

I believe that I have negotiated the sale of more acres of land for exclusively grazing purposes than any other man living in Texas.

I have made my last move and I want to be buried in a plot of ground west of the Pecos, and I want my grave to be marked by a slab out of the marble mountain that I own a controlling interest in. This mountain contains four hundred acres of solid marble rising for three hundred feet above the plain. How far down into the earth the marble sinks nobody knows. In this huge mass there are, according to the Californians who have a contract to work the quarry, forty-two distinct shades of marbling, graduating from snow white to midnight black. I used to think that I might some day be able to erect in San Antonio a hotel of marble devoted to the use of trail drivers and other cowmen. My idea was to put it on the site occupied by the old Southern Hotel, once headquarters for the cattle world of the Southwest. I guess now that the cowmen's hotel of marble will never be, but just the same the old trail drivers deserve marble halls with tiled floors and frescoed walls. Yet, deserving or undeserving, I and they were but creatures of circumstance—the circumstance of an unfenced world. I salute them all. *Vaqueros, amigos, pasen buenas noches!*

APPENDICES

APPENDIX A

(BIBLIOGRAPHY OF SOURCES USED IN THE PREPARATION OF CHAPTER V)

It was the original intention of the author to cite authority for every statement made in this chapter, which contains much not familiar to the public; but the manuscript became so cluttered with "ditches of footnotes" that the plan was altered. However, the authorities used in preparing the chapter are listed below. The chief sources have been newspapers and government documents.

Civilian and Galveston Gazette, incomplete file, 1844–1873.

Corpus Christi *Gazette,* Mar. 29, Apr. 12, Apr. 24, May 31, July 12, Nov. 29, Dec. 20, 1873; Jan. 3, Jan. 10, Feb. 7, May 16, June 13, June 20, July 25, 1874; July 24, Aug. 7, Sept. 11, 1875.

Dallas *Daily Herald,* 1874.

Dallas *Weekly Herald,* 1872–1878, particularly Aug. 14, 1875.

Galveston *Daily News,* 1873 and 1877–1881, particularly the following issues, usually under the head of "State Items": Feb. 6, May 8, May 9, Sept. 3, and Nov. 21, 1873; May 17, June 13, Aug. 10, Aug. 12, Sept. 2, and Sept. 4, 1877; Jan. 27, July 25, Aug. 7, Aug. 20, 1878; July 4, 1879.

Galveston *Weekly and Tri-Weekly News,* 1844–1858 (incomplete files), particularly the issue of Aug. 14, 1855.

Nueces Valley Weekly, Corpus Christi, Texas, 1857–1858, particularly Nov. 7, 1857.

Western Stock Journal, Pleasanton, Texas, 1873–1875.

Sen. Ex. Documents No. 21, 36th Cong., 1st Session; No. 24, 36th Cong., 1st Session; No. 2, 36th Cong., 1st Session; "Difficulties of the Southwestern Frontier," Ex. Doc. No. 52, House of Representatives, 36th Cong., 1st Session; "Claims of the State of Texas," Ex. Doc. No. 277, House of Representatives, 42nd Cong., 2nd Session; "Troubles on the Texas Frontier," Ex. Doc. No. 81, House of Representatives, 36th Cong., 1st Session.

In the library of the University of Texas there is a volume, perhaps privately bound, entitled *Texas Frontier Depredations*. Its extraordinary contents are as follows: "Depredations on the Frontiers of Texas," Ex. Doc. No. 39, House of Representatives, 42nd Cong., 3rd Session, said document containing "Report of the United States Commissioners to Texas, Appointed under Joint Resolutions of Congress, Approved May 7, 1872"; "Depredations on the Frontiers of Texas," Ex. Doc. No. 257, House of Representatives, 43rd Cong., 1st Session, "Texas Frontier Troubles," Report No. 343, House of Representatives, 44th Cong., 1st Session, including "Testimony Taken by the Special Committee on Texas Frontier Troubles, Appointed . . . Jan. 6, 1876."

Supplementing the last named volume is a privately issued pamphlet, rather voluminous, entitled "Memorial of the United States, Number 230, before the General Claims Commission of the United States and Mexico, under convention concluded September 8, 1923. . . . United States of America on behalf of Richard J. Kleberg, Sr., etc. . . . Richard King vs. United States." Most of the evidence in this highly interesting Memorial is taken from testimony made at Brownsville in 1872, at which time King, Kenedy, and many other ranch people of Southwest Texas were seeking damages from the United States for failure on the part of the government to have protected American property against Mexican depredations.

Texas Almanac, issues through the '60's and '70's.

Trail Drivers of Texas, San Antonio, 1920, Vol. I, pp. 185–187; Vol. II (1923), pp. 456–459.

Bonnet, W. A., "King Fisher," *Frontier Times,* Bandera, Texas, July, 1926, pp. 36–37.

Breakenridge, William M., *Helldorado,* Boston, 1928, pp. 104–105.

Cox, James, *The Cattle Industry of Texas and Adjacent Territory,* St. Louis, 1895, 393, 395, 398, 430.

Ford, John S., *Memoirs,* unpublished, in archives of the Library of the University of Texas.

Gatschet, Albert S., "The Karankawa Indians," in *Archaeological and Ethnological Papers of the Peabody Museum,* Vol. I, No. 2, pp. 49–51.

Graves, H. A., *Andrew Jackson Potter,* Nashville, Tenn., 1890, 250–251; 332.

Jennings, N. A., *A Texas Ranger,* N. Y., 1899, pp. 82–204.

Johnson, Frank W., *A History of Texas and Texans,* edited by Barker and Winkler, Chicago and New York, 1916, Vol. I, pp. 474, 512, 515.

Merriman, Eli, in Corpus Christi *Caller,* Dec. 13, 1925.

Morris, Leopold, "The Mexican Raid of 1875 on Corpus Christi," *Quarterly* of the Texas State Historical Association, Vol. IV, pp. 131–132.

Ramsdell, Charles, *Reconstruction in Texas,* N. Y., 1910, Chapter III.

Roberts, Dan W., *Rangers and Sovereignty,* San Antonio, 1914, pp. 95-104.

Santleben, August, *A Texas Pioneer,* N. Y., 1910, pp. 71, 116, 157.

Sowell, A. J., *Rangers and Pioneers of Texas,* San Antonio, 1884, pp. 193–196.

Sowell, A. J., *Early Settlers and Indian Fighters of Southwest Texas,* Austin, 1900, pp. 530–535; 683–691.

Stevenson, Laura May, "Early History of Eagle Pass" (with bibliography and sources), Dallas *Morning News,* Nov. 6, 1927.

Sumpter, Jesse, *Memoirs,* unpublished, from the library of Frost Woodhull, San Antonio.

Sutherland, W. G., in Corpus Christi *Caller,* Aug. 31, 1924, also in private letters to the author.

Interviews with Walter Billingsley and George W. Saunders, San Antonio; R. C. Barfield, Mrs. R. J. Dobie, and Joe McCloud (colored), Beeville; S. N. Hardy, Austin; John Young, Alpine; J. W. Hargus, Asherton; J. O. Luby, San Diego; Forrest Clark, Alice; Harbert Davenport, Brownsville.

APPENDIX B

(THE STOCK RECORD BOOKS OF ATASCOSA COUNTY, TEXAS)

Three of the massive volumes that contain the stock records of Atascosa County, with skips, from 1868 to 1876, are in the hands of George W. Saunders, San Antonio, Texas. They are to be placed by him in the Witte Museum of that city. They contain invaluable accounts, many of them rather informal, of the cattle business of Southwest Texas during the years they cover.

An example of informality is contained in the record of a herd of cattle sold by F. M. Mansfield to W. S. Hall (one of the coast packers), December 25, 1874, the cattle to be butchered at Fulton. In the itemized description of the cows and beeves occur the following entries:

1	*72*	∞	"old cripple"
1	*H2*		"old scalawag for hide"
1	*9L*		"cripple for hide"
1			"old sway back"

The peculiar figure following the brand, which looks like a figure 8 lying down, represents a pair of ears and gives the ear marks. A "scalawag" is a worthless "cut back," generally wild and old.

In the books are posted sales from adjacent counties as well as from Atascosa County. A bill of sale from La Salle County, dated January 30, 1875, shows an interesting collection of Mexican brands.

The most extensive cowman of Atascosa and McMullen counties was W. J. (James) Lowe of Dog Town (now Tilden), and the records of his transactions occupy hundreds of pages.

The following entry is typical:

"State of Texas
"County of McMullen

"Know all men by these presents that we the undersigned have this day sold unto Burnett and Cassidy cattle in the following marks and brands this the 28th day of April, 1874."

Ninety-six head of cattle are listed according to brand, mark, age, and class (beef, cow, 1-year-old, 2-year-old, and 3-year-old). The record shows that 38 of the cattle were sold by James Lowe; 28 by J. G. Heritage; 11 by John R. Weaver; and 19 by James Martin. Several dozen brands are listed, and any owner of any brand on any of the cattle sold would, upon examining the record, know exactly to whom to go for payment of his animal. Beeves valued at $12; cows, at $8.

After the description of the cattle is this entry:
"State of Texas
"County of McMullen

"This is to certify that I have this day examined a herd of ninety-six head of cattle for Burnett and Cassidy and the foregoing bill of sale contains a true and correct list of the marks and brands on said animals, this the 28th day of April, A.D., 1874. Said cattle are to be driven to Indianola.

"Given under my hand and seal of office—James Martin, Deputy Inspector of Hides and Animals for Live Oak County."

INDEX

INDEX

Abilene, Kansas, cow town, 23, 86, 96
Adair, John, of J A Ranch, 136, 139
Adams, Andy, cowboy chronicler, xv
Adams, Charlie, author, 256
Adobe Walls fight, 133
Agarita, 192
Agua Dulce, 62, 118
Alamo, 45, 47, 76
Alexandria, Mo., 40
Allen and Poole, stockmen, 28
Alpine, Texas, xi, 278
Altita, 221
Alvarado, Atilano, 58
Amargosa, 192
Animas, Rio de las, legend of, 154
Antelope, 140, 147, 151, 171, 174
Apaches, 46, 166
Aransas Creek, 78, 79
Arkansas, razorback home, 30–42 *passim*
Armour, packer, 29
Army troops in the Southwest, 52, 53, 59, 67, 157
Arrington, Captain G. W., ranger, 141
Astronomy, cowboy, 92–94
Atascosa County, 76, 77, 105, 107
Atascosa Creek, 210, 213
A. T. & S. F. railroad, 154, 156
Austin, 63, 65, 85, 183

Baca, Elfego, 165
Bad men, 43–68, 84, 125–126, 133, 134–135, 189–190, 216–220
Badger fight, 172
Bagdad, Mexico, 54
Baker, cowman, 140, 146
Bandana, 131, 173, 194, 213, 234, 248–249
Bandera, 105
Bandits, 43–85

Barbed wire, xii, 111–112, 188, 225
Barboquejo, chin-strap, 193
Barfield, R. C., old timer, 62
Barlow's Ferry, 205
Barnes, Will C., author, 240
Barrow, Henry, cowhand, 13
Bass, Sam, outlaw, 130
Beall, Sebastian, frontiersman, 68
Bean, Roy, judge, 274
Bear, 140, 242
Beaver Lake, 123, 124, 125, 128, 185
Bee County, 78, 79, 80, 81, 179, 205, 209, 211, 213
Beef: price of, 23; "salt junk," 25; jerky and mess, 28; for hogs, 33–34; called "wohaw," 89; barbecued, 213
"Beef biscuit," 28
"Beef books," 106
Beeville, 62, 80, 81, 263
Belton, 101
Benavides, Refugio, captain of Mexican militia, 60
Benton, Frank, author, 157–158
Bevins, Will, 278
Big Bend, xi, 278
Big Canyon ranch, 278
"Big Steal," xi, 111, 205–215
Billie, race horse, 179
Billingsley, Walter, trail driver, 62, 196
Billy the Kid, xi, xii, 148, 150, 156–169, 275; character, 166
Bishop, vigilante, 76
Blackjack, 180, 182
Blanconia, 73
Blocker, J. R., cowman and roper, 247
Blocks Y and H ranch, 278
Boggas, Frank, minuteman, 74
Bonneville, Captain, xiii
Bonney, William. *See* Billy the Kid

291

INDEX

298 INDEX

134, 140; married to Mexican, 153; soldiers, 162; impudence, 175
Negro Sunday School, 75
Nesters, xiii
Newton, Tommie, trail driver, 88
Nichols, A. M., cowman, 209, 212, 213
Nichols, J. M., cowman, 211
Noakes Raid, 62
Noel, Theophilus, quoted, 33
Nueces County, 24, 84, 94, 113, 190
Nueces River, 41, 43, 44, 45, 53, 56, 68, 82, 109, 112, 113, 115, 119, and passim throughout
Nuecestown, 60, 61, 62, 73
Nunn, Bill, cowhand, 229–231
Nye, Bill, humorist, 222

Oakville, 81–82; Tribune, 109 n.
O'Connor, Tom, cowman, 114
Ocotillo, 191
Oklahoma, 130, 136
Old Time Trail Drivers' Ass'n, 11
O'Phalliard, Tom, 163
Ord, General E. O. C., 54
Oso Creek, 62
Outlaw cattle, 13 ff., 112–113, 199–201
Outlaws. See Bandits, also Bad men
Ozona, 128; Kicker, 270

Packeries, 21–29, 40
Palo Alto, 118; battlefield, 68
Palo Duro Canyon, 139, 140, 147, 174
Panhandle of Texas, 139 ff., 154, 173, 244
Papalote River, 80
Paradise Valley, 139
Parr, Archie, cowboy and senator, 121
Payaso, noted horse, 101, 112, 115, 116, 123–126, 128, 146, 150, 152, 153, 154, 160, 254; death, 170
Peacock ranch, 210
Pease River, 133, 135, 139, 141, 142, 146, 147, 170, 172
Peat, Jake, murdered, 77
Peckerwood Pete, 241
Pecos River, 128, 156, 161, 164, 165, 245, 264, 272–276 and passim throughout

Pendencia Creek, 43
Penascal, murders at, 58–59, 69
Pettus, Buck, cowman, 68, 107–108
Pial, 247
Picketwire River. See Rio de las Animas
Piedras Negras, 46, 222
Piedras Pintas, 58
Pierce, J. T., Oakville citizen, 81
Pierce, "Shanghai," cowman, xii, 27–28, 111, 112
Pike's Peak, 170
Plains, the. See Panhandle
Platte River, xi, 86, 100, 121
Pleasanton, 108, 214
Plum Creek, 4, 130
Pope, Lee, brasadero, 217, 221
Porter, Lake, fiddling cowboy, 91
Porter, Sam, cowman, 209, 213–214
Porter, Sydney (O. Henry), 85
Potros, 10, 237. See Horses
Potter, "Fighting Jack," preacher, 64
Prairie dogs, 89–90, 98, 174
Prairie fire, 268
Prickly pear, 118, 195, 202; poultices of, 198
Pryor, Ike, trail driver, 34, 89
Pulliam, John, cowboy, killed, 64
Purgatoire River. See Rio de las Animas

Quail, Mexican, 192, 198
Quintanilla Creek, 229
Quitaque, 140, 146, 147

Rabb, Lee, cowman, killed, 118–119
Rabb, Mrs., her string of Mexican ears, 119
Rachal, Albert, cowman, 214
Rachal, D. C., cowman, 112, 214
Ramadero, 195
Ranches: distances between, 53; how established, 139–140. See also under ranch names
Rancho Saco, 113, 114, 116, 118
Range, open: customs and conditions on, 100–116, 137–144; changes today on, 261